MAFIACRAFT

AN ETHNOGRAPHY OF DEADLY SILENCE

HAU
Books

Hau Books are published by the
Society for Ethnographic Theory (SET)

www.haubooks.org

MAFIACRAFT

AN ETHNOGRAPHY OF DEADLY SILENCE

Deborah Puccio-Den

Hau Books
Chicago

To Judge Giovanni Falcone,
the first anthropologist of the mafia

Contents

List of Figures

Figure 1: Exhibition "Mafia & territory," 1978: Impastato, center. (Source: Photo Archive, Centro Siciliano di Documentazione Giuseppe Impastato. Photographs displayed on the poster by Letizia Battaglia.)

Figure 2: Cover of the catalogue of the *Mafia Oggi* (Mafia Today) exhibition. (Source: Photograph by Franco Zecchin.)

Figure 3: National demonstration against the mafia. (Source: Photographs displayed on the poster by Letizia Battaglia.)

Figure 4: Posters bringing people face to face with the mafia. (Source: Photo archive Centro Siciliano di Documentazione Giuseppe Impastato.)

Figure 5: Camorristi, masked as witches, preparing lines of coke. (Source: Photograph by Mauro D'Agati.)

Figure 6: Kids, one of them holding a weapon, play games in a rundown neighborhood of Naples. (Source: Photograph by Mauro D'Agati.)

Figure 7: Tattoos on skin and rocks. (Source: Photograph by Mauro D'Agati.)

Figure 8: "The mafia kills, so does your silence – Peppino Impastato's comrades," anti-mafia demonstration (Source: Photo archive Centro Siciliano di Documentazione Giuseppe Impastato).

Figure 9: Young Peppino Impastato (front row, third from right) holding the arm of his father (a mafioso), walking alongside one of Baladamenti's brothers. (Source: Family archive Felicia Bortolotta Impastato).

Acknowledgements

It would be impossible to thank individually all those who have contributed, in one way or another, to making this research life-path called Mafiacraft an incredible experience, intellectually, scientifically, politically, and humanly.

First of all, I wish to express my gratitude to Giovanni da Col for accompanying this project from the outset and giving it a proper life with his coining of the neologism Mafiacraft. The reader of this book will comprehend the critical role of words in bringing an idea to life. More than a word, Mafiacraft is a paradigm for reframing the "mafia" as an anthropological topic.

This paradigm was initially discussed on the occasion of the publication of a colloquium in *HAU: Journal of Ethnographic Theory*, curated by Mariane Ferme and supplemented by insightful comments offered by such prominent and esteemed researchers as Michael Herzfeld, Marco Santoro, Jane Schneider, and Harry Walker: their input prompted stimulating discussions that have substantially enriched Mafiacraft as a research program. The issues they raised have given flesh to the conclusion of this book.

The first version of the manuscript was discussed in December 2018 on the occasion of my "accreditation to supervise research" (HDR) defense with the members of its jury: Nicolas Dodier, Béatrice Fraenkel, Michael Houseman, Salvatore d'Onofrio, Catherine Perret, and Daniela Piana. I am grateful for their wise and encouraging remarks.

During the editing process at HAU Books, the manuscript entered a new phase of its life thanks to the accurate and creative work of the reviewers. I could not have dreamt of better commentators than those selected by the members of HAU Books editorial team. One of them, Peter Geschiere, waived anonymity, and Mafiacraft is indeed deeply in-debted to the profound renewal of witchcraft, achieved by this eminent anthropologist, for defining the contours of this new paradigm. The edi-torial collective of HAU Books should also be credited for the improve-ment of this volume, particularly Hylton White who took charge of the editorial process in delicate times, during which he was able to carry it out despite all the difficulties linked to the Covid-19 pandemic. I also thank Nanette Norris, managing editor, who showed unwavering sup-port for this project, and Caroline Jeannerat, copy editor, whose thor-ough proofreading of the manuscript was another invitation to improve it. During all the different steps of this path, I could also rely on the con-stant availability of my English teacher, Andrea Talmud, and of Sébast-ien Le Pipec, English tutor at the École des hautes études en sciences sociales (School for Advanced Studies in the Social Sciences, EHESS) in Paris, whose acumen and refined knowledge of the English language were valuable for upgrading my work.

Over the last three years, this research program has been discussed with my students in my EHESS seminar "Anthropologie de la mafia, pour une anthropologie politique du silence." I warmly thank them for all that their current fieldwork, awareness, and criticism offered to the testing of Mafiacraft as a paradigm for founding a political anthropology of silence. The EHESS and the Centre national de la recherche scienti-fique (National Center of Scientific Research, CNRS), the institution I am affiliated with, provided strong support for the defense of this set of methodological and theoretical proposals.

Outside France, I was able, in Italy, to rely on the expertise of Um-berto Santino, director of the Centro Siciliano di Documentazione Gi-useppe Impastato (Sicilian documentation center Giuseppe Impastato, CSD), and of his wife, Anna Puglisi, who both founded the indispensa-ble No Mafia Memorial (Palermo): not only could I count on their skills and on a documentary fount unique in the world, but they also provided me with the historical black-and-white photographs published in this book. I would like to thank them and photographers Paolo Chirco, Pino Manzella, and Guido Orlando for their generosity, as well as artist-pho-tographer Mauro D'Agati, who offered me the copyright of his magnifi-cent photos on the Neapolitan camorra, photographer Franco Zecchin for the right to reproduce his photograph on the catalogue of the exposi-tion "Mafia Oggi," and photographer Shobha, who agreed that one of her photographs would be used for the cover of this work in exchange for a donation to her foundation Mother India School.

I could not have written this book without the commitment and generosity of so many anti-mafia activists, but I am much indebted to the anti-mafia judges, such as Maurizio De Lucia, the public prosecutor of Messina, Gaetano Paci, former prosecutor from the Anti-mafia Directorate of the District of Palermo, Roberto Scarpinato, the public prosecutor of Palermo, and Antonio Balsamo, from 1995 to 2007 judge at the Court of Palermo and now a judicial expert in European law, human rights, and international legal cooperation in criminal matters for the United Nations.

I dedicate my book to Judge Giovanni Falcone and this shall make evident the importance I attach to his vocation as a judge who revolutionized thought on the mafia as a political and social phenomenon. The epistemological gesture I propose by Mafiacraft owes him immensely: may this book be a small offering in recognition of his grand sacrifice.

Permissions

Chapter 1 is based on the article "Juger la mafia: Catégorisation juridique et économies morales en Italie (1980–2020)" published in *Diogène* (3–4, no. 239–240, 2012), available online at doi: 10.3917/dio.239.0016. Translated and re-edited by Sage Publications as "Judging the Mafia: Categorization under Law and Moral Economies in Italy (1980–2010)." Used by permission of the publisher. Chapter 2 is based on the article "The Sicilian Mafia: Transformation to a Global Evil," published in *Ethnográfica* (12, no. 2, 2008), available online at doi: 10.4000/etnografica.1763. Used by permission of the publisher. Earlier versions of chapter 3 were presented at the "MAFIAs: Realities and Representations of Organized Crime" conference, John D. Calandra Italian American Institute, New York, 2014; and at the "Anthropological Legacies and Human Futures" congress, European Association of Social Anthropologists, Milan, 2016. Chapter 4 is based on the chapter "The Anti-mafia Movement as Religion? The Pilgrimage to the Falcone's Tree," published in *Shrines and Pilgrimage in the Modern World: New Itineraries into the Sacred*, edited by Peter Jan Margry, in 2008. Chapter 5 is based on the chapter "'Difficult Remembrance': Memorializing Mafia Victims in Palermo," published in *Grassroots Memorials: The Politics of Memorializing Traumatic Death*, edited by Peter Jan Margry and Cristina Sánchez-Carretero, in 2011. Used by permission of Berghahn Books. Chapter 6 is based on the article "L'ethnologue et le juge: L'enquête de Giovanni Falcone sur la mafia en Sicile," published in *Ethnologie française* (31, no. 1, 2001), available at doi: 10.3917/ethn.011.0015. Translated and re-edited by Cairn International "The Ethnologist and the Magistrate: Giovanni Falcone's Investigation into the Sicilian Mafia." Used by permission of the publisher. Chapter 7 is based on the articles entitled "De la responsabilité" and "De l'honneur à la responsabilité: Les metamorphoses du sujet mafieux," both published in *L'Homme* (3, no. 223–224, 2017). "De la responsabilité" was translated by Cadenza Academic Translations as "On Responsibility" (https://www.cairn-int.info/article-E_LHOM_223_0005--on-responsibility-htm). Used by permission of the publisher. Chapter 8 is based on the chapter "Mafia: état de violence ou violence d'État? L'affaire Impastato et la requalification concomitante des groups subversifs et de l'État en Italie (1978–2002)," published in *Quaderni* (no. 78, 2012). Used by permission of the publisher. Chapter 9 is based on the chapter "On Intentionality in Mafia Crimes," published in *Truth, Intentionality and Evidence: Anthropological Approaches to Crime*, edited by Yazid Ben-Hounet and Deborah Puccio-Den, in 2017. Used by permission of Routledge. Chapter 10 is based on the article entitled "'Dieu vous bénisse et vous protège!' La correspondance secrete du chef de la mafia sicilienne Bernardo Provenzano (1993–2006)," published in *Revue de l'Histoire des Religions* (228, no. 2, 2011). Used by permission of the publisher. The conclusion is based on the article entitled "Invisible Things" published in Hau Journal in 2019, available online at doi: 10.1086/706547. Published with permission by the publisher. I warmly thank all the publishers who granted me these permissions.

Personages

Abate, Ida: schoolteacher, collected testimonies for the beatification of Judge Rosario Livatino

Aiello, Michele: doctor, accused of participation in a mafia association, 2008

Alberti, Gerlando: member of Cosa Nostra

Andreotti, Giulio: Italian politician, charged in 1993 with external complicity with a mafia association, cleared in 2004

Badalamenti, Gaetano "Tano": mafioso of Cinisi, accused as instigator of the murder of Giuseppe Impastato, 2002

Bartolotta Impastato, Felicia: mother of Giuseppe Impastato

Basile, Emanuele: captain of the carabinieri, worked with Borsellino, killed in 1980

Battaglia, Letizia: anti-mafia photographer

Borsellino, Paolo: anti-mafia judge, killed in the Via d'Amelio bombing on July 19, 1992

Brusca, Giovanni: *pentito* (repentant mafioso), known for having pressed the detonator of the bomb causing the Capaci massacre

Buscetta, Tommaso: pentito, informant of Giovanni Falcone

Calderone, Antonino: pentito

Calò, Pippo: mafia boss accused in the Maxi Trial

Caponnetto, Antonino: anti-mafia judge, creator of the anti-mafia pool

Chinnici, Rocco: anti-mafia judge, inventor of the anti-mafia pool, killed by the mafia on July 29, 1983

Contorno, Salvatore: pentito

Costa, Gaetano: prosecutor, murdered by the Mafia in 1980

Cucuzza, Salvatore: pentito, passed away in April 2014

Cuffaro, Salvatore: politician, President of Sicily 2001–2008, accused of favoring the mafia in the Aiello Trial

D'Agati, Mauro: artist and photographer of a Camorra group

Dalla Chiesa, Carlo Alberto: general, assassinated on September 3, 1982

De Lucia, Maurizio: prosecutor from the Anti-Mafia Direction of the Palermo District during the Aiello Trial

Di Lello, Giuseppe: anti-mafia judge, member of the anti-mafia pool

Dolci, Danilo: Italian sociologist, anti-mafia activist (1924–1997)

Falcone, Giovanni: anti-mafia judge, killed in the Capaci massacre on May 23, 1992

Finazzo, Giuseppe: builder close to Gaetano Badalamenti, suspected of having ordered the murder of Giuseppe Impastato

Giuffré, Antonino: pentito

Greco, Michele: Palermo mafia boss, accused in the Maxi trial

Guarnotta, Leonardo: judge

Guttadauro, Giuseppe: doctor and mafioso, head of Brancaccio neighborhood

Impastato, Bortolotta: mother of Giuseppe Impastato

Impastato, Giuseppe: anti-mafia activist, killed in May 1978

La Torre, Pio: regional secretary of the Italian Communist Party, conceptor of the 1982 Rognoni–La Torre law, assassinated in April 1982

Livatino, Rosario: anti-mafia judge, murdered by the mafia association called Stidda in 1990, beatified in 2020

Meli, Antonino: judge

Messina Denaro, Matteo: considered as the current head of the Sicilian mafia

Morvillo, Francesca: magistrate, wife of Giovanni Falcone, killed with him

Mosca, Gaetano: jurist

Orlando, Leoluca: former member of Christian Democracy, founder of the anti-mafia movement La Rete, Palermo mayor in late 1980s, 1993–1999, 2012–2021

Paci, Gaetano: prosecutor from the Anti-mafia Direction of the District of Palermo

Palazzolo, Salvatore: pentito

Palazzolo, Vito: mafioso, accused of the murder of Giuseppe Impastato as accomplice of Gaetano Badalamenti

Palizzolo, Raffaele: Sicilian politician, indicated for the murder of Emanuele Notarbartolo, 1902

Pintacuda, Ennio: Jesuit priest

Pitrè, Giuseppe (1841–1916): folklorist

Provenzano, Bernardo: mafioso, right-hand man of Totò Riina, head of Cosa Nostra from January 1993 until 2006, when he was arrested

Puglisi, Anna: scholar, wife of Umberto Santino, co-founder of the Centro Siciliano di Documentazione Giuseppe Impastato and of the No Mafia memorial

Puglisi, Pino: priest of Brancaccio, murdered by Cosa Nostra in Brancaccio on September 15, 1993, beatified in 2017

Riina, Salvatore: mafioso, head of Cosa Nostra, arrested January 1993, succeeded in Cosa Nostra by Bernardo Provenzano

Santino, Umberto: anti-mafia activist and scholar, founder of the Centro di Documentazione Siciliano Giuseppe Impastato and of the No Mafia memorial

Scarpinato, Roberto: anti-mafia judge, examining magistrate of the Andreotti trial

Sciascia, Leonardo: Sicilian intellectual and writer

Signorino, Domenico: judge in Palermo who took the first statements from family members in the investigation of the murder of Giuseppe Impastato, committed suicide in 1992

Vitale, Leonardo: Cosa Nostra's first pentito

Zecchin, Franco: anti-mafia photographer

From witchcraft to "mafiacraft": Shifting paradigms

> The mafia? What is the mafia? Something you eat? Something you drink? I don't know the mafia, I have never seen it.
> —Mommo Piromalli, the 'Ndrangheta boss*

> The mafia? What is the mafia? A brand of cheese? Tell me what it is because I have no idea!
> —Gerlando Alberti, member of Cosa Nostra†

Mafiacraft is a neologism pointing to a new method of ethnographical inquiry and a new form of theorizing the mafia phenomenon. Its novelty consists in adopting a stance of methodological agnosticism about what the mafia is and in focusing on how the mafia was crafted—supposing that this crafting, triggered by the silent nature of the mafia and the "mafiosi," has had ontological consequences for the way it *exists*. Most studies of the mafia have endeavored to answer the question: "What is the mafia?"[1] In so doing, researchers in the social sciences have become an integral part of

---

* Quoted in Nicaso (2010: 12).

† Quoted in Padovani (1987: 9).

1. I invite the reader to consult in particular Umberto Santino (1995), an important book that summarizes the bibliography on the mafia. More recently, Santoro (2007) has pointed to the overabundance of research studies

1

what they set out to study and define: a cognitive event shaped by silence, a performative non-speech act fed by the endless process of questioning it produces. In these studies, silence is regarded as a veneer (a "veil," a "blanket," a "wall") that conceals the essential reality to be discovered: the Mafia. Overcoming the silence will "expose" the Mafia as it really *is*. The methodological assumption that informs my own work is that the "mafia" is not a social fact fixed once and for all, ready to be studied or "exposed" by social scientists. I argue that the comforting perspective "that the object already exists in some form of language, only requiring translation from one language to another or from orality into writing" (Hirschauer 2006: 422) does not apply to "mafia studies." Indeed, the "mafia" can be used as a magnifying glass to tackle one of the social sciences' conundrums: how do we put into words "the silence of the social" (Hirschauer 2006: 423)?

The term "silence" is not used here in terms of its common, everyday meaning. It is rather an analytic framework that refers "to a mute challenge for description to 'make something speak' that resists verbalization" (Hirschauer 2006: 423n13). Sociologist Stefan Hirschauer (2006: 423) uses it to draw attention to "verbalization methods [that presuppose] that people have specific knowledge that can be extracted by means of questioning." But, he asks, what kind of ethnographic relationship is possible when only one side is audible (Hirschauer 2006: 435)? What theoretical and methodological problems emerge when ethnographers cannot access the object itself? Approaching a mute entity such as the mafia through the social sciences entails taking into account the object's ontology. Dealing with "mafiosi" places us in the same embarrassing position as ethnographers dealing with voiceless beings manifesting themselves by means of meaningless sounds, symptoms, and signals. We cannot expect that mafiosi give an answer to the question "What is the mafia?" We cannot describe the mafia "as it is" by taking a phenomenological approach (Crotty 1996: 202), in view of the difficulty of providing empirical data. As anthropologists, we are required to keep preconceptions at bay, adopting an epistemological stance of "suspension of belief" (Vivilaki and Johnson 2008) about assumed knowledge and assumptions.[2] But, as ethnographers, we can do something useful: we

---

on the mafia, counting about 450 books published in fifteen years. Santoro (2015) provides an update on contemporary studies of this issue.

2. This is the path followed by medical scientists tackling uncertain physiological phenomena. See Atkins et al. (2013) on medically unexplained physical symptoms.

may seek to grasp the multifarious ways in which all sectors of society have dealt with what is unsaid, what is avoided by means of silence, what is kept silent. It is precisely the attempt to describe this *work* that is at the heart of the Mafiacraft project.[3]

I propose that the labor of diagnosing the mafia, which lies at the core of the anti-mafia movement and of anti-mafia justice, forms an inherent part of the mafia phenomenon as a whole. Mafiacraft, thus, includes the analysis of two forms of "work": the mafia work (or, more accurately, the silence) and the anti-mafia work of interpreting, reading, fighting, and judging this silence. The paradigm thus focuses on interactions between society, the judiciary, the state, and what all these bodies call the "mafia," rather than isolating the latter as a pathology, a deviance, an anti-state, or whatever is separated from the state as a legitimate way of being and living together. These interactions are characterized by the fact that one of the two parties involved in the communication is silent—we should possibly say "mute"—obliging the other to establish a never-ending diagnosis, always precarious because never validated by the counterpart.

We may compare this situation to the experiences of physicians and patients with medically unexplained physical symptoms. Confronted by an indecipherable illness and suffering "in silence" because of this diagnostic uncertainty, the patient—and in parallel the anti-mafia force—may "create divergent narratives" in order to explain "unfathomable symptomology" (Atkins et al. 2013: 3). Until they have available a proper vocabulary through which they can share their concerns with others, patients "exist in separate silos of awareness" from the medical practitioners—as anti-mafia campaigners exist in "separate silos of understanding" from the mafia—even as both are "tackling the same situation" (Atkins et al. 2013: 5–6). It is to produce such a vocabulary that the cognitive effort or "work" that I name Mafiacraft was launched, with a consistent part of the Italian society, including some mafiosi (the so-called *pentiti*), in an attempt to find appropriate words and shared categories to describe this undiagnosable,[4] untreatable, unexplained (and thus devastating) social and political "symptom" called "the mafia."

This operation recalls the cognitive mapping proposed by Frederic Jameson (1991: 54), an aesthetic and ethical project capable of

---

3. "Work" is one of the meanings of the word *craft* in Mafiacraft, which defines the guidelines for my research program.

4. In a previous work, I analyzed the political and social implications of the nosographic representation of the mafia as a "plague" (Puccio-Den 2009).

"connecting seemingly disconnected or fragmented parts of changing and different experiences into one well focused entity" (Shuqair 2019: 361). In a similar fashion, Mafiacraft is an attempt at cognitive mapping: it aims to describe how a range of widespread illegal practices (aggression, extortion, smuggling, money laundering, fraud, murder) and social phenomena (corruption, poor governance, territory degradation, market deterioration) have been publicly "grouped" or "counted-as-one" (Badiou 2005: 4), by lawyers, artists, activists, politicians, journalists, or plain citizens who identify the mafia as a special kind of criminal association and a mafioso as a member of a mafia-type association. Cognitive mapping and Mafiacraft share another feature: both address a "subject" that "does not exist" (Jameson 1990: 347). Does this mean that mafiosi have a point when they challenge those asking whether they had been part of the mafia (as in the epigraphs above) to produce evidence of its existence? Is it their way of raising the ontological issue of *orders of reality* in which things and beings *exist*? Recalling Hirschauer's (2006: 414) central thesis that "ethnographic writing puts something into words that, prior to this writing, did not exist in language," we might wonder about the role of ethnographic writing in stabilizing "things" which *do not exist* in the language of the very people or groups we study (those we call "mafiosi" do not identify themselves to this social and legal category, neither do they speak about "mafia" when they refer to their association). Nevertheless, the writing process that was undertaken by the anti-mafia movement has had ontological implications for the mafia object that cannot be ignored.

How does the use of speech and silence define social spaces? In a study on public discourse in the 1970s, Shirley Ardener (1975: viii–ix) argues that, because this tended to be characteristically male-dominated and the appropriate language registers seemed "encoded" by males, women were at a disadvantage when wishing to express matters of particular concern to them. One of the contributors to her edited book, Edwin Ardener (1975a, 1975b), drew on the concept of "muted group" as suggested by Charlotte Hardman to speak about women's lack of communication skills to portray their own world in their own words (see also S. Ardener 1975: xii). This notion of a muted group functions as an umbrella term: other groups in society may also be effectively muted. This pioneering feminist work[5] provides a critical conceptual framework

---

5. It is noteworthy that, during my first fieldwork on female carnivals and gender construction in Europe, I experienced how women found a way of expression in forms other than direct expository speech (Puccio 2002).

with which to view the mafia as a muted group. Just as the women and men in Hardman's models and "counterpart models," the mafia and the state seem to operate in different political and conceptual spaces. This is certainly due to the absence of what Shirley Ardener (1975: ix) calls the "suitable code." Therefore, what Mafiacraft endeavors to tell are narratives of codes and translations, of encoding and deciphering, of silencing and *voicing*.

The mafia, as we saw, cannot be directly and empirically perceived. As a muted group, it also has no "independent existence": it can only take form when "clothed" (Ardener 1975: xx) in cultural patterns of behavior and communication shaped by society and the state. One of these cultural patterns, in my view, is *omertà*, silence, shaped by the state in order to grasp an elusive language practice *on its own terms*, one somewhat acritically adopted by "specialists" of the mafia phenomenon, thereby carelessly falling back on conventional moral and intellectual understandings of silence. Mafiacraft, in turn, points out the gap between the academic discourse on the mafia, on the one hand, and the everyday experience of the latter's silent presence in the life of activists, photographers, citizens, lawyers, and magistrates.

Feminist theory seems to offer possible ways forward in the particular field of research designed as mafia studies. But a distinction must be made. If we simply apply Shirley Ardener's framework to describe the mafia as a muted group, we run the risk of remaining trapped in a binary model. Mafiacraft is rather based on the assumption that there is a strong interconnection between mafia, on the one hand, and society and the state, on the other. Indeed, Mafiacraft will not consider society and state as separate entities, to ensure that it does not succumb to the pressure of the "state effect" to conceive the state as a "free-standing object, located outside society" (Mitchell 2006: 169). In Ardener's words, the "dominant group" and the "dominant model" together form the "dominant structure." It follows that the "muted group" and the "counterpart model" together form a muted or "subdominant structure" (S. Ardener 1975: xxii n 4). Sociological and even anthropological research on the mafia tend to describe it as a "sub-culture," and *omertà* as one of the main expressions of this sub-culture, a negative expression of the self, a passive resistance to the state. These studies can indeed be valuable. Nevertheless, by locating the mafiosi in the overall ideological framework of the dominant culture, they miss the *specific forms of agency* mafiosi may deploy by the performative use of silence. A genuine anthropological survey ought to be concerned with what silence is on the terms of its users:

5

what is at stake when people use silence instead of words as a social skill, when people "give up on words" (Basso 1970)?

Mafiacraft carefully examines the modalities of action, language, and silence of both the "speaking" and the "muted" groups through the study of their relationships. It is important to underline that this relationship has not been unvarying. It has changed over time, according to specific *situations* this book describes and analyzes. In 1970, anthropologist Keith Basso analyzed certain types of situations in which members of western Apache society "gave up on words." These situations—minutely, ethnographically described, where silence appeared as a socially shared behavior—were all marked by ambiguity about the status of the people involved, by uncertainty and unpredictability. This book takes up Basso's (1970: 214) challenge to study more widely such "acts of silence" and the "social contexts where silence occurs," by developing them further from the point of view of political and moral anthropology.

Omertà as a folk "act of silence"?

Before embarking on this enterprise, it is necessary to question widely accepted ideas about silence, or its local expression, *omertà*. In the rhetoric of folklorist Giuseppe Pitrè (1841–1916), aimed at defending Sicily against Italian attacks, *omertà* (the quality of being a man or *omu*) is a performative, and basically positive, non-speech act against the law and its representatives (demonstrating that a real man does not need to be protected by the law). Mafiacraft conceives silence as a communication tool between mafia and the state, rather than as a local means to resist the nation state. Refusing to talk does not necessarily signal the impossibility of interaction between mafia members and state representatives. Instead, *omertà* appears to constitute an alternative non-verbal route through which another modality of communication might be established. This modality of political action, the powerful act of non-speech, can be used by mafiosi as a political strategy as well as by members of the state itself. Considering silence as a political practice to be observed and studied is thus a way to de-ideologize it. The very object of Mafiacraft is not "the silence" as such, nor the speech acts and writing events (Fraenkel 2002) aimed at fighting it: it is the meaningful and unexplored realm that lies between these two poles, between silence and speech (Kidron 2009: 19), between the mafia and the state.

Basing her conclusions upon a long tradition, in the wake of Pitrè, anthropologist Maria Pia Di Bella (2008: 75–86) postulates that *omertà*, a mafioso's supreme attribute, has been rooted in a continuum and constitutes the extreme growth-point of a local culture, encapsulated within a relationship of defiance toward a central state perceived as being foreign or inimical. Nearly a century before her analysis, political scientist Giuseppe Alongi ([1886] 1977: 5) declared that the "ways in which the Maffia [sic] seeks to inhibit the legal process"—since the notion of *omertà* precluded approaching the justice system to resolve disputes—simply exacerbated the reticence of all Sicilians, or almost all of them, to have recourse to the law. As a folk act linked to popular Sicilian culture, *omertà* blinds us to the fact that power is built not only on language (Barthes 2005: 12) but also on silence. By deconstructing *omertà*, this cultural category shaped by folklorists, sociologists, and anthropologists, Mafiacraft examines how this unpredictable and unfathomable symptom called "the mafia" was diagnosed by the state and, concurrently, how it was itself occulted by the same ambiguous entity. Here Mafiacraft intersects with "statecraft," pointing up the powerful techniques through which the state creates *things* by naming them (Bourdieu 2012, quoted by Santoro 2019), at the same time as obliterating whole swathes of reality by denying them the legitimacy to *exist*.

"What is the mafia?"

Since the unification of Italy in 1871, certain phenomena—such as impunity for crimes (as when committed with the complicity of political power or by organized crime with the capacity to exert territorial control and sustain military-style operations), violent "protection," assassinations not easily ascribed to their perpetrators, intimidation, and other "silent acts"—have been classified by public authorities, local governments, the media, and social scientists (but never by those directly affected) under the common denominator of the "mafia." In reaction to this invisible threat, political scientists, not differently than public officers, investigators, and prosecutors, have endeavored to develop theories aimed at solving the following puzzle: "What is the mafia?" My aim here is not to produce an exhaustive analysis of the publications that have dealt with this issue. The output is indeed voluminous. Rather, the very profusion of ideas compulsively addressing the mafia is part of my research focus: namely, the *uncertain phenomenon* whose very existence was speculative for more than a century until the concept of the "mafia" was introduced into the Italian penal code. The Rognoni–La Torre law, promulgated in 1982, stipulates that the mafia is a criminal category and a special form of criminal association. The law chose this definition from a range of conflicting interpretations of the question, "what is the mafia?" I use the term "Mafiacraft" for a new form of inquiry that, rather than seeking an answer to this question, focuses on the questioning process itself, which includes explanations given by the social sciences, the law, legal proceedings, and at the grassroots level. What are the consequences of this questioning process on the ontology of the silent "things" it endeavors to define? More generally, what happens when a silent phenomenon, which may *exist* "only in its own moment of occurrence" (Geertz, quoted by Hirschauer 2006: 417), is solidified by its "inscription" in another order of reality? Is this process always fruitful or can we identify some "blind spots" where the fleetingness of the social action *resists* its *fixation* into a stable empirical referent?[6]

At this point, I would like to make clear a distinction I propose between specific examples of the social and criminal relationships defined by the state as mafia-type organizations—Cosa Nostra, 'Ndrangheta, Camorra, Sacra Corona Unita, if we confine ourselves to Italy—and the "mafia" as a broader social, cultural, and political phenomenon whose contours are blurred by silence (that is where part of its performativity lies). Mafia-type associations, wherever they are located in the world, can be studied and compared as particular types of secret societies (Simmel 1906) or, following Gambetta (1993), as a particular form of organized crime that produces and trades in private protection; organizational analysis may thus be preferred over any other perspective (Catino 2019). But the mafia phenomenon needs to be studied in a broader framework that includes epistemology as well as cognitive sciences and law, with the methodological suspension of the "what it *is*" question and a focus on how this type of questioning has reshaped social and political reality. This is not to say that the mafia is not a social fact but that its changing contours not only make it difficult to say what exactly it is but also carry the political essence of the problem. The work of setting and resetting these contours lies at the core of the Mafiacraft project.

---

6. Hirschauer (2006: 436) warns that "the verbalization of the silent does not come without a basic transformation of the object."

The manner in which the "mafia question" was raised in Italy entailed not only innovative forms of mobilization, substantial modifications in the structure of the justice system, and fundamental changes at a political level, but also new forms of knowledge. Changing epistemological frameworks and paradigm shifts to approaching and conceptualizing the phenomenon of the mafia led to the transformation of judicial categories, moral values, current practices, and codes of behaviors. The relationship between legal and illegal, the boundaries between licit and illicit, the conditions governing social and political life, and the very essence of humanity were challenged by the question, "what is the mafia?" What is the broader cultural and intellectual context in which the mafia became a subject of law, capable of bearing the burden of responsibility (Puccio-Den 2017a)? The criminalization of the mafia in 1982 profoundly altered the ontological conditions of this research topic and was not without consequences for the practice of anthropology. Before this watershed moment it is possible that anthropologists did not fully recognize the odd situation that required them to produce an ethnography of "something" that *did not exist.* Twenty-four years after the publication of his monograph, *The Mafia of a Sicilian Village* (1974), Anton Blok returned to his field site of Contessa Entellina. His position as an outsider, the fact that he showed only an indirect interest in the mafia (initially his research was on traditional land tenure systems), and probably also lack of mastery of the local languages (Italian and Sicilian) allowed him to engage in the patient work of silent observation which, coupled with an accurate study of the archives, provided data for reconstructing the history of several families that formed "the backbone of the rural mafia" (Blok 2001a: 62). But it is indeed not clear if there was consent or discrepancy regarding the local use of the term "mafia," the way it appeared in written sources produced by the state, and the meaning it had for the so-called mafiosi.

It was not until the 1980s that *pentito* (repentant mafioso) Tommaso Buscetta explained that "the word mafia is a literary creation. The real mafiosi are simply called 'men of honor'; their association is called Cosa Nostra" (Arlacchi 1992: 15). In so doing, Buscetta engaged his counterpart, Judge Giovanni Falcone, in a genuine ethnographic relationship. Buscetta opened up new ways for Judge Falcone to grasp the mafia, which crystalized in the "Buscetta theorem," a controversial yet effective description of what the mafia is. Following the example of this magistrate—to whom I dedicate this book—I do not assume a dominant position as a social scientist but rather acknowledge the "critical competencies" and skills of actors (Boltanski 1990), assigning to myself the task of describing their intellectual, cognitive, and moral universe through their deeds and actions.

Two other anthropologists studied social reform and transformation processes in rural Sicily, elucidating the birth of the local mafia by the conflicts that erupted between local interest groups and centralized power after the unification of the Italian state in 1861. In their monograph of Sambuca (1976), Jane Schneider and Peter Schneider took into account not only economic factors but also cultural patterns such as honor and friendship, local customs, and Mediterranean values. Analyzing speech regimes that made the mafia *exist* in local inter-knowledge networks—in which they were, for better or worse, involved, just as many other inhabitants of Sambuca were—was but a side interest of their work. But many years later, during an interview I conducted with them in Palermo in 2002, they remembered their occasional participation at banquets or other ceremonies held by local figures known as *intisi* (mafiosi). What was a possible way of doing fieldwork for them in the early 1970s became formally forbidden after 1982 when being an *intiso* became a crime. The law marked a point of no return for the anthropology of the mafia by situating it in the realm of criminal studies, moral and political anthropology, and legal anthropology..

My ethnographic inquiry came "after Falcone," that is to say, at a historical moment when the epistemological and moral conditions of all research on the mafia had already changed profoundly compared to the first fieldwork conducted by foreign anthropologists in the 1970s. Mafiacraft takes up the epistemological model founded by Falcone and the methodological approach pursued by the anti-mafia judges in their inquiries in order to analyze the way in which the latter structure the question, "what is the mafia?" Here epistemology and ethics converge, since the answers that were found to this question, from one inquiry to the next and one trial to the next, completely altered the "moral economies" (Fassin 2009) of Italian society.

The belief that drives Mafiacraft is that the mafia phenomenon deserves to be approached by adopting a wider, interdisciplinary perspective, which takes into account its specific epistemology and ontology. Works by such folklorists as Pitrè ([1889] 1944), convinced of the local anchorage of the mafia, drew on the "traditional culture" of Sicily (proverbs, beliefs, and practices). But to overlook the political nature of the mafia, reducing it to a mere cultural fact, is to miss its essence. Sociologists, generally speaking, neglected to ground their theories in empirical data, "difficult to harvest," and more importantly, they also failed to subject the categories of "mafia" and "mafioso" they used to critical scrutiny, limiting themselves to using them as they appeared in the sources (Arlacchi 2007). Ethnography, risking being swamped by the theorizing, almost disappears in their works. Historians thought they would bypass this limitation by accessing archives, but failed to question the historical conditions of the categorization process generated by the introduction of the words "mafia" and "mafioso" into the Italian political language (Lupo 1999, 2007). More recently, some anthropologists conducted participant observation in Sicilian villages marked by the historical presence of the "mafia," believing that meeting some "mafiosi" would enrich their experience (Rakopoulos 2018). Yet they fell into their own trap because of their lack of understanding of the social (and legal) contexts and situations of "talk and silence" they encountered (Puccio-Den 2019a), and for failing to comprehend the logical paradox that meeting a member of a secret (and criminal) society creates. Thus, the "mafiosi" presence (and possibility of meeting them) in fieldwork remains highly speculative, as fleeting and elusive as the presence of "witches" in other contexts.

Faced with this evanescent object, another line of anthropological inquiry is available even though it has received less attention: the ethnographer can explore the "mafia" by indexing the conjectures and speculations around this mysterious entity, describing the acts (social, judicial, or graphic) performed in the attempt at "breaking the silence" in and around this secret phenomenon, and at solving the multiple problems linked to its indeterminacy (impunity, invisibility, irrepresentability).

Ethnographing the silence

My inquiry began in the mid-1990s when I conducted participant observation while personally engaged, as an Italian citizen, in the political struggle against the mafia, incorporating, in at least some respects, the principles of activist research as delineated by Charles Hale (2001). I believe that my insider status as a Sicilian woman facilitated my entry into my fieldwork as I was introduced not simply as an anthropologist but also as a person sharing the same concerns and values regarding the anti-mafia struggle for justice. But this methodological choice was also linked to the moral discomfort and practical difficulty of describing "from the inside" a secretive criminal world. In contrast, doing an ethnography of the anti-mafia movement and interviewing anti-mafia judges and allies was not always effortless but was at least possible.

First I undertook ethnographic fieldwork on the practices of anti-mafia activists. I then widened the perimeter of my research to include the practices of anti-mafia judges who were facing the same problem, namely how to expose a silent and hidden phenomenon. From a certain point in Italy's contemporary history onward, descriptions of the mafia phenomenon became part of the legal framework of judicial responsibility. In this stage I examined the investigative tools and devices developed by the judiciary and the actions of civil society as joint endeavors, not only to demonstrate that the *mafia exists* but also to get a sense of *what it is made of.* The data collected made clear that another line of research was necessary, namely one of anti-mafia photography as a political and cognitive act to fix the meaning of the mafia in images.

I have interpreted both the practices of the anti-mafia movement and of mafia trials as social and cognitive attempts—forms of cognitive mapping—to grasp an unsettling phenomenon that gains some of its power of fascination from its capacity to elude any form of definition. The logocentric paradigm on which the social sciences are based must allow effective representation of "silence as a medium of expression, communication, and transmission of knowledge" (Kidron 2009: 7). Since I realized that the anti-mafia movement and anti-mafia trials relied on the power of words and images to dispel the frightening, nebulous threat borne by the word "mafia," I deduced that the performative power of silence relies on the possibility of maintaining this state of troubling confusion. For several years, I observed protests and demonstrations, analyzed pedagogical devices and practices of remembrance, followed criminal investigations and legal proceedings, and consulted pieces of expertise, deeds, and other legal documents. This fieldwork was carried out and inspired by the consciousness that all these practices for fighting and judging the silence were, in fact, shaped by it. Through these activities, steered toward transforming the tacit traces of the mafia into explicit texts of its harmful presence in the world, it may be possible to grasp the way in which the mafia *works* silently. Are materially objectified symbols of this "plague," embodied forms of witnessing, practices of anti-mafia memories, and the mute interactions of mafiosi with the judiciary valid ethnographic *evidence* of the silent life of the mafia? All these endeavors, only partly successful, have evidenced how silence *resists* its translation into shared knowledge, public experience, and narrative processes.

I use the term "Mafiacraft," therefore, as a program for studying a range of activities and practices that reveal the relationship between the shaping of knowledge models, the transformation of moral and judicial categories, the modification of political structures, and the renewal of forms of mobilization. A top-down and a bottom-up logic exist in the anti-mafia project, and Mafiacraft is a way of connecting them in order to examine the multifaceted process of allocating responsibility for mafia misdeeds. From this point of view, Mafiacraft shares with witchcraft a special attention to "systems of accountability," as they were outlined by Mary Douglas (1980: 59) on the basis of E. E. Evans-Pritchard's work on the Azande and the Nuer, by describing the inferential chains, socially and mentally shaped in order to attribute unexplainable events occurring in "areas where uncertainty needs to be reduced." When tracing responsibility—to use Douglas's expression in relation to mafia crimes (Douglas 1980:12)—Mafiacraft intersects with witchcraft.

Mafiacraft vs witchcraft

The dominant paradigm in the social sciences, recalling the work undertaken by a historian such as Carlo Ginzburg, establishes a more or less explicit link between inquisitorial procedures of witch-hunting and anti-mafia inquiries: both procedures create categories (witches and mafiosi, respectively) aimed at "criminalizing" social behaviors, forms of relationship, and ways of acting. This representation is shared by a broad cross-section of civil society, yielding to the romantic view of the mafia as a cultural fact, under the guise of critiquing the state. But, this view prevents critical thinking and political awareness. It misses its target because the mafia as seen across its history is not an expression of local culture subdued by the state but rather a political configuration in which the state is actively involved, and which the state strives to safeguard.[7] By focusing its attention on the state's acts of silence (see, in particular, chapter 9), Mafiacraft is an inverted paradigm of witchcraft. Nevertheless, recent innovative work shows that in many settings across the world witchcraft is rooted in the intimacy of the house, the family, and the neighborhood but also provides secret openings to the outer world. It

---

7. See the work of Umberto Santino (1992, 1994, 1995, 1998, 2000a, 2000b), whose approach to the mafia phenomenon is shared by anti-mafia Judge Roberto Scarpinato (Lodato and Scarpinato 2008), many anti-mafia magistrates (Di Lello 1994), and many Italian researchers, such as Alessandra Dino (2009).

flourishes at the intersection between national and local government systems, exposes the contradictions of the growth but also neoliberal weakness of the state (Geschiere 2013), thus offering a striking parallel with the mafia.

When lawyers tried to define "what the mafia is," they approached the mafia through its *manifestations*: unlike social researchers, they did not essentialize this "thing" ("our thing," Cosa Nostra) but rather took the viewpoint that certain forms of behavior *manifest* its *presence*. The presence of this conduct or the use of these "methods" were taken to prove—in law, if not in fact—an individual's membership of a mafia-type association (Article 416 *bis* of the Italian Penal Code), the latter seen as the *logical* consequence of the former (if someone belongs to the mafia, then the mafia exists). However, these behaviors defining what a mafioso (and consequently what the mafia) *is*, remain no less difficult to prove. More than acts, these behaviors are *non-acts* or acts that are not (necessarily) realized, such as *intimidation* (silent threats, effective because they use words in a minimalistic way); *non-words* or words unspoken, such as in *omertà*; and *subjugation*, a *condition* all the more terrifying for the lack of words it implies in the mafia world. The Rognoni–La Torre law nevertheless marked a considerable advance at an ontological level since it amounted to a *tautological demonstration* of the existence of the mafia (Turone 2008: 25), in law and in fact. At this level of analysis, Mafiacraft is close to witchcraft, both paradigms concerned with the way in which the legal system qualifies certain behaviors in order to provide the ontological foundation to social categories with uncertain contours (the witch or the mafioso). In both cases, the law plays a founding and structuring role, by punishing the maleficent power of words, which constitutes the very substance of this type of phenomenon (Favret Saada 1980), or the deadly force of silence, which constitutes the essence of the mafia. We may then ask ourselves the following question: is the mafioso not like the witch for being unjustly blamed for an *indirect* action whose evidence is only conjectural?

When we consult the court documents, we can note the colossal effort made by the prosecuting judges to establish precisely, on a case-by-case basis, the *connection* between silent acts of speech and harmful actions, silent mafia orders, and spectacular mafia murders. But there is an essential element that distinguishes witches from mafiosi. Where the "witch is the effect of a speech act" (Siegel 2006: 219), the mafioso *goes beyond words*: he acts with *real* weapons. "The boy was not a witch before he was called one," states James Siegel, anthropologist of witchcraft

(2006: 218); neither was the mafioso, we might say. Nevertheless, the latter was not only using the power of silence to *symbolically* dominate their fellows. What precisely do the mafiosi *do*—besides *intimidating, keeping silent* and *silencing, subjugating* and *being subjugated* to an authority other than the state (calling into question its very sovereignty)—to deserve the penal attention of prosecuting judges and the alarm of citizens? Mafiosi kill, defraud, attack, whitewash, pollute, alter, corrupt, ruin…in other words, they are inscribed in the real, manipulating and modifying it, and leaving *traces* that can be constituted as *proofs* of action, not generically harmful but criminal according to the norms in force in our democratic states.

Some eminent voices have drawn parallels between anti-mafia justice—or the fight against terrorism, which inspired its proceedings—and the inquisitorial system (Ginzburg 2002; Sciascia 2002). However, the judicial struggle against the mafia did not criminalize "innocent" popular practices, as in the case of the nocturnal agrarian cults of Friuli, transformed into "witchcraft" by the Inquisition (Ginzburg 1983), or the elucubrations of a literate miller, transformed into "heresy" by the same repressive institution (Ginzburg 1980). Anti-mafia justice, supported by the anti-mafia movement and in the same liberating spirit, revealed the *connection* between certain *proven* crimes and certain individuals who evaded any criminal qualification and judicial control, sometimes with the assistance or complicity of the state. The social and legal *work* that Mafiacraft follows makes it possible to absorb this discrepancy between a "signifier totality" and a "signified" reality. This is the main difference with witchcraft: "there is always a non-equivalence or 'inadequation' between the two, a non-fit and overspill which divine understanding alone can soak up" (Lévi-Strauss, quoted in Siegel 2006: 214). "Witchcraft accusations succeed as poetry does, summoning up a word before there is a thing" (Siegel 2006: 228); mafia accusations, in contrast, succeed in summoning up a word *after* there was a *thing*. Witchcraft is a technique for dealing with the "uncanny," to cast it in Freudian terms, as Siegel (2006: 229) did; Mafiacraft describes the deductive and symbolic process of attributing a fixed meaning to the uncanny ability of some people, namely the "mafiosi," to dominate without effective power.

Mafiacraft takes into account the renewal of this conceptual framework by anthropologists such as Siegel and Peter Geschiere, whose innovative findings were achieved by paying attention, on the one hand, to the political implications of the cognitive operations involved in witchcraft and, on the other, to the way it has been formulated in indigenous languages. Both categories—the witch and the mafioso—arise during moments of *crisis* in which the definition of social reality has lost its meaning. Remember that the mafia phenomenon is linked with the overturning of power relationships entailed by the birth of the modern Italian nation-state. Geschiere's work on Cameroon (Geschiere 1998, 2000) has shown to what extent witchcraft, rather than being a manifestation of local tradition, is an expression of the complex political relationship entangling villages and the African state: a way to deal with growing social inequality, wealth accumulation processes, and the change of political elites burgeoning in the wake of modernization (Geschiere 2005). Siegel's (2006) work on witch-hunts in Java after the fall of Suharto depicts these as a process of "naming the witch." By adopting Claude Lévi-Strauss's "quasi-linguistic point of view," Siegel (2006: 2–3) explains witchcraft as "an attempt to make expressible something which ordinarily could only be suspected": namely, the undetermined menace of death. Looking for an answer to unanswerable questions (Why me? Why now?), people "find the witch to whom the event is attributed": they identify a name for the setback "which happen[ed] for no reason, and therefore proceed[ed] from no place namable." But this "attempt to name something unnamable" is not always successful; it can fail. When this occurs, the negative event remains "behind any possibility of signification," "leaving 'witch' as a concept without a content" (Siegel 2006: 8–10, 2).

Let us recall the provocative answer given by Cosa Nostra member Gerlando Alberti when questioned by the police in the early 1980s about the mafia: "The mafia? What is the mafia? A brand of cheese?" In Italy, the process of attributing responsibility for "mafia crimes" entailed the attribution of a name, a shape, a structure, a physiognomy, in a word, a *body* capable of *incarnating* the "mafia," following the conceptions of personhood prevailing in western Christian societies. The question at stake—similar to the one raised in the epigraphs above (for provocation is always meaningful in the mafia world)—is how to *incarnate* the invisible, how to provide a body for "something" that you can neither see nor touch, that you cannot "drink nor eat," that is only a label covering a vacuum of evidence—the mafia—a concept without content, we might say. Christians have created rituals to drink and eat the Body of Christ, and mysteries to solve the mystery of the presence of God in His absence.[8] How can one provide this volatile and

---

8. I explore the issue of the incarnation in Puccio-Den (2009).

mysterious "thing" some call the "mafia" with a "body of evidence" fit to bear the burden of responsibility? The purpose of this book is to describe the successful process of "naming the mafia" by giving this "floating" concept a fixed content. From 1982 onward, the word "mafia," a "signifier with indefinite, infinite references," to quote Siegel (2006: 10) again, was stabilized by the law. From this moment on—as we will see in the second part of this book—every anti-mafia trial put this definition to the test.

Witchcraft arises when the certainty of the conventional link between a "signifier" (witch) and a "signified" (harm, for which he or she is supposed to be responsible) fails. Meaning is no more taken for granted for such words as "witch," so that "its usage has to be established each time" (Siegel 2006: 219). Mafiacraft starts when the uncertainty of the signified linked to the signifier (the mafia) is removed. A closer look at the word "mafia" reveals that, since its origins, it has been tightly connected with the semantic field of witchcraft. Indeed, the first occurrence of this term (*Maffia*) appears in a document of 1658 as the nickname of a sorceress, "magàra', thus a woman devoted to magical practices" (Sciascia 2013: 16). Since then, the most variegated origins, etymologies, and meanings have been attributed to the word, some of them carrying negative connotations (arrogance, from the Arabic *mahias*; or cavern, where seditious people meet, from the Arabic *maha*), others positive ones (protection of the weak, from the Arabic *mahaf^at*; or beauty, courage, superiority, from the Greek *morphē*). What is important here is not to establish the correct etymology but to point out, first, the extreme variability of meanings attached to the word "mafia," and, second, that its transmutation from a positive to a negative signification occurred with the creation of the Italian nation-state in 1861, a change in meaning that Pitrè ([1889] 1944: 292) deeply regretted. From this moment onward, the term "mafia" is intended to mean a criminal underworld, as in Giuseppe Rizzotto's play *I mafiusi de la vicaria* from 1863 where the term "mafioso" was used for the first time. In 1865, the phrase *delitto di mafia* (mafia crime), as used by the prefect of Palermo, Filippo Antonio Gualterio, already indicated a form of organized crime where the order to kill is dissociated from the execution of the murder, leaving the motive of the killing obscure.

At a certain point in Italian history, a number of specific political situations were labelled as being "mafia," thus raising the issue of "what is the mafia?" Answering this question required not only paying careful attention to the arguments developed by anti-mafia prosecutors and the models they shaped but also to the various tools that social actors from many professional and cultural backgrounds employed to produce *evidence* of the mafia. The line of inquiry pursued here traces the links between these grassroots activities and the allocation of mafia liability by state institutions. This book is divided into two parts to highlight the distinction between these two arenas, the social and the judicial, investigated during different phases of my research. But rather than keeping these two spheres separate, I have decided to collate them into this volume in order to emphasize the considerable overlap between these two different kinds of processes for allocating social and legal responsibility. The definition of the mafia as formulated by prosecutors and lawyers eventually prevailed, but the capacity of other social actors—including mafiosi, as we see in chapter 10—to produce their own conceptions, traces, and proofs of the mafia's existence, and their skill in shaping and managing alternative meanings and frameworks of responsibility (or irresponsibility), should not be ignored. Mafiacraft follows the various stages—including the setbacks, blows, forward and backward leaps—of this creative process of detecting and naming the unnamable and its damaging powers by describing the nexus of the singular events that caused harm.

However, the attempt at understanding what is said *about* the mafia—like in the case of witchcraft (Siegel 2006; 22)—must not overshadow what is left unsaid, and especially *how* it is left unsaid. The mafia owes its power of fascination to our inability to grasp it fully. Every trial opens but also limits this cognitive performance. Mafiacraft follows the work that the word "mafia" performs, from the maximum expansion of an "evil" corresponding with the Evil (or with the Divine Providence from the point of view of the mafiosi, as we will see in the last chapter), to the extent permitted by law, describing how the indescribable and indecipherable political experience called the "mafia" was successfully identified, even if the latter continues to generate inexplicable harms, leaving the mafia as something that we may fail to recognize. This action of silencing or "invisibilizing" acts of political violence is more akin to the methods used by dictatorial regimes in Central and Latin America to *conceal evidence* of bodies that "disappeared" rather than to procedures invented to *create the evidence* needed to legally prosecute "popular culture."

There are two categories of misconceptions in mafia studies: the essentialist assumption, that the mafia *is* something and that this can be exposed, and the constructivist presupposition, where it is considered a *mere construction* (possibly a legal one). Mafiacraft adopts a stance of methodological agnosticism equidistant from both of these "beliefs" and rather sets itself the task of following the work of how bodies of evidence of the mafia's existence and nature are produced (or hidden). For this reason the body and embodiment play a central role in Mafiacraft.

Mafiacraft: An embodied history of silence

Statements, claims, moral issues, or paradigms do not just float in the air; they are incarnated in bodies and objects. In 1992, when two judges, Giovanni Falcone and Paolo Borsellino, were murdered after their success in gaining legal confirmation for the Buscetta theorem (an innovative framework of responsibilities introduced to prosecute mafia crimes), tens of thousands of people demonstrated in the streets carrying banners and flags bearing the phrase, *Le vostre idee camminano sulle nostre gambe* (your ideas walk on our legs). These bodies in movement substantiated the theorems and principles that the two magistrates had upheld. Civil society came to support the judiciary, its criminal justice reports, and sentences or legislation when it came to assigning mafia's liability relying on many and various "writing events" (Fraenkel 2002).[9] Mafiacraft follows the judicial, graphic, literary, and moral processes of naming and identifying the workings of the mafia in a social body inhabited by silence. Part I—on naming the mafia—prompts the reader to engage with anti-mafia activism not only through direct ethnographic observation but also through ethnographic material that gives concrete or ontological anchoring to the abstract idea of the mafia. Part II—on judging the silence—traces and maps how responsibility for the violent power of the mafia is attributed, by examining inquiries, trials, and "affairs," and brings to the forefront other actors, such as anti-mafia judges, pentiti, and non-repentant mafiosi.

Mafiacraft is a theoretical enterprise that draws on a wide spectrum of ethnographic material that shows how moral stances, cognitive categories, and political emotions are embodied in things and objects without which they could not *exist*. In this sense, the issue of the mafia's existence

---

9. My focus on the material support of statements is grounded in the notion of "writing acts" as derived from Austin's speech act theory (1962), following the path set out by French anthropologist Béatrice Fraenkel (2007).

itself contains and generates the issue of the social existence of every-thing and anything that cannot be directly and empirically experienced (friendship, love, God) save through traces of *evidence*. Studying the mafia confronts us with the methodological dilemmas and theoretical difficul-ties of doing ethnographic research in situations where words are of no use to understand what is at stake. In such situations, the ethnographer can use reflexivity as a tool to grasp what they experience within silence. As in a hall of mirrors, the contradictions and conundrums experienced during fieldwork of what is silent provides openings onto much broader theoretical issues for anthropology. Thinking reflexively about responses to the question "What is the mafia?" may also be useful to highlight oth-er contexts of action whose meaning is not fixed or where the relation-ship between words and things is unbalanced. Rooted in a questioning of ritual action and theatrical performances (Puccio 2002; Puccio-Den 2009), nourished by other parallels and ongoing works on dance and art as forms of social action that becloud the relationship between the signi-fier and the signified (Puccio-Den forthcoming), the mafia, seen from an anthropological point of view, is not an altogether different phenomenon because of its criminal status, which is also a situational and historical effect of its recent classification as such in the Italian penal code. The mafia is probably not a brand of cheese, but the mafiosi are correct in challenging us to reflect on our ways of labeling reality.

The Mafiacraft project aims to reach the mafia beyond the reflective screens of the state and society as the entity it deals with does not of-fer its own self-representation. In chapter 10, I will give deeper insight into the moral world of the mafiosi through the rare traces they them-selves produce. Nevertheless, a study of a "muted group" (be they women, ethnic minorities, or mafiosi) ought definitively not to be a subordinate kind of social anthropology. Mafia challenges many assumptions and principles of the modern state, leading to study other values, behaviors, and models present in obscured and secret worlds, by developing new strategies of inquiry capable of hearing their specific tongue: silence. It is also a challenge for general anthropology in dealing with the "non-verbal dimension of social reality" (Hirschauer 2006: 436), which entails a seri-ous engagement with the consequences of our scientific language: How do we translate into words practices that do not need words to *exist*, practices that are tacit, unspeakable, or ineffable? How do we document silence (Kidron 2009)? What scope and force does silence have? How does it resist, contend with, or capitulate to the strength of words or the force of law?

Mafiacraft is an anthropological life project, a body of work on the mafia and the anti-mafia movement and justice that has taken shape over a long period of time, interwoven to create a unique tapestry in which the diverse elements enrich and support each other, arranged into a new kind of creative thinking. In so doing, I abide by the model established by Falcone's inquiry in Sicily (Puccio 2001): for the magistrate, the breakthrough was elicited not from conducting new investigations but from allowing all pieces of the jigsaw to fall into place. Under the rubric "Mafiacraft," I return to the research I have been carrying out over the last twenty years, including both ethnographic studies and epistemological reflections. My aim is to understand silence as a special form of agency or *regime of action*. As in the case of the secret, which cannot exist without leaving "secretions" (Zempleni 1996), silence cannot *exist* from either an ontological or a social point of view without leaving *traces*. Ethnographing silence through the verbal and non-verbal traces it leaves behind reconnects with Judge Falcone's key idea, the cornerstone of his revolutionary methods of investigating the mafia. Hopefully his legacy will allow us to improve the methodological skills required to tackle other silent objects.

A compass for the Mafiacraft reader

As previously mentioned, one methodological difficulty in undertaking research on the mafia is the absence of any commonly agreed definition of what the mafia actually *is*. This raises issues when it comes to defining the focus of study, demarcating a specific fieldwork site, or adopting a suitable methodology. Confronted with a plurality of interpretations, ethnographers may choose one over the others for the sake of credibility, or try to solve this conflict by acknowledging that it is part of the issue they wish to address: an elusive and fleeting phenomenon marked by *ontological uncertainty*. A starting point for a deeper understanding of the mafia phenomenon was, for me, when I began compiling an inventory of all available definitions and mapped their relevance in the social space. This allowed me to see how they were indexed to specific social, political, juridical, or scientific positions. Some trends could be at least partially attributed to a particular historical or political condition that affected the shaping of anti-mafia knowledge. These circumstances constituted an object of research in themselves. I placed special emphasis not only on contextualizing these statements about the mafia but also on identifying the conditions of intelligibility of the word "mafia" itself: what makes a verbal statement audible, understandable, acceptable, plausible, credible, or worthwhile in a certain context?

From the middle of the 1980s, texts, images, photographs, letters, theatrical and festive performances, books, police reports, and judicial acts all seemed to speak the same language, pointing to the responsibility of the mafia, its damaging nature, its dark side. Through these practices, anti-mafia activists not only substantiated the mafia's "existence," they also gave meaning to it. Cosa Nostra, "Our Thing," was no longer "our" thing: it was a social and political evil, and sometimes even an absolute and transcendent Evil. But all these *processes of responsibilization*, even if and when connected, should not be confused as phenomena situated at the same level. They did *exist* but—as the mafia—they operated at different levels of reality or in different spaces, tiered between fiction and reality. This implied understanding not only the power of symbols but also the *process of symbolization* per se: How do symbols work? What can they do and what can they *not* do? This issue would later contribute substantially to the recognition of the mafia as an ideology, drawing on religious symbols to create legitimacy, as examined in chapter 10. But at this stage, symbolization was a way to comprehend how people speak—and how they find new languages to speak—about traumatic, silent events. This question led to further ethnographic fieldwork on the role played by judges in the construction of a new paradigm for understanding and describing the "mafia plague," returning to the ontological issue and the question of proof. In the following, I give a sketch of each of the ten chapters and provide a first theoretical frame for the reader.

The ontological issue and the question of proof

Any procedure aimed at bringing the mafia to justice is based on the ontological presupposition that the mafia *exists*. The object of chapter 1 is to reveal the work of legal categorization and judicial testing that lawyers, judges, and experts were forced to carry out in order to substantiate this claim. This statement had consequences for the ontology of the people and entities on whom it is applied. Like the witch who "does not exist until he is pronounced" (Siegel 2006: 219), the mafiosi, and subsequently the mafia, changed status when they were named, when "what one suspected but could not name takes shape" (Siegel 2006: 220). This chapter shows what the implications of this assumption are for the "moral economies" of Italian society. I have borrowed this concept— revisited by Didier Fassin (2009) from the original sense of the word "oeconomia" as used by Edward P. Thompson (1991)—for its capacity to describe the organization of a social space in which moral norms, values, emotions, and sentiments are at play, and within its ambit to study the linkage between the different forces and actors involved. While taking into account the whole range of spheres involved in the mafia prob- lem (political, judicial, and media arenas along with many others), this chapter concentrates on the way in which the trials of the mafia and the mafiosi contribute to structuring the Italian moral landscape, mobilize ethical categories and their links with political values, and propose dis- tinctions between what is acceptable and what is not within the Italian body politic.

The controversies sparked off by these trials in the courtroom or, prior, in the chambers of examining magistrates demand a clear defini- tion of what is politically and morally at stake with any specific defini- tion of the mafia or its presumed members. The dissociation between instigator (the person who gave the order for a crime) and its executor, peculiar to mafia criminal action, had the effect of obscuring the very structure of the crime. It was necessary to rely on the knowledge of individuals aware of this structure—thus, necessarily, insiders to the mafia, given the organization's secret nature—to respond appropriately to the question "What is the mafia?" They could supply the names of others connected to whatever specific bloody event by allowing a new reading of those events within a much larger criminal project. This new paradigm for describing the mafia, the Buscetta theorem, postulates that the mafia association Cosa Nostra has a unitary and hierarchi- cal structure and is managed by the Commission, a decision-making assembly whose members decide on what murders need to be carried out.

The first court case against Cosa Nostra as such, the *Maxiprocesso* (Maxi Trial), initiated by Falcone and Borsellino (1986–1987), put the Buscetta theorem to the test. One of the obstacles to curbing mafia crime was not only the fact that the crime scenes often remained hidden—re- maining undiscovered by the state, as in so many ordinary crimes—but that these scenes were also often incomplete, leaving in the shadows what anti-mafia judge Roberto Scarpinato called the *ob-scene*, in a play on the Latin etymology of the Italian word *osceno* to mean both that which is offstage and that which is abominable: the space where deadly orders are issued from the top down and deadly resolutions are taken and acted upon. It is at this level that silence acts most effectively. These backstage areas frame the crime because without them and what happens within them the crime would more than likely not have taken place. According to some anti-mafia judges, it was this level—structuring and matrix-like at the same time—that judicial action needed to address if the anti-mafia struggle was to be effective and lasting.

A more audacious vision of the mafia as a highly organized criminal network supported by various sophisticated non-criminal powers (economic, financial, political) required the adoption of new legal tools constituting a new challenge for existing moral categories. Mafiacraft follows the work undertaken by lawyers and magistrates to soak up the "signifier surfeit" (Lévi-Strauss 1987: 63) of the word "mafia" by finding other mafia-related legal categories which *fit* the gray area around criminal facts. Nothing is ever definitely acquired because, as in the case of witchcraft, "there is another, still greater force, that remains unnamed"—in the case of the mafia conceptualized as "the third level," the political one. Nevertheless, the ontological issue was settled. In witchcraft, the "copula 'is' links anything with anything" (Siegel 2006: 228); in Mafiacraft the failure to signify was at least partly reduced: the mafia *is* something, and the mafia *is* or *exists*, even if its meaning remains controversial and needs to be tested anew in every trial.

The question "does the mafia exist" can also be answered by drawing on special kinds of imagery whose power to testify to the truth is socially recognized (Chapter 2). I use photography and an examination of the photographer's position as co-creator of a new iconography of the mafia to analyze the role that photography plays in constructing a visual order of mafia injuries (Chapter 3). I examine the shaping of the anti-mafia movement as a "witness community" to what exactly the mafia is (Chapter 4). And I discuss the difficulty of stabilizing the meaning of the word "mafia" by institutionalizing an anti-mafia memory without silencing a substantial part of the phenomenon (Chapter 5).

Reframing the mafia

During an initial phase of my inquiry, while I was shelving the issue of "what the mafia *is*" from an essentialist viewpoint, I explored the ways in which social perceptions of the mafia have shifted over time, first in Sicily and then in mainland Italy. Chapter 2, on reframing the mafia, accounts for this investigation. For an extended period prior to the law putting up its definition of the mafia, the debate was not structured around two different "persons" or entities, namely the state and the mafia. As with witchcraft, "there was no longer a second person who could mark the reception of one's speech and so confirm the existence of the I of the speaker. At that point, language was not delimited but unlimited, so that it meant everything and the opposite" (Siegel 2006: 227). This changed in the early 1980s when the mafia, considered a Sicilian way of being, a cultural trait, or a set of values (even positive, for some people), was increasingly identified as a form of social, political, and religious evil. But the term "perception" should not be misleading. My concern was not to grasp the social representations of the mafia but to launch an ethnographic survey into the different materials, devices, and tools used by diverse categories of social actors (from activists to artists, citizens to prosecutors, writers to politicians) in support of their claims. Mafiacraft is a material history of moral ideas, sensitive to their shifting over time.

Of course, there were spheres of competencies and areas of expertise that had to be investigated separately. But there were also interconnections that needed to be illuminated so as to discover the cognitive frame underpinning judicial inquiries, social mobilizations, and artistic performances: What was the relationship between the new theoretical models for explaining the mafia, as elaborated by the anti-mafia judges, which exposed its ramifications in and outside Sicily, and the new forms of anti-mafia activism forging social and political links across Italy? Was there a connection between the criminalization of the mafia as a social pathology and more fictional devices that drew on the historical and mythical image of the plague in order to depict the mafia as the symbol of political decay? What was the connection between the emergence of a new anti-mafia iconography that placed the struggle against the mafia within a religious frame, the blooming of devotional practices surrounding assassinated anti-mafia magistrates, and the birth of a new literary genre, the anti-mafia biography (or perhaps even the anti-mafia hagiography)?

Photographing the mafia

Many legal proceedings against the mafia took place before 1982, but they were never able to prove the existence of the mafia simply because the mafia *did not exist* in the Italian Criminal Code. As we saw above, it was only determined as a criminal organization with the Rognoni–La Torre law that was promulgated in 1982, in the wake of the killing of

General Carlo Alberto Dalla Chiesa. Sicilians as well as Italians were now forced to take a stand on the definition of the mafia, and to define their positions with respect to this "special type of criminal association." But before this legal revolution, how could one put on stage such a non-presented or unpresentable phenomenon as the mafia? Moving from an unofficial state of existence to an official one meant that new visual technologies began to have a huge impact on "moral economies." In chapter 3, on photographing the mafia, I consider the key role that the media played, by sketching how iconographic language transformed itself since the 1970s, examining how photo-reporters shifted their positions over time, and scrutinizing the political commitment implicit in the act of "photographing" the mafia, this silent, hidden, secret, and criminal phenomenon.

Photographing the mafia should be considered as a militant act deployed against the performative force of silence that acts as a sensory and emotional regime: if you do not see a reality, you suffer less. The spectator is not merely a viewer but someone likely to commit to a cause (Boltanski 1993). The reporter (journalist or photographer) is one type of spectator, an eyewitness who relates a story through statements and images to another spectator, a viewer, who amplifies with the emotional content he or she experienced. These statements and images express a particular concern for a topic, paving the way for a new mode of engagement. Emotions, senses, and thoughts produced by photographs thus built up a new moral community and created new narratives to tell what the mafia *is*.

Grassroots process of responsibilization

In chapter 4 I turn to grassroots processes of allocating responsibility for mafia deeds and crimes. Immediately after the Capaci massacre on May 23, 1992—which cost the lives of Judge Falcone, his wife Judge Francesca Morvillo, and three of their bodyguards—the magnolia tree in front of the assassinated judge's apartment was turned into a shrine. The Falcone Tree, as it came to be called, had become a place of devotion. Palermitans were joined by people from all over Italy in "pilgrimaging," as they said, to the shrine. Letters, writings, drawings, photos, and objects typical of "spontaneous shrines,"[10] such as candles, flags, sweets, and teddies, were tied to the trunk of the tree or laid in the flowerbed where

---

10. On sites of death and tragedy, see Jack Santino (2006).

the magnolia took root. For several years, I interrogated these objects as privileged testimonies of anti-mafia practices of mobilization.

On a global scale, the Falcone Tree can be compared to other memorial sites and graves, places of non-confessional pilgrimage that demand a reappraisal of this term and its boundaries, located between the secular and the religious (Margry 2008). But this was not the only appropriate point of comparison. Spain after Franco's dictatorship, dealing with the traumatic memory of the civil war, offered another case study and fieldwork site in which a tree—an oak this time—was used as metaphor and as point of connection structuring a fractured and wrenched society. In this country of Christian Europe, left-wing groups mobilized religious language, iconography, and symbols (Puccio-Den 2009). Closer to home, on Monte Pellegrino, overlooking the city of Palermo, letters and writings were placed on the altar of the city's patron saint, Saint Rosalia, during the annual pilgrimage on the anniversary of her death (Puccio 2007). By associating the memory of Falcone with the symbol of the tree, the anti-mafia activists situated the judge within the genealogy initiated by the Passion of Christ and used by saints, founders of monastic orders, and martyrs (Donadieu-Rigaut 2005: 205). But there is much more to it than that. Etymologically, a "martyr" is a witness (of God). Bearing witness means affirming the value of something through one's actions and words. The cult surrounding Judge Falcone constituted a fieldwork site for studying the grassroots production of *traces* of the mafia's existence. Writings and drawings, left by the "pilgrims" to Falcone's Tree, testified to an unprecedented situation in Sicily: the urgency to *bear witness*, at a time when mega-trials and legal proceedings were running against the mafia. It was in the literal sense that the commitment that "your ideas walk on our legs," undertaken with slain Judge Falcone, began to be honored as it was drawn onto banners and flags displayed at anti-mafia demonstrations. Pilgrims were "witnesses," not only in the Christian but also the legal sense. By moving and mobilizing themselves, by leaving their written testimonies, by *being there* they were demonstrating their support for the anti-mafia cause. Participating in this "literacy event" meant also bearing witness to the Buscetta theorem, confirming the existence of the mafia as a unitary, centralized criminal organization and denouncing its political supports.

Fleeting words, fleeting worlds

Looking to expand the scope of my research from a particular site—the Falcone Tree and the related Falcone Foundation—to the entire city, I

studied the ways in which anti-mafia history was inscribed in the topography of Palermo. In chapter 5, I examine the "fleeting words" of the
city, makeshift memorials that spontaneously emerged at the scenes of
murders perpetrated by the mafia. What was the relationship between
these spontaneous forms of commemoration and the commemorative
program instituted by the Italian state? In a broader context, what was
the public policy on writing about mafia victims?

There were essentially two aspects to this policy: one was educational,
involving educational activities in primary and secondary schools across
Sicily and Italy, while the other was based on town planning initiatives
that involved naming streets after mafia victims and, in the case of the
most prominent of these victims, erecting monuments in their names.
I examine these two aspects through, on the one hand, the pedagogical
initiatives inspired by the figure of Judge Falcone and, on the other, the
street-naming procedures in Palermo and the controversies it sparked.
In this chapter I explore Paul Ricœur's concept of *inscription*, the placing of a message, written or graphic, onto a physical medium (Ricœur
2000: 183). For this, I draw on Ricœur's emphasis of the relationship
between writing and space (Ricœur 2000: 527), which evokes Pierre
Nora's concept of *lieu de mémoire* (Nora 1984–1992).[11] I explore inscription in the broader sense of the word as a commemorative practice in the
Palermitan space, shedding light on the link between remembrance and
the place to which this remembrance is attached. How are family-scale
commemorative initiatives complemented by the commemorative policy
implemented by local authorities?

Even years after the Capaci massacre, letters and drawings were still
being laid down at the Falcone Tree, pinned to the bark, wrapped around
the trunk as far up as the arms would reach, placed on the ground before
it, and wedged between its roots. How could the persistence of these
writing practices be explained? How could we understand the meaning
of offerings, initially inspired by the heightened emotions after the mafia
attack, now that remembrance of the assassinated judge, organized and
shaped by the Giovanni and Francesca Falcone Foundation, had taken
on more institutionalized contours? Could the unsettled and shifting
forms of Judge Falcone's commemoration stabilize, and perhaps become

---

11. This concept of *lieu de mémoire* (place of remembrance) was first introduced
to the social sciences by *Les lieux de mémoire*, a work in several volumes
published under the supervision of Pierre Nora between 1984 and 1992.

fixed, through the institutionalization process launched by the Falcone Foundation?

For the fieldwork I consulted archived graphic materials held at the Falcone Foundation. Grounding my argument in the premise of the performativity of writing in post-traumatic contexts (Fraenkel 2002), I investigated not only what these writings *said* but also what they *did* (Austin 1970). I also used biographies of Falcone—produced by journalists with the help of citizens who played the role of "witnesses"—that aimed to reveal the dark, contentious, and controversial side of anti-mafia remembrance, erasing the internal conflicts within the government and its institutions in order to create national heroes. I considered the anti-mafia literature not as neutral but as a form of *political action*, a monument erected against acts of silencing stemming from different sectors of the state. The state and the judiciary were split into two fronts, as was the judiciary, both being the stage of a profound revolution which was above all a knowledge revolution.

From traces to proofs

As indicated above, judges and citizens have experimented with innovative modalities of mobilization and inquiry to provide an ontological basis for a social fact that *did not exist*. Some crimes (assault, murder) could be attributed to individuals on the basis of *signs* (weapons, drops of blood, personal items) traceable back to the executors, based on standard procedures for producing legally valid evidence. But activists and prosecutors understood perfectly well that the anti-mafia struggle revolved around words, definitions, descriptions, and statements. Judges, lawyers, and campaigners, aware of the performativity of silence, tried to oppose this through the force of words, on banners and placards, arrest warrants and sentences, or in anti-mafia laws. In chapter 6 I investigate how traces were turned into proofs acceptable as evidence in court.

Indeed, the most important anti-mafia judge did not merely anchor his control strategy in the power of words. The entire Falcone method is, in fact, a *heuristic of silence*. Because he himself was Sicilian, the judge knew what silence is made of and wherein its power lies; but he also knew its loopholes. Mafiosi do not speak—but they act, and their acting leaves *traces*, traces that can, where applicable, be transformed into *proof* of their criminal acts. The first phase of anti-mafia inquires sought to follow the mafia money trail left in national and international banking systems: this led to the first case filed and won against the mafia in the early 1980s, the Spatola Trial. While anthropologists of the period published monographs on the mafia in Sicily (Blok 1974; Schneider and Schneider 1976) based on field research and localized archival holdings, prosecuting judges formulated new responses to the question "What is the mafia," leading to the emergence of a model of globalized crime. This pioneering legal framework was aligned with the new social perception of the mafia as a global Evil, finding a shared matrix in the image of an epidemic contamination.

In reality both local and global models are pertinent for describing mafiosi action, which articulates the local and the global according to its own particular criminal or cultural logic (Campana 2011). Legal inquiries were indeed able to rely on their capacity to closely track the criminal action of the mafia worldwide, by virtue of the intrusive capacity of the judicial police and the empirical materials available. Thus, even today the "Falcone method" comprises a set of investigative techniques followed by the anti-mafia judiciary in Italy and abroad, especially in the United States, thanks to the contacts Falcone established during the time he spent with the FBI. Moreover, it has been adopted by teams of researchers (sociologists, anthropologists, and criminologists) who reconstruct mafia networks using mathematical models based on actions (criminal and non-criminal) and communications linking the mafiosi among themselves. Setting out from the same question, "What does the mafia *do*?," anthropologists such as Paolo Campana and Federico Varese in the world's most prestigious university and research centers apply mathematical methods of network modeling to mafia communication systems.[12]

This empirical and pragmatic approach was not the only condition for renewing knowledge about the mafia. Falcone realized that the first battle against the mafia would have to be conducted within the judiciary itself: factions, compartmentalized knowledge, infighting, the withholding of information and data by individual bureaus of investigation all posed obstacles to the perception of a phenomenon whose unitary nature was beginning to be inferred. Here too the monographic survey had to give way to a conceptual model more adapted to the reality

---

12. One of these investigations specifically targeted certain Camorra groups linking the Naples region with the Scottish city of Aberdeen, using wiretaps of telephone conversations between Camorrists as an empirical database (Campana 2013).

under study, namely a network of criminal groups united by shifting relationships but nonetheless constituting a single organization.[13] Falcone thus became one of the first promoters of a method of collective inquiry, joining a powerful work structure, the "anti-mafia pool," inherited from antiterrorism efforts. For the first time, judges in Sicily shared the results of their investigations on the mafia among themselves, and this pooling of knowledge broke the mafia silence, itself constructed of partial knowledge and missing pieces (Dino 2013).

None of this would have been possible, though, without Judge Falcone mastering the mafia language, that is the silence, its expressive possibilities, nuances, and inflections: the language of gestures, the facial mimicry, the unsaid, the metaphors (or the art of saying one thing under the guise of another), the hanging phrases and pauses, the implicit, and the tacit part of social rules. This mastery of the local codes of communication created the conditions of possibility for an unprecedented dialog between Judge Falcone and pentito Buscetta. This is a good example of how a genuine interactive process shapes culture and its transmission (Clifford and Marcus 1986). The encounter of Falcone and Buscetta led to a complete renewal of the interpretive paradigm of the mafia phenomenon, one that social science researchers should have acknowledged and that should have pushed them to revise their own theorizations concerning the mafia. Mafiacraft draws all the consequences from this breakthrough, adopting the same pragmatic and empirical approach to answer the question "What is the mafia?" by using the terms of the people concerned.

From honor to responsibility

Drawing on Lévi-Strauss, Siegel (2006: 210) argued that "witchcraft, held responsible for the insupportable and inexplicable travails of the world, says that society is innocent." This process for identifying and holding accountable those responsible for something unnamable is not performed using the first person: indeed, the witch "speaks in another persona" (Siegel 2006: 216). Applied to the mafia, when a man of honor

---

13. This had been predicted by some of the verdicts issued by pioneering magistrates who would pay for their intuition with their lives, as Cesare Terranova, assassinated in 1979 for being the sole signatory of the sentence handed down in the Catanzaro trial in 1968 that hypothesized the unitary nature of the mafia.

kills, he never does it for himself or for personal gain but "in the name of Cosa Nostra," for the shared interests of a third person, an impersonal one: "Our Thing." On this point there is a convergence between the witch, who "does not come into being with the speaker, the first person,...[but] with the third, or more accurately with multiple third persons." Indeed, in witchcraft "there is a failure to inhabit one's own speech because in a sense, there is nothing (or no one, no defined entity, yet still someone from whom speech issues) to do the inhabiting" (Siegel 2006: 224–226). The mafia presents a very similar configuration: men of honor say they act for the whole, not for their own interest; hence the difficulty for anti-mafia prosecutors to allocate responsibility and to hold such a fleeting entity accountable. Thus, when in February 1986 a trial was opened in Palermo against the mafia, it was the Cosa Nostra association as a whole, as a being in itself, that was in the dock and not only its members as individuals. In chapter 6 I investigate how it was possible for the Italian judiciary to conceive charges against the mafia as a unitarian organization. In chapter 7, I analyze what happened when Cosa Nostra's members were ordered by the Italian judiciary to assume the personal responsabilities corresponding to their roles of murderers or murder's instigators.

The shared practices of murdering carried out by the men of honor allow us to pose the question of *action*: What is a collective action? How are action and speech, death and the order to kill connected? What does it mean, concretely, to share the same criminal purpose, to be *part of* Cosa Nostra? What is an actor or an author of a criminal act? And, to what extent, ultimately, is a subject, an individual, responsible for his or her own actions? This is a long list of anthropological questions that the presence of the mafia raised for society as a whole and for which anti-mafia judges tried to find pragmatic responses. A huge amount of work was required for saying, "he is a mafioso," and for allocating the responsibility borne by the word "mafia" after its introduction into the Italian Penal Code. The burden of proof fell only on those who took charge of this unilateral process of nomination of unnamable powers, the magistrates, with the help of pentiti, like the former man of honor Buscetta.

What is the meaning of the phrase "man of honor," so important to these men who would never label themselves as "mafiosi"? Can an anthropology of law and justice, including its concepts and practices, contribute to the renewal of *honor*, such a classical notion in the anthropology of the Mediterranean (Albera, Blok and Bromberger 2001)?

From rumor to truth

Before accusations of witchcraft are addressed to the person concerned, they circulate in the third person. Thus Siegel (2006: 230) explains: "'Muki is a witch' is a communication whose force rests, tautologically enough, on the simple ability to pass from person to person rather than on a reference to a meaning." The same can be said for mafia accusations. Over a long period, saying that a certain person was a mafioso was only possible in the form of a *rumor*. This triggers the question of what changes in regimes of speech and silence are necessary for these kinds of rumors to become a legal truth with a precise legal meaning? Chapter 8 uses the Impastato affair as case study to examine this question.

On May 9, 1978, a corpse, blown to bits by an explosion, was found on the railroad tracks at the station of Cinisi, a provincial town outside of Palermo. The police concluded that it was a kamikaze attack: the person whose mutilated body lay on the tracks, Giuseppe Impastato, the local representative of the Democrazia Proletaria, a far-left party suspected of terrorist activities, had been trying to blow up the railroad tracks when the bomb went off and killed him instead. But the version that circulated around town was quite different. His mother captured it with these words: "The people of Cinisi immediately said, No! Peppino [her son's nickname] was not capable of committing such an act! Peppino spoke out against the mafia, described them as they were, which is why Badalamenti [whom Impastato had accused of being a mafia leader] had him killed" (Ebano 2005: 106). One night, Giuseppe's comrades planted a sign at the crime scene carrying the following in large black letters: "GIUSEPPE IMPASTATO ASSASSINATO DALLA MAFIA QUI. 9 MAGGIO 1978. ORE:01,30" (Giuseppe Impastato killed here by the Mafia, May 9, 1978, at 01:30). The accusation by Giuseppe's comrades and family of Gaetano Badalamenti, a notorious mafia boss of Cinisi, for having ordered the crime was proven in court twenty-four years later when he and Vito Palazzolo were accused for having been the instigators of Impastato's murder. In the meantime, Impastato—labelled first a "suicide bomber" and then a "terrorist" who aimed to harm the state and made to look responsible for his own death—was finally recognized as a "victim of the mafia." My work involved following these phrases, or scraps of phrases, step-by-step, as they passed from one space to another—from street to court, Cinisi to Palermo, the local setting to the national, the event itself to the defense of a cause—in order to ascertain how they became transformed and, in turn, themselves transformed the status of people and entities concerned.

It is precisely this change of scale and arena that places us firmly in the frame of what Élisabeth Claverie (1992, 1994, 1998) has identified as the political form of the *affair*,[14] a device that allows for the overall "increase in the degree of generality" of a single case (here the death of a young anti-mafia activist) and makes possible that a single event be transformed into the emblem of a common cause, namely that of the anti-mafia. The political form of the affair, inherited from the Enlightenment, allows us to think about the reversibility of judicial truths and simultaneously acts as a "testing of the state" (Linhardt 2012), a moment for requalifying all the people and entities involved, including the Italian state, which the anti-mafia struggle helped unify and centralize.

Microscopic and macroscopic changes, articulated in a highly complex game, gradually led to the indictment of those found responsible, the "mafiosi" Badalamenti and Palazzolo. However, what amounted to a Copernican revolution in how responsibility was accorded for mafia actions was primarily indebted to a transformation in the epistemological frameworks used to make sense of the mafia phenomenon. The Impastato Affair exemplifies the results of Mafiacraft in one single case study: to establish that Badalamenti and Palazzolo had indeed been responsible for Impastato's murder, it was necessary to rethink the model used to describe mafia action. Action had to be redefined as not just *committing* crimes but also *inciting* crimes. Silence appeared here as a stratified, diversified, and layered substance: not a wall, as it had often been described, but a veil of multiple layers that needed to be lifted one by one to answer the question, "What is the mafia?" and solve all other moral and political conundrums posed by this issue. Mafiacraft has carefully followed each step of these operations, showing how simple words can enable a reformulation of the social and political order.

Following the phrases implies following the actions that these phrases *make exist*: Impastato's comrades had to conduct a counter-investigation and present evidence that was previously ignored or evaluated in a biased manner to the Palermo prosecutor's office, a body that was less compromised than the Cinisi police that, like other local authorities, colluded with the mafia. Transformations were needed within the judiciary, enabling the emergence in the main towns of Sicily of a new generation of prosecuting judges, ready to listen to the unheard and to make this

---

14. Ferrando, Puccio-Den, and Smaniotto (2018) provide an overview of publications on the *affair*, translated from French to Italian, with an introduction on the critical return of this notion.

audible, plausible, and credible. These judges had to have the proficiency of rephrasing the demands for revenge and honor by Impastato's mother and brother in terms of justice; changes had to be made in national politics and the judiciary to discredit political power and reveal its entanglements with the mafia; the terms "mafia" and "victim of the mafia" had to be accepted into Italian legislation and acquire a legal and judicial meaning; the term "terrorism" had to be assigned to mafia actions, after spectacular attacks had made evident the menace posed by the mafia for society as a whole; the wide majority of citizens had to support the anti-mafia cause and no longer associate it with extremism and political marginality.

But for all this to be possible, it was necessary for the anti-mafia movement not to remain silent but to speak and write publicly, using all available media: books, brochures, flyers, photographs, newspaper articles, law articles, denunciations, judgments. Mafiacraft considers all these media, without rating them, trying to grasp, beyond the messages that they convey, the discursive registers on which they *act*. Their performativity lies in their successful linkage between a certain kind of criminal profile (embodied in particular individuals) and the signifier "mafioso." That is what makes the difference with witchcraft, in which "the person to whom the term 'witch' is applied is the object of an unsuccessful naming" (Siegel 2006: 230). In witchcraft, "the constant circulation of such rumors attests to the inability to satisfactorily attach words to referents" (Siegel 2006: 225). In Mafiacraft the same operation of creating and fixing meaning is successfully achieved by the judiciary. Nevertheless, there are still areas of uncertainty, especially in the "gray zone."

From intention to crime

As strange as it may sound, a mafia action is a bad deed justified with the good intention of "doing justice" (a paradox explored in detail in chapter 10). Siegel's (2006: 220–221) frequently quoted claim with regards to witchcraft that "he did not know he was a witch. He has no malevolent intentions" could easily fit the mafiosi too due to their shared ontology. Just as witchcraft, the mafia is "both me and not me" (Siegel 2006: 224). Anti-mafia judges have to deal with criminal actions that *do and do not* belong to their perpetrators, the latter situating the compelling origins of their actions *elsewhere*, such as within Cosa Nostra, Divine Providence, the Gospel, or Justice.

Nevertheless, after the Maxi Trial and the Capaci massacre and Via d'Amelio bombing, no one in Italy could ignore that the mafia *existed* and that its aims were criminals. In this new moral and mental environment, how could one establish the intentional nature of the unlawful conduct regarding mafia-related crimes? Taking as a starting point an empirical case of legal proceedings—the Aiello trial—Chapter 9 describes how a definition emerged of the inner truth—the intent of a mafia act—and how it was proved. It asks what elements are deemed to be genuine, conscious, and probative and what part they play in judgment, mediation, arbitration, and the perception and characterization of an "act" (not necessarily a murderous one) as a mafia crime. "Participation in a mafia association" (Article 416 *bis* of the Italian Penal Code), external complicity in a mafia association (*concorso esterno*), and assistance provided for someone linked to the mafia association to avoid police investigations (*favoreggiamento aggravato*) are based on a conception of the criminal as someone who participates in, contributes to, or abets crime *in the full knowledge and cognizance of their acts*. But is the mafioso who lives in *assoggettamento*, a condition of subjugation that we might also translate as de-subjectivation[15]—someone acting like a soldier or a robot—aware of the actions he carried out when he was granted no insight into their background and wider circumstances?

A wider question then arises in relation to the issue of responsibility discussed above: How do we describe the action? Elizabeth Anscombe (1958) pointed out that intention, instead of being a private event of a psychological sort, a preliminary to the act, is a discursive operation implying social practices and rules. According to Quine (1960), shared social norms are used to assign reasons and intentions to an action. Inquiring into the intention or reason for an action is a hermeneutic, interactive operation for assigning meaning. A single act can be described from different angles, and this is exactly what happens in court. But are such reasons the actual causes of the action? Are they not always retroactive justifications that have little explanatory power about the chain of mental states and physical and social processes that caused a certain act to be performed instead of another?

Where magistrates, experts, and the police have the task of inquiring into the causes and motives of a mafia-type criminal act, Mafiacraft follows the successive (material and cognitive) operations that lead to the formation of a judgment of intentionality in mafia trials. Moral

---

15. I thank philosopher François Athané for suggesting this translation of the legal and psychological concept *assoggettamento*, thus opening new perspectives for approaching it anthropologically (personal communication).

questions crop up, even for legal practitioners (judges or jurists) who—by bearing the burden of proof even as they are required to find a "psychological truth"—become genuine philosophers. Both the social scientist and the magistrate necessarily intervene after the event, or the criminal act. What guarantee do they have that their retrospective constructions match the truth? For this to happen, it would be necessary to postulate that what actors *say* about their actions coincides with what they *believe* about them. However, nothing could be less certain for mafiosi whose intentions remain unknown even to themselves before being formulated, possibly for the very first time, when they are interrogated during a trial. What appears to be at work are forms of knowledge or *unawareness* that are not conditional on verbalized existential experiences: rather they are conditional on silence as the experience of the unspeakable. This is also a key to explain the disavowal of mafia crime. Knowledge of the mafia is ineffable until the mafioso reflexively narrates his experience, losing its essence forever.

Usually the actors rely on a common, shared stock of knowledge and aptitudes that help them find their bearings in the world and interpret ordinary events (Garfinkel 1967). But what if judges and the accused do not share the same tools for thinking and talking about faults, crimes, and sanctions? Adjustments are continuously made to bridge the gap between these two spheres, as it happens in local contexts where a plurality of norms generates tension between different normative and legal systems. That was exactly what happened at the Aiello Trial: a confrontation between mafia norms and the state justice system about the *consciousness* of mafia related crimes. A surprising archive allows addressing the issue of the consciousness and awareness of evil from within Cosa Nostra.

The ultimate proof

An anthropology of traces, Mafiacraft examines in chapter 10 the written evidence for the existence of the mafia as produced by mafiosi themselves. During the Aiello trial in 2005, when I was collaborating closely with the public prosecutor responsible for scrutinizing the case of fraud perpetrated by a distinguished doctor with the help of the head of Cosa Nostra, Bernardo Provenzano, I had in my hand the *pizzini* (letters) sent by the latter to the various members of the criminal association from 1993 onwards when he took over its directorship. These secret texts, discovered by the criminal police, are valuable ethnographical material if we aim to answer the question "What is the mafia?" from a mafioso point of view. These letters, concerned with matters of racketeering, extortion, and violence, were strewn with religious references and all surprisingly ended with the formula: "May God bless you and protect you!" We know how the framework of superstition has weighed on witchcraft (Geschiere 2005, 2010). These letters point to the fact that the same applies to the mafia. Chapter 10 undertakes a critical analysis of categories such as *omertà*, honor, and superstition, in an effort to grasp what they encompass for the mafiosi.

The methodological premise for this interest in mafiosi religiosity has to be deontological in nature, a premise that might be quite obvious to the anthropologist but that may be worth reasserting when the object of one's research consists of a criminal association: the premise is to attribute a sense of morality even to those whom we consider, according to our own mental and cultural scheme, as the worst of the worst among humans,[16] an approach that Falcone himself urged for (Falcone and Padovani 1997). This allows us to avoid two major epistemological obstacles: the folklorization of mafia religious practices—reducing them to mere superstitions and thus emptying them of meaning and depth—and their derision, by asserting a cultural superiority above such declarations of Christian faith by these men of honor, a derision that would prevent us from understanding the origin, function, and *raison d'être* of these practices. The sneer that spontaneously appears on our lips when we encounter Provenzano's famous *pizzini*, with their recurring invocation of Catholic saints, should not lead us to dismiss these practices as simply instrumental in nature. We should rather see it as a warning, pointing to our radical estrangement from the inner world of the mafioso, and an enticement to study, for example, the relation between a certain way of writing and a particular approach to commanding[17] that bases its power in a transcendent order.

Even more than alerting us to the religious practices of the mafia, Provenzano's *pizzini* provide the ultimate proof of the validity of the Buscetta theorem: for the first time, anti-mafia judges could attempt to answer the question "What is the mafia?" by drawing on sources that had

---

16. The need to acknowledge the moral competence of the actors under examination is put forward in particular by the pragmatic approach in the French sociological tradition (see especially Boltanski 1990).

17. Historian Yves Cohen (1997) did something similar with respect to letters by Joseph Stalin.

been (unwittingly) provided by men of honor who were in active service and not by pentiti. The network of correspondents in Provenzano's correspondence reshaped the physiognomy of the Sicilian mafia, reframing power relationships within what was now recognizable as a unitary, centralized, and indeed very efficient organization.

As the story was told by Falcone, the mafia holds out a mirror to the state. But it does not recognize itself pursuing this search for meaning. How mafia silence has stimulated the search for meaning to a (in some sense always arbitrary) political order is possibly the very object of Mafiacraft.

PART I: NAMING THE MAFIA

CHAPTER I

Does the mafia exist?

The history of a question

"I don't know what that means," stated Carmelo Mendola in 1883, defendant in the Amoroso trial, to the question put to him by the chief trial judge: "Were you not part of the mafia?" (Lupo 1988: 463). A century later, a police officer posed the same question. Gerlando Alberti, who had just been arrested, answered: "The mafia? What is the mafia? A brand of cheese?" (Padovani 1987: 9). Despite having been accused of murder more than once, this mafia boss was regularly acquitted "for want of proof." The law had pursued him for nearly twenty years but was unable to charge *U Paccaré* (the Imperturbable One), as he was known, for being a mafioso, as this category had no penal relevance yet, nor as co-responsible for the murders he had ordered and arranged from within the mafia association. Though the principle of co-responsibility was certainly enshrined in the Italian penal code,[1] it was extremely difficult to prove the causal link between the person who ordered a murder and those who actually carried it out. At this point in time, no description was available in law of this secret society, its goals and internal functioning, the links

---

1. Indeed, the principle of equivalent conditions (Art. 110 of the Italian penal code) gives formal recognition to the co-responsibility of all those who participate in the same offence, whether it be as an accessory, by commission, or by collaboration. This principle equally applies to homicide (Art. 575 c.p.).

between its members, or the manner in which they undertook to commit a criminal offence.

The first descriptions of the mafia phenomenon appeared after the unification of Italy in 1861, in reports of state agents charged with studying social issues in the Mezzogiorno, Italy's southern part. Their conclusions were contradictory: on the one hand we have a report dating to 1865 in which Filippo Gualterio, then prefect of Palermo, defined "the so-called mafia" as "a properly constituted association, furnished with proper statutes and with the capacity to provide services, including those to political parties" (Dickie 2006: 49–50); on the other we have Bonfadini, rapporteur of the Parliamentary Commission of Enquiry into the Social Conditions of Sicily of 1877, who refuted that this form of "instinctive solidarity" based on violence, deceit, and intimidation had any structured or organized character (Marino 1964: 53). A third report, based on a private parallel enquiry undertaken by Leopoldo Franchetti and Sydney Sonnino (Franchetti [1877] 1993), two young right-wing intellectuals, supported Gualterio's assessment in its assertion that there existed an organization that was in effective control of the region, having infiltrated even its public institutions.

Legal descriptions of the mafia in the twentieth century were no more uniform. In the early 1930s, the Sicilian magistrate and criminologist Giuseppe Guido Lo Schiavo (1899–1973) firmly maintained the idea of the criminal and associative nature of the mafia, whereas the Sicilian attorney G. M. Puglia considered it as nothing more than an expression of local culture (quoted by Turone 2008: 5n4). In the late 1940s, jurist Gaetano Mosca identified the "mafia spirit" as comprising certain behaviors ("self-esteem, pride, arrogance") embedded in social relationships, from that "collection of small associations pursuing different goals, ones which, quite frequently, cause their members to engage in marginally illegal activities and are, sometimes, truly criminal" (Mosca [1949] 2002: 4). In the 1960s, jurist Francesco Antolisei, author of a celebrated manual of penal law (1966), defined mafia conduct as illicit and immoral without being necessarily criminal and did not see it as arising out of any form of organized crime. Mosca had pre-empted this point: "I have nearly reached the end of my speech, and I have not made any mention of any form of organization by which all the elements of the mafia, or better, of the mafia bands, are joined together and disciplined. I have not mentioned it for the simple reason that such a form of organization *does not exist*" (Mosca [1949] 2002: 54, emphasis added). The jurist does admit that "occasionally, two or more bands, whether neighboring or distant, unite to commit an 'offence'" (Mosca [1949] 2002: 29). However, since the proper character of a criminal association, such as defined in the Italian criminal code, was the permanence of association for criminal ends, not attributing a permanent character to the mafia organization amounted to exempting it from any possibility of being quashed and left it floating in a legal vacuum.

Constrained by its incapacity to pursue the mafia in terms of being a criminal association, the justice system turned its attack to individual mafiosi. But, since this category too was absent from the criminal code, such persons could only be pursued for crimes that they had personally committed and that engaged their individual responsibility. Establishing proof for these crimes was rendered problematic by the dissociation between those who had ordered the crime and those who had carried it out, a mode of operation characteristic of the mafia (Mosca [1949] 2002: 42). This is the reason why several homicide trials between the late nineteenth and late twentieth centuries were invalidated. The most famous of these was the 1904 trial accusing Sicilian politician Raffaele Palizzolo of having been behind the murder of Bank of Sicily director general Leopoldo Notarbartolo, stabbed to death on a train by two railroad workers. Acquitted for "insufficient evidence," Palizzolo declared fearlessly:

> If by mafia you mean the sense of honor taken to its extreme, generosity of spirit which confronts the strong and is indulgent towards the weak, a loyalty towards friends which is stronger than anything else, even death; if by mafia you mean these feelings and these attitudes, even with their excess, then you are dealing with distinctive markers of the Sicilian soul. I declare I am "mafioso," and I am proud of being one! (Renda 1997: 26).

This definition of the mafioso as supreme expression of the Sicilian character echoes folklorist Giuseppe Pitrè's declarations made on the occasion of the same trial in an effort to protect Sicilian culture from attack by "northerners" who, by equating Sicily with the mafia, threatened to criminalize the whole island. In his writings Pitrè deplored "the sad fate to which the term mafia has been condemned, a term which still yesterday expressed good and innocent things but which is now forced into representing bad things," and claimed that mafia in its original sense was synonymous with "beauty, grace, perfection, excellence,…the sense of what it [is] to be a man, self-assurance, even taken to the extent of audacity, but never arrogance, never hubris." Most noteworthy was his declaration that "the mafia is neither a sect nor an association. It has neither rules nor statutes.... The mafioso is neither a thief nor a brigand" (Pitrè [1889] 1944: 291–292). In terms of this definition (that focused on what they are *not*), the mafia and the mafioso were beyond the reach of justice.

It is easy to see how, in order to be operative, judicial descriptions had to find an effective way to counter these cultural definitions, which were given authority by scholars such as Pitré and were widespread among the local population. But until the end of the 1960s, the intuitions held by judges and police dealing with these offenders and claiming the organized and structured character of their crimes remained purely conjectural. Certain jurists, such as Vincenzo Manzini ([1908–1919] 1983), perceived the mafia as an organization which was not only immoral but also committed to crime. But beyond this, it still had to be proven that a person associated with the mafia was by definition involved in the criminal program pursued by this association. The proof was difficult to establish as long as the state of belonging to the mafia organization, and the acts that this membership implied, remained covered in secrecy (Chinnici 2006b: 60–61). This secrecy was not only maintained within the mafia but also extended to large parts of the population through the law of *omertà* or silence. Neither did perpetrators confess to their deeds nor did families and friends of victims lay complaints against them. Even if those responsible for the atrocities were known by everyone—for the secret was indeed an open one—their names circulated only by *rumor*. In a few rare cases, examining magistrates, such as Cesare Terranova, tried to work around the intrinsic limits to an anti-mafia enquiry and had dossiers drawn up for trial. But these judicial procedures proved fruitless, systematically resulting in the acquittal of the majority of accused for insufficient evidence[2]—an outcome that did not prevent Terranova's assassination in 1979.

The mafia's impunity was perpetuated for yet another reason, as explained by the anti-mafia magistrate Giuseppe Di Lello (1994: 55): for the most part the judges of this time belonged to the same social position as the large landowners, the well-to-do or the politicians whose interests were defended by these "violent entrepreneurs" (Blok 1974), the

---

2. See, for example, *Sentenza contro La Barbera Angelo + 116*, December 22, 1968, Assizes Court of Cantanzaro (Justice Pasquale Carnavale). Commissione Parlamentare antimafia, Documentazione allegata, 8th Legislature, doc. XXIII, 1/X, v. 4, t. 17: 1230–1232.

mafiosi. This limitation, which extended well into the late 1970s, prevented that a satisfying answer could be found for the question "What is the mafia?," with the system of power implicitly relying on that fact that any possible solution for the problem would be ignored. The difficulty of laying a charge against the mafia as a criminal organization led a number of other magistrates to ask a different question. Rather than asking "What is the mafia?," they began to consider what kind of offenders the mafiosi are, what they *do*, and in what way their acts are contrary to law. They thus shifted from an ontological question to a set of pragmatic ones. This approach allowed the development of new techniques of investigation that were capable of circumventing *omertà*. Their victims and accomplices might well remain silent, but their activities left clues that could be read and interpreted, veritable signatures that allowed a link to be traced back to the authors of the crimes:

> Although mafia crimes can be programmed in the secrecy of the so-called "mafia commission" and carried out by unknown killers, the investment of mafia wealth must necessarily take place in the open, according to certain unavoidable laws of the market, and drawing on the cooperation and intermediary role of individuals who do not necessarily belong to the mafia themselves, thereby leaving indelible traces which just need to be sought and tracked down. (Chinnici 2006b: 67)

These new methods of enquiry, which Judge Rocco Chinnici set out in January 1983—six months before his assassination—before the Associazione Nazionale Magistrati (ANM, the national association of Italian magistrates), had been used by Judge Giovanni Falcone during the Spatola enquiry in the late 1970s. Following the traces that the clearance of checks, the transfer of funds, and other financial transactions by the Gambino and Spatola-Inzerillo mafia families had left in the banking system, and constructing a map of the drug trafficking that linked these two Sicilian families with the United States and Canada, Falcone was able to establish—once the obstacles that national legal systems put in the way of his enquiry had been overcome—the international dimension of mafia criminality. The mafia was no longer just a cultural abstraction, a product specific to Sicily, but a transnational network of traffickers linked by blood ties and economic relationships.

This new model, constructed by deductive logic after a labor of investigation as minutely detailed as it was monumental, was validated by the verdict handed down in 1982 in the Spatola trial with the conviction of the accused.[3] This unprecedented success damaged the mafia's air of impunity and brought a new climate of confidence to the Sicilian magistrates engaged in the anti-mafia battle. Di Lello (1994), an anti-mafia judge in his own right, describes a historical and social shift taking place, from judges effectively turning a blind eye to them engaging in a fight to curb the mafia and risking their own lives. This new generation of magistrates emerged from an internal reform of the Italian magistracy, which broke up the former system defined by class loyalties and corporatist hierarchies, and gave greater powers to the examining magistrates—rather than the courts of appeal and the supreme court (a court of cassation)—and to judges of criminal courts—rather than of civil courts (Vauchez 2004: 25–67). This change had already led a number of judges, who had conducted criminal enquiries and drawn up indictments against left-wing and right-wing terrorist networks that were active during a period that came to be called the Years of Lead (1960s to 1980s), to attract national attention and assume a role of expertise in the social sphere (Vauchez 2004: 50). In the early 1980s, it was anti-mafia judges like Chinnici who publicly spoke about the relations between the mafia and drug-trafficking and its role in national and international crime, and who brought up the thorny question of the relationship between the mafia and politics. They did so not only within the legal sphere but in speeches at schools and universities, at clubs like the Rotary, or in settings that involved the Catholic church that had become increasingly sensitive to the mafia question.[4] Explaining the nature of the mafia was another way in which these judges fought against a phenomenon that drew its strength from prevailing secrecy.

The early 1980s thus marked a turning point in the elaboration and promotion of new jurisprudential solutions and unprecedented probatory strategies in the anti-mafia field, strategies borrowed from the fight against left-wing and right-wing terrorism where they had proven successful. The magistrates in northern Italy who had managed to dismantle these terrorist networks had done so by coordinating their investigations on a national scale to ensure the effective sharing of information, by instituting specialist work teams called pools, and by drawing on the cooperation of pentiti, "repentant" terrorists (Vauchez 2004: 69–169). In

3. *Spatola Rosario + 119*, decision of the examining magistrate Giovanni Falcone, January 25, 1982.
4. Chinnici's speeches were published by Zingales (2006).

the early 1980s, anti-mafia judges set up an initial judicial pool whose purpose was to bring together all mafia dossiers into a single wide-ranging enquiry that could illuminate the significance of criminal acts that had occurred at distinct times and places but which could be supposed to form part of a single criminal enterprise. The sharing of the results of the various enquiries brought to light the manner in which mafia crimes were coordinated at regional and national levels. As a consequence, the pool magistrates called for a law that would give official recognition to what they had discovered empirically: "Since the mafia exists as a criminal and crime-generating reality," declared Chinnici at the International Congress on "Mafia and Power," which took place in Messina in 1981 (2006a: 28), "the legislator cannot be exonerated from recognizing this fact and thus from enacting a new category of offence." When asked what characterized the mafia in contrast to other criminal organizations, Chinnici (2006a: 28–31) identified four such attributes: secrecy, total loyalty between associates, the connection between mafia families, and its relationship with the structures of power.[5] In it he provided a first outline of a law characterizing the mafia, which would lead, in 1982, to the formal establishment of the offence of "association with the mafia."

The birth of the mafia as a criminal offence

The creation of the offence of "association with the mafia" (*delitto di associazione mafiosa*) came in response to the necessity of giving a fixed definition to a social phenomenon whose parameters were ambiguous, ranging from the culturalist explanation that it expresses the archetypal Sicilian way of being to the criminological definition of it as a loose association of malefactors. We noted above how the difficulty of proving the existence of durable links between mafiosi and of demonstrating knowledge of criminal plans within their association rendered inoperative judicial attempts to impute to mafiosi the offence of belonging to a criminal association as foreseen by the penal code.

The Rognoni–La Torre law, promulgated in 1982 to define the mafia association in its specificity, is an extension of Article 416 of the penal code which defines criminal association. The legislation postulates that what characterizes the mafia association in comparison to simple

---

5. Speech by Chinnici to the international Congresso Mafia e Potere (Mafia and power), Messina, October 19–23, 1981.

criminal association are its methods, and notably three of these: intimidation, *omertà* or the "law of silence," and subjugation. As a consequence, any individual may be defined as mafioso who derives advantage from the power of intimidation emanating from the capital of violence inscribed in his association, even if this violence is not exercised in a systematic fashion; who protects his organization by exercising silence, or by imposing silence on his environment; and who lives in a relationship of submission toward an institution that takes precedence over the state, thus one like the mafia. Clearly, such mafia-related behavior was predicated on the presupposition that the mafia has an existence. Much more than being a legalized instrument for the repression of the mafia phenomenon, the Rognoni–La Torre law represented the act by which the existence of the mafia was recognized in law and socially. Mafia-type behaviors would henceforth be punished *as such*, with little attention given to whether the object achieved through these behavior's was legal or illegal. Mafiosi were now subject to a penal sanction of between three and six years imprisonment on the basis that the elemental fact of belonging to the mafia, proved by their conduct, was now defined as an offence (Turone 2008).

This law circumvented the need for ontological proof of the mafia by putting the focus of evidence on mafia-type methods. Nevertheless, these methods remained difficult to prove. How could intimidation be demonstrated in the absence of evidence from the victims, and how could submission to mafia authority be shown without confessions of those thus subjected, in a context where both victims and mafiosi upheld the law of silence? What the magistrates lacked was therefore a framework that would allow them to encompass both the mafia and mafiosi.

The Buscetta theorem

In the early 1980s, the magistrates of the anti-mafia pool collected a considerable volume of data on mafia criminality in Sicily. However, as long as the collated data was captured in a single dossier, it remained difficult to interpret. Enveloped by silence, a practice exercised even by anti-mafia prosecutors, the mafia's broad internal dynamics remained opaque. This weakness in the arsenal of the anti-mafia investigators was to be overcome when several mafiosi—the number of which would steeply increase over the course of the 1980s—decided to reveal their secrets to the judges. They were called the pentiti—repentant informers—borrowing a term from the previous decade for turncoat political terrorists who had begun to collaborate with the Italian state. The motivations of these pentiti were various (Puccio-Den 2014). More than a sudden crisis of conscience, a generic desire for revenge, or simple opportunism, we should mention the fear of being murdered by former associates turned enemies in the course of the "second mafia war" that broke out within the mafia, provoked by the rise to power of the Corleonese clan. Anti-mafia judges such as Falcone and Borsellino envisaged the role confessions could play in the construction of a new tool for repressing the mafia phenomenon. It was essential for the anti-mafia judges to shelter their sources from criticisms of insincerity as this could have delegitimized their evidence that was so critical on the judicial level (Falcone 1994: 33–65). The media came to call this model the Buscetta theorem, after pentito Tommaso Buscetta whose confession enabled Judge Falcone to indict Cosa Nostra in what came to be known as the Maxi Trial, the biggest ever trial against the mafia. The trial, which took place in Palermo between February 10, 1986, and December 16, 1987, was the demonstration of this theorem in action.

The pentiti offered "a key to the interpretation of the inner process of the mafia phenomenon" and corroborated the observations made by the magistrates (Stajano 2010: 27). The Maxi Trial's examining magistrates were careful to use the pentiti's evidence not as primary evidence but only to confirm information already established through other enquiries. More generally, the judges rejected the use of the term "the Buscetta theorem" as this would have suggested a type of *inductive reasoning* that relied on the testimony of a mafioso. The mafia, now recognized as a criminal macrostructure, required the creation of a special ad hoc tribunal. It necessitated the construction of a bunker where the 475 accused could be tried and the safety of all could be ensured. The colossal dimensions of this trial reflected the heights of its ambition, as rendered explicit in the terms that inaugurated it: "This is the trial of the mafia organization referred to as Cosa Nostra, a very dangerous criminal association which, by the use of violence and intimidation, has spread and does spread death and terror."[6]

The indictment extended to 8,607 typewritten pages, and was signed off on November 8, 1985, by Falcone, Borsellino, Di Lello, and Judge Leonardo Guarnotta. It began with the observation "that the mafia

---

6. *Ordinanza-Sentenza contro Abbate Giovanni + 706*, Office for the Investigation of Penal Trials, High Court of Palermo, 1985, p. 713.

association exists, to which entry is by the ritual swearing of an oath of allegiance that the new inductee, from that moment, declares himself ready to pursue the goals of the association, among which are absolute loyalty between members, as well as to respect a set of rules of behavior whose principles are blind obedience to leaders, complete secrecy and the law of silence." Three years had passed since the promulgation of the Rognoni–La Torre law, a period marked by feverish work to construct an argument capable of bringing to trial the top bosses of the Sicilian mafia. Its starting point was a description of the mafia that Buscetta's theorem allowed to be rendered formal: a secret society, with initiatory rituals, permanent in character, centralized, and with a fixed hierarchy (and not dispersed in autonomous "families"). On this basis, the examining magistrates argued that the members of its governing body—the Cupola (Commission)—be held responsible for all homicides committed as part of a single criminal purpose, thus making it unnecessary to establish the direct involvement of each leader in every one of the murders.

The court passed down nineteen sentences for life imprisonment and prison terms amounting to more than two thousand years. But these sentences, which validated the Buscetta theorem, immediately faced several forms of criticism, both from within the judicial world and outside. Sicilian intellectual and writer Leonardo Sciascia, for example, sharply attacked the anti-mafia judges, accusing them of blurring the elementary rules of the democratic state and being driven by their own egocentrism (see Sciascia 2002). The subsequent election of Judge Antonino Meli to head the Office of Investigations of Palemo's prosecution service, above that of Judge Falcone who had also applied for the position, led to the dismantling of the anti-mafia investigations, thus annihilating the work of the anti-mafia pool and the conceptual elaboration of the unitary mafia model. This vision was once again damaged in 1990, when the judges of the Appeal Court came to a different conclusion on the Maxi Trial convictions on the grounds of an "uncircumventible principle of our legal system: the strictly personal character of criminal liability" (U. Santino 1992: 126). But a significant twist occurred in January 1992 when the Italian Supreme Court reaffirmed the Buscetta theorem by confirming the verdict and the sentences handed down at the initial High Court trial. For its part, the mafia showed its response to the trial and verdicts in the assassination of Falcone on May 23, 1992, and that of Borsellino less than two months later, on July 19. For the Italian citizenry, the Capaci massacre and the Via D'Amelio bombing, for which the mafia adopted a modus operandi previously known from political terrorist attacks in the 1970s and 1980s, became the blatant proof of the mafia's existence (Lupo 2007: 46).

The Maxi Trial marked an epistemological turning point for the way in which the mafia phenomenon was perceived. Descriptive models that social scientists developed in the 1970s and 1980s on the basis of archival records (Hess [1970] 1998) or anthropological and sociological fieldwork (Schneider and Schneider 1976; Blok 1974; Arlacchi [1983] 2007), postulating the association to be non-structured, opportunistic, and discontinuous, were shown to be obsolete. The judges firmly established their expertise on the mafia question (Vauchez 2004: 101–109), agreeing that the mafia was a unitary criminal organization, a status that had both judicial and scientific veracity.

During the compilation of the indictment for the Maxi Trial, Falcone had taken care to avoid extending enquiries into the links maintained by mafiosi with the outside world, for fear of diluting the mafia's specifically criminal character. He rather concentrated on searching out forms of liability that were clearly definable under the penal code.[7] But if the objective of the examining magistrates was to isolate the mafia as a "social problem" (Blumer 2004) and to circumscribe this "disease" so as better to "treat it," the results of their investigations in Sicily and in Italy more widely uncovered

> the well-camouflaged and thus all the more insidious capacities for insertion of the mafia element into vast sectors of society, at the heart of which they [the mafiosi] succeed in bringing about that entanglement of collusions and complicities that constitutes the fertile ground on which the mafia entity has for a long time been able to prosper, grow stronger, and become more widespread.[8]

Chapter 5 of the indictment in the Maxi Trial, entitled "Close contacts in the social, political, and economic spheres," is entirely devoted to these forms of "organic compenetration" (U. Santino 1992: 113–114). Although the judges' understanding of the mafia phenomenon rejected

---

7. From 1982, Falcone (1994: 221–228) emphasized the necessity of meticulously reconstructing "the most explicit criminal aspects of the mafia organization," which must take priority over an investigation of "networks of complicity and connivence."

8. *Ordinanza-Sentenza contro Abbate Giovanni + 706*, Office for the Investigation of Penal Trials, High Court of Palermo, 1985, p. 1204.

the culturalist paradigm and looked at the criminal organization separate from its surrounding society, the evidence they assembled revealed a multilevel structure with a complex pattern of relations with the outside world (U. Santino 1992: 117): at the basis were the "actual executants of the offences"; the second level was made up of "behind-the-scene instigators, being the heads of the mafia families"; the third level was politico-financial in nature, constituting the "sphere of relationships between the mafia and the political." The jurist Mosca had already suggested a similar differentiation in 1904, in relation to the murder of Notarbartolo, where he separated the murderers proper (the instigator Palizzolo and the actual perpetrators) from the crowd of swindlers who benefited from Palizzolo's acquittal and from the "tolerators"—those who consented to the fraud and so, actively or passively, abetted the fraudsters (Mosca [1949] 2002: 64). Another major advance was achieved at an ontological level: henceforth it was known not only that the mafia *existed* but what it *was*. The anti-mafia trials of the 1990s would attempt to give juridical qualification to this system of relationships.

The "third level"

From 1972, the date of the first report of a Parliamentary Anti-mafia Commission, the mafia was officially identified as being not only a criminal, secret association, but "a part of the structure of public power" (Pepino 2005: 18). During the 1980s, the mafia question increasingly became the basis of public denunciations by political personalities and the press, and by activist movements that incriminated in particular the Christian Democracy party but also the other governing parties, notably the Italian Socialist Party. In the early 1990s, politicians who were found to be colluding with the mafia to ensure their re-election were brought to trial (Briquet 2007: 82). The revelation of political complicities that benefited the mafia was therefore nothing new; what was unprecedented, however, was their transcription into relevant categories of penal law.

In 1993, the Palermo prosecutor's office asked the Italian senate to lift the parliamentary immunity of Giulio Andreotti, a senator for life for the Christian Democracy party, so as to authorize the pursuit of investigations against him. Due to the outcry triggered by the assassinations of Falcone and Borsellino, parliament was unable to refuse this request despite the fact that Andreotti had been a leading figure in Italian politics since the end of the Second World War and had served as prime minister seven times. Andreotti was to be accused of the offence of "association with the mafia." In 1994 the charge was changed to one of "external complicity with the mafia association Cosa Nostra" (*concorso esterno*), an offence which did not necessarily imply that the accused was a formal member of the association but that he made "a conscious contribution to the maintenance and strengthening of the association"[9] (Grosso 1994: 194).

The indictment against Andreotti was made in a long narrative[10] that weaved a pattern of the politicians, financiers, entrepreneurs, and mafiosi who were in some way linked to the Christian Democracy senator. Andreotti challenged the imputation, arguing that this contained a "sort of collective crime performed by the Sicilian Christian Democracy Party" (Andreotti 1995: 5). His line of defense led him to minimize the mafiosi's capacity to harm others—"We knew that they were not angels... but they nevertheless did not represent a national danger" (Lupo 2007: 47)—and allowed him to withdraw behind a wall of ignorance: of the mafia in general and of eminent members of his party playing a role in that criminal association, whether as associates or as accomplices (Lupo 2007: 68). It was not only the status of the accused that was on the line. At stake was a new account of Italy's history, "the true history of Italy" (Montanaro and Ruotolo 1995), read from the perspective of its dark and *ob-scene* side,[11] that was asking to be recognized and accredited by the judiciary.

On October 23, 1999, the Palermo High Court acquitted Andreotti for "insufficient evidence."[12] The existence of relationships between the Christian Democracy senator and various notables of the political, economic, and financial world linked to the mafia had been amply demonstrated; but Andreotti's actions were not considered significant from the penal point of view, to the extent that it could not be proven that he had an "awareness of the nature of [these] links" (Pepino 2005: 38). The court concluded that "there was not sufficient proof that senator

---

9. This juridical category was created through the application of Article 110 (which defined "cooperation toward the commission of a crime") to Article 416 *bis* of the penal code.

10. For an abridged account of the 1,915-page case against Andreotti, see Arlacchi (1995).

11. It was during the Andreotti trial that prosecutor Scarpinato coined this term, in a play on the etymology of the Italian word *osceno*, to designate the hidden scene of power.

12. The judgment was published in Pepino (2005).

Andreotti had acted with full awareness and intent to bring a significant contribution to the mafia association for the purpose of maintaining and reinforcing the organization of this association" (Pepino 2005: 76). This judgment was reversed on appeal: "Andreotti was fully conscious of the fact that his Sicilian interlocutors maintained friendly relations with certain mafia chiefs." The Appeal Court held on May 2, 2003, that the defendant had "a veritable participation in the mafia association, which was noticeable and prolonged over time" (Pepino 2005: 142), which corresponds precisely to the offence of "external complicity" (Pepino 2005: 147). But this judgment, confirmed by the Italian Supreme Court in 2004, also affirmed that the "availability of the accused to mafiosi was not extended beyond 1980" (Pepino 2005: 42) and since offences committed before this date fell outside of the statute of limitations, the defendant was acquitted. Barely escaping the silence, the "true history of Italy" was still unspeakable.

Throughout the trial was marked by controversies—within the judiciary, the media, politics, and academia—as to whether the indictment was well founded. Consigning the Andreotti judgment "to the court of history" (Pepino 2005: 142), the Appeal Court bequeathed to society the question of the boundary between politics and morality. If the relationships, certified to different degrees, between the senator and political personalities linked to the mafia did not make the accused liable before the law, they nevertheless put his political liability into question (Macaluso 1995), a concept that in itself is defined by law. The Italian constitution (Art. 95/2) applies political liability to a group of people, in contrast to the principle of individuality that applies in criminal liability. In other words, a leading politician, even if he is not criminally responsible for the acts of his lieutenants, must answer for the behavior of third parties to whom he is linked for political reasons and may face political sanction for these behaviors (Neppi Modona 1994: 186). In fact, on April 6, 1993, the Parliamentary Anti-mafia Commission—which since its origins had been investigating the links between the mafia and the political system—signaled "the potential political liability" of Andreotti and pronounced on the incompatibility of his actions with the democratic order.[13] However, in 1994 the First Republic, the political system that had been in place in Italy since 1946, collapsed in the wake of the political scandals brought to light by the *Mani pulite* (clean hands)

---

13. Report of the Parliamentary Anti-mafia Commission compiled by Deputy Luciano Violante, approved by the 9th Legislature, p. 29.

investigation that implicated the whole political class that had been in power in Italy since the end of the Second World War. The new political figures to come to the fore, such as entrepreneur Silvio Berlusconi, launched a campaign against the judiciary that also attracted the support of the parties of the left. In the context of this political crisis, with the political balance being rewritten upon a unanimous rejection of the supposed practice by anti-mafia judges of "filling in the policy gaps," the Italian parliament did not judge it timely to take the recommendation against Andreotti on board.

The outcome of the Andreotti trial had the effect of calling into question the faculty of the magistracy to bring the law to bear upon the gray zones of the power nexus between the mafia and the political sphere. Nevertheless, this trial did create the precedent of a judicial investigation into external complicity, which could potentially be used to pursue other politicians. A certain number of judges began to consider going after certain powerful persons that others before them had chosen not to investigate, on the basis that the penal treatment of relationships between the mafia and the political domain had now been placed in the domain of what was feasible.[14]

The "white mafia"

The Andreotti trial brought about a split within the Anti-mafia Directorate[15] at the Palace of Justice in Palermo—nicknamed the "palace of poisons" after the climate of suspicion and conspiracy that had poisoned Falcone's last years. Several magistrates were put off investigating mafia crimes by what they considered both a judicial and a political failure in the Andreotti case, at the same time as Andreotti was being absolved by a public increasingly hostile to what it considered as political trials. They began to question whether they were compelled to indict leading politicians for "external complicity with a mafia association." It was this hybrid

---

14. I am borrowing the term *jouable* (feasible) from Violaine Roussel (2002: 113) who uses it in her analysis of activist judges who enquired into the political scandals in France during the 1990s.

15. The Direzioni Distrettuali Antimafia (DDA) structure was created in 1992 at the initiative of Falcone, with offices in all Italian cities with a Court of Appeal. These units, which carry out judicial anti-mafia enquiries, are coordinated by the Direzione Nazionale Antimafia (DNA), located in Rome.

penal category, also described as a "legal monster,"[16] that now came under scrutiny: the ability to apply the offence of association to someone who is not linked to the organization in any formal way.

Every trial that was lost arrested the progress of the anti-mafia investigators, who were accused of fomenting judicial plots for political ends. Tracing a demarcation line between political and moral truth, on the one hand, and the—always partial—judicial truth, on the other, a group of prosecutors opposed to the Andreotti trial judges were content to establish a minimal indictment, without trying to fulfill the role of experts of the social world that the examining magistrates in the 1980s had taken on.[17] But their adversaries considered the relation between the mafia and the political domain to be structural and saw in it the root of the mafia problem. In their view, handing down light sentences did not take account of the gravity of that intertwined nexus of relationships with normal society, which gave the mafia its specific character in comparison to other criminal associations. It was in these peripheral connections that the vital organs of the mafia resided, they claimed. It was therefore in this sector that intervention was necessary if effective action was to be made with regard to this phenomenon, and in this sense the concept of "external complicity with a mafia association" was the only juridical category that could be mobilized. The political cost of such an accusation should matter little in the face of the binding nature of penal action, which was a fundamental principle inscribed in the Italian constitution.

Beyond these judicial controversies, the ups and downs of these trials demonstrated that although the question of "what is the mafia?" has found significant clarification in the judicial sphere, the question of "who is a mafioso?" still remains unclear. How should one measure the degree of criminal involvement of an individual who is not formally part of the mafia association? How might one measure the degree of awareness of such an involvement? This is the same problem confronting magistrates hearing cases for racketeering: What charges should be brought against

---

16. This term has been used in the media and in the parliamentary debate about the Italian Supreme Court decision of March 9, 2012, to quash the conviction of Forza Italia senator Marcello dell'Utri to seven years imprisonment for "external complicity," used to discredit the standing of the offence and the judges who made use of it.

17. One should recall that a new code of judicial procedure was adopted in Italy in 1989 and that, under this new system, which is by nature accusatory, the examining magistrates have been replaced by the public Ministry of Justice.

business people who have been brought—sometimes even forced—to pay a "tax" to criminals, but who finally end up associating with these, accepting their investments, laundering their money, taking "friends of friends" into their businesses, and ultimately benefiting from the criminal economy (control of markets, rigged calls for tenders, intimidation of competitors, preferential tariffs, etc.). Many entrepreneurs who would have been seen as victims in the extortion trials of the 1960s were now from the 1990s onward accused of being accomplices, of granting external complicity, even of associating with the mafia, depending on the extent of their participation in the criminal enterprise. Herein lies the interest of the anti-mafia trials: they are laboratories that permit us to observe how the moral economies have changed over the last forty years in Italy.

The "white mafia," these interlocking relations between mafia criminality and the dominant political or economic class, is as old as the mafia itself, just as is the presence of the liberal professions, such as the medical profession, within Cosa Nostra. The "Operazione Ghiaccio," an antimafia investigation initiated in 2002 thanks to the avowals of the pentito Antonino Giuffré, revealed the complex pattern of interconnections and complicities around well-known doctor Giuseppe Guttadauro, who was the mafia boss of Brancaccio, one of the Palermo neighborhoods with the greatest mafia concentration. There are numerous examples of mafioso doctors, ranging from Melchiorre Allegra, who left some evidence in 1937 of his involvement in the association, to Michele Navarra, head of the Corleonese family from 1940 to 1958. The medical profession has always been particularly appreciated within Cosa Nostra because it opens up possibilities for meeting people, influencing voters, discovering secrets, and creating networks. Telephone tapping and electronic surveillance of Guttadauro's office revealed how it was frequented during the by day by Palemo's well-to-do and by night by killers, receivers, and drug traffickers. Step by step, a name which repeatedly appeared led to the prosecution of another famous Sicilian doctor, Michele Aiello. The press referred to the *mafia bianca* (white mafia) in order to speak about this "white coat" mafiosi, stressing the change in the regime of violence compared to the bloody 1980s and 1990s, a violence that was only whitewashed in the early 2000s.

The Aiello trial, which will be analyzed in Part II, allows us to examine in greater detail the interrelations between the mafia and all sectors of society, including the Anti-Mafia Specialized Police Services. Aiello was one of the wealthiest medical practitioners in Sicily and was accused of extensive fraud at the expense of the Sicilian health system. Pentito Giovanni Brusca, examined as a witness during the Aiello trial, stated that he had received a *pizzino* from Bernardo Provenzano—letters by which the head of Cosa Nostra, who was fleeing from justice, communicated with his associates (see chapter 10)—asking him to treat the Sicilian medical entrepreneur "as if he was the same person as he was."[18] This letter constituted an irrefutable proof that Aiello belonged to the mafia association. This opens the question of whether anti-mafia prosecutors should not apply the criteria for affiliation that were used internally to the mafia and consider as mafiosi only those individuals who had been ritually inducted into the association or were considered as thus by its members (for example, when they call someone "the same person," "the same thing," "Our Thing," Cosa Nostra). Or, alternately, should they not adopt a more complex vision of this phenomenon and seek to punish what is the most harmful for society, namely those interfaces that nourish mafia criminality?

These judicial issues will be addressed in the second part of this book, after examining in this part a number of additional facets of the multifaceted process of naming the mafia. The legal process of constructing a signifier for the word "mafia" that we analyzed in this chapter was supported by the work of activists, artists, writers, and photographers, using the witnessing power of images and texts to demonstrate the mafia's existence.

---

18. Penal Trial n° 74/05 r.g. indicting Aiello Michele, Rome, session of June 7, 2006. I attended several sessions of the Aiello trial in Palermo and had at my disposal the transcript of the whole trial, recorded and transcribed by the Cooperative of Indictment Services O.F.T.

CHAPTER 2

The mafia as a plague

From Falcone's new theoretical model to the grassroots anti-mafia fight

A brief iteration of the changes that had occurred in the legal sphere allows us to fully understand the shifting moral and cultural landscape of social, political, and religious behavior toward the mafia. When Judge Falcone started his career at the end of the 1960s, the mafia was, so to speak, non-existent (Falcone and Padovani 1997: 104). In other words, the tragic and violent events that marked Sicily at the time were attributed to rival gangs and no connection was recognized to exist between them (Mosca [1949] 2002: 4). The commonly held view was that the mafia, rather than a criminal organization or an association with a strict code of conduct, was a Sicilian way of being, feeling, and behaving—thus an attitude, not an organization (Pitrè 1994: 287–297). Until the early 1970s, journalists, magistrates, and policemen who dared to speak of the mafia as a criminal association were systematically silenced, murdered, discredited, or driven out of the public sphere (Lodato 1996). As Falcone recalled: "In the spirit of the time, I sensed an institutional culture that denied the existence of the mafia" (Falcone and Padovani 1997: 39).

The situation changed when, in the late 1970s, prosecutors at the Palermo court appointed Judge Falcone to investigate the Spatola case related to fraudulent activities between the United States and Sicily. It was at that point that the examining magistrate, unable to find direct evidence or witnesses ready to break the Sicilian law of silence, invented what is now known, and still used, as the financial investigation.

By using bank receipts, plane tickets, pictures, and digital prints he unearthed a dense network of conspiratorial ties and an intense traffic in drugs between the Spatola and Inzerillo families in Palermo and the Gambino family in New York. In this manner, Falcone exposed the international character and worldwide spread of the mafia, as well as the seriousness of this phenomenon. For, as Sciascia (2002: 48) remarked, "drugs was not 'one homicide', but a vast and continuous network of homicides; a multinational company of crime, similar to terrorism."

The Spatola case, which culminated in the arrest of some fifty people and the murder of Prosecutor Gaetano Costa—who initiated the case—produced a sense of the unitary character of the mafia. This was soon confirmed from the inside by the testimony of pentito Buscetta which radically changed Falcone's investigation, revealing the imperceptible ties binding together a vast array of criminal events across Sicily, all of which were controlled and executed by a criminal organization that its members called Cosa Nostra. As the investigation progressed, it began to reveal a network, a structure, and view of the unitary character of mafia emerged on the basis of the Buscetta theorem.

The new vision of Cosa Nostra as a unitary and pyramidal criminal association, administered by the Commission and controlled by a head, confirmed the initial intuition captured by the legal category that was created in the 1982 Rognoni–La Torre law, namely "the crime of association with the mafia." Under Article 416 *bis*, which led to the murder of its promulgator (Ruta 2014), Falcone and Borsellino organized the Maxi Trial. The verdict of this trial, reached in 1987 and validated by the Court of Cassation (the highest appellate court in criminal affairs) in 1992, confirmed the Buscetta theorem.

But the pentiti confessions also revealed another truth, adding a moral dimension to the mafia phenomenon: being part of Cosa Nostra also involved torture, dissolving corpses in acid, and assassinating children. The descriptions of murder and violence given by these former men of honor at the Maxi Trial were transmitted on television day and night, and were reported on in detail by the five hundred journalists attending the trial. Sicilians who had not experienced the horrors of the mafia in their own lives or had refused to acknowledge them were now confronted by this reality day after day. They started to feel concerned by what they began to identify as a "civil war" among them, wreaking havoc on the country, especially as the attacks that targeted judges and state representatives also hit bodyguards and civilians. The methods used by the mafia, increasingly described as terrorist in nature, broke the silent consensus that had surrounded the mafiosi and led to alarm and protest among civil society. For the first time there were public demonstrations staged against the mafia (Schneider and Schneider 2003) and people at last began to pluck up the courage to write the simple word "MAFIA," in bold letters, black on white.[1]

The bloody Palermo Spring

During the second half of the 1980s, the fight against the mafia became a political struggle, thanks to Palermo's new mayor, Leoluca Orlando. A member of Christian Democracy, he launched a vast campaign of moral reform and unveiled the ties between his own political party and Cosa Nostra. In 1989, he pioneered a radically new approach in Italian politics, that of integrating representatives of the Italian Communist Party into his council. Indeed, the collapse of the Berlin Wall late that year opened up new avenues for communication between Catholics and communists, who were consequently able to unite their forces in the name of a common cause: the anti-mafia fight for justice.

This new political era, which became known as the Palermo Spring, entailed a broad project of transforming civil society, the renewal portrayed with the symbol of spring. The aim was to reform Sicily's economy and regenerate its political system by subjecting both to close judicial scrutiny. In this context, the city of Palermo, as the first "victim" of the mafia, appeared as joint plaintiff in the Maxi Trial. But the Palermo Spring was to end in bloodshed, as anti-mafia judges, policemen, and politicians were murdered one after the other. Sicilians' new optimism and confidence collapsed even further with the assassination of judges Falcone and Borsellino within less than two months of each other in 1992, in attacks of unprecedented violence.

But the anti-mafia movement continued. Following these tragic events, people began to leave pledges to continue the anti-mafia fight at the "magnolia leaf" fig tree standing in front of Judge Falcone's private home, turning it into as a shrine.[2] "One can rip out a flower, but not

---

1. Many photographs of this period show the importance of writing the word "mafia" in characters as large as possible, and even to photograph this word during demonstrations.
2. The tree is a Ficus macrophylla f. *columnaris*, commonly known as the Moreton Bay fig, but easily confused with trees in the Magnolia genus,

the Spring," one of the pledges stated (Amurri 1992: 46). In 1993, in the wave of support for the anti-mafia cause and emotion that did not break off after the murder of the two judges, Orlando was re-elected mayor of Palermo, which led to a new political era, the so-called Palermo Renaissance. This appellation referred not only to Orlando's project of civic renewal but also to his hosting and sponsoring of a circle of artists, intellectuals, and writers after the fashion of the Italian Renaissance princes.[3] In this way, the mayor promoted a new "culture of lawfulness" through a variety of cultural programs—including theatre, exhibitions, musical performances, literary festivals, scientific and festive events—in order to "grow the anti-mafia culture" (to cite the rhetoric of the time). This culture was deeply impregnated with religious language, to which I now turn.

Sacrifice for the city

One of the most spectacular civic events sponsored by Orlando is doubtless the celebration of Saint Rosalia. Revived under the patronage of the Palermo city council in 1994, this celebration developed prodigiously and rapidly, spectacularly increasing its previous attraction of thirty thousand spectators to five hundred thousand, half of Palermo's population, in just one year. That means that large parts of left-wing, atheist, even anti-clerical part of society took part in this religious celebration. We need to find an explanation for this.

To answer this question we can explore how the new *Festino* interpreted and reinterpreted the iconography and hagiography of the medieval hermitess Rosalia in light of the political context of the anti-mafia struggle (Puccio-Den 2009). The legend recounts that during a violent epidemic of the plague in Palermo in 1624, Saint Rosalia's relics were rediscovered and, after they were carried around the city, miraculously halted the plague. As a result, Saint Rosalia became the patron saint of Palermo, celebrated as the savior of the city. Under Orlando's

---

hence one of its nicknames is "magnolia leaf" fig tree. I use the term "magnolia" to refer to the tree, however, as this is the way it is commonly referred to in the literature around Falcone.

3. See Fabre and Puccio (2002) for an examination of how, some ten years later, some of these artists, writers, and intellectuals assessed their civic, moral, and political experiences during this time.

administration, the themes of the curing of the plague and Palermo's liberation from the mafia were closely intertwined, through repeated references in the media, mayoral speeches, sermons by the cardinal, and leaflets distributed during the festival. This discourse gave a new political and civic meaning to the stage production of Saint Rosalia's legend during the *Festino*.

The image of the saint with a crown of roses was chosen to be illustrated on the festival's posters and leaflets. The rhetoric of revival, common to so many political ideologies, led local authorities to underscore the specific iconographic symbol associated with Saint Rosalia: the singular attribute of this virgin, signified by her name, is her crown of roses. The roses capture Saint Rosalia's representation of spring. In this role, Saint Rosalia evidently constituted the best guarantee as promoter of the Palermo Spring. Indeed, Orlando came to identify himself, and be identified by others, with Saint Rosalia in several ways. First, and most spectacularly, he appeared on stage together with the statue of the saint covered with roses during the central act of the *Festino*, called the Redemption. Second, and more importantly, the mayor's life itself embodied the hagiographic model of Saint Rosalia. Like many other anti-mafia leaders, he had to withdraw from the world for safety reasons, leading a secluded, austere, and solitary existence and sacrificing his private happiness in the name of his ideal. His life was placed in parallel to that of Saint Rosalia who, in the twelfth century, renounced the pleasures of the court she enjoyed as Norman aristocrat and devoted her life to prayer and contemplation on a secluded mountain overlooking Palermo. In the 1990s, hagiographic biographies of anti-mafia judges, activists, or politicians became a new literary genre (La Licata 2002; Lucentini 2003).

In the iconography, Saint Rosalia is often depicted as a Christ-like figure contemplating the cross. Seventeenth-century imagery portrayed her holding a mirror in which the reflection of Jesus Christ invited her to follow him as a spouse and as a model to the world (Gerbino 1991). Yet in the stage representation of her legend in the 1990s, it was the mayor of Palermo who faced the saint, like her mirror's reflection, in a scene entitled "Wedding of Saint Rosalia." In this way he identified himself as the Saint Savior. Indeed, many Sicilians viewed Orlando as a Messiah, whom they expected to free them from the hegemony of the mafia, this transcendent form of Evil. Such identification was supported by the fact that the mayor's biography, as well as that of the murdered anti-mafia magistrates, was compared to the Passion of Christ. This religious theme was reinterpreted within a political code—striking parallels with how mafiosi interpret their political actions and criminal deeds in a religious code (see chapter 10).

Another motif common to the triptych of anti-mafia heroes, Saint Rosalia, and Christ is the acceptance of death as an ineluctable fate. In the iconography of Rosalia, who died at the age of thirty, this is generally represented by her smiling and a skull being placed close to her. This image corresponds closely to the fate of these men and women who dared to confront Cosa Nostra and had to pay for it with their death. As Falcone stated in his last interview: "The thought of death is always my companion" (Falcone and Padovani 1997: 15). "Remember that you will die" is the motto and the common fate of the judges who survived— "walking corpses," as they characterized themselves (Lucentini 2003: 122)—their lives inexorably marked by the inevitability of a premature death. Accordingly, the iconography representing them captures a sense of melancholy with its use of black and white as dominant colors (Battaglia 1999), echoing the theme of one of the most famous paintings in Sicily, the *Triumph of Death*, in which a skeleton rides a white and black horse.

The mafia as "martyrdom"

The most popular photographic image of Judge Scarpinato, the magistrate pursuing the Andreotti case, depicts him as a hermit, an ascetic man of justice standing on a rooftop terrace, surrounded by bodyguards with lethal weapons that both protect and isolate him. The picture was taken by photographer Letizia Battaglia, a protagonist of the Palermo Spring (Battaglia 1999: 124–125). In her book entitled *Passion, Justice, and Freedom*, she deliberately chose to insert some images that represent the Passion of Christ among depictions of the violent deaths of murdered judges, politicians, or policemen, thereby fixing the latter tragic representations in terms of the stylistic Christian codes applied to the former (Battaglia 1999).

Falcone and Borsellino's assassinations inaugurated a new era in which the death of the judges at the hands of Cosa Nostra gained the absolute value of a "sacrifice." Far from weakening their aura or attesting to their vulnerability as mortals and to their failure in undermining the power of Cosa Nostra, the attack on their bodies transformed them into martyrs. Several proceedings were opened in the attempt to have them, and other victims of Cosa Nostra, canonized by the Catholic church.

Among them, Father Pino Puglisi, priest of Brancaccio and murdered by members of Cosa Nostra in September 1993, was beatified in 2013. But the murdered priest was not the only figure of the anti-mafia fight sacralized by the Vatican. During a visit to Agrigento in south-western Sicily in May 1993, Pope John Paul II declared Rosario Livatino, a young judge assassinated by the members of the mafia-type Sicilian organization called Stidda, as "a martyr to justice." Soon after, Livatino's beatification hearings began and, as testimonies were feverishly gathered and biographies flourished, this magistrate became another Christ-like figure. In December 2020, Pope Francis recognized Livatino's martyrdom.

Even when they are not advocated for beatification, the assassinated judges inspired practices drawing from the religious sphere. As we will examine in more detail in chapter 4, Falcone has been, since his death, the object of a civic cult. As such, the gestures performed around the Falcone Tree, such as prayers, offerings, donations of valuables, and, above all, the writing of letters, clearly derive from Catholic devotional practices already studied in other contexts (Albert-Llorca 1993; Puccio 2007). On drawings, still tacked to the Falcone Tree many years after his death, the judge is represented as an angel, as Christ, as Saint Rosalia advocating for Palermo.[4] In letters, he is addressed as if he could hear the writers "from the heavens," as if he had been proclaimed a martyr in a Catholic beatification process. As one poem puts it: "You are my saint; pray for us" (Amurri 1992: 65). Many poems draw on the terminology of the cross, faith, justice, sacrifice, and martyrdom. To this day, messages are placed at the Falcone Tree on the anniversary of Falcone's death on May 23, with thousands of young people travelling to Palermo in what they call a "pilgrimage" to participate in a commemorative ceremony. As Falcone's biographer writes: "Citizens have learned to view this magnolia with a devotion that is similar to that expressed toward St. Rosalia's sanctuary on Mount Pellegrino" (La Licata 2002: 67).

Beyond these retrospective reconstructions, however, the judges' perceptions of their own practices can help us to specify more precisely the ties that link them to Saint Rosalia. Before his assassination, Judge Livatino argued that, in order to judge men, one has to be *above* civil society and therefore stand *outside* society (Abate 1997: 61–74). Rosalia's experience as a hermitess was the very condition that enabled her to intervene in civic life, transforming her into the "advocate of Palermo." Likewise, both Falcone and Livatino have become figures of sacrifice for

---

4. These images are published in Puccio-Den (2009: 283–4).

the city. And in order to achieve their project of salvation, the saint, and the judges needed to lead an ascetic life. In other words, their engagement in the world required that they detach themselves from the world and renounce worldly goods. As such, the ascetic and civic dimensions coexist within judicial practice, revealing the intrinsically religious character of justice in the anti-mafia fight.

Based on this analysis of the iconography that was developed in support of the anti-mafia cause, often drawing on the past and on religion to support this civic fight for justice metaphysically, I now turn to an examination of anti-mafia photography as a new art of seeing and representing the mafia and of fixing a negative meaning to it once and for all, in black and white.

CHAPTER 3

How to photograph something that does not exist?

Anti-mafia photography as a political and cognitive act

When I began studying the mafia, I decided to take into account the whole range of interpretations of the mafia phenomenon that were being produced in society, in order to analyze which prevailed over the others, relying on which media. In the previous chapter, we analyzed how (and why) anti-mafia iconography used religious artifacts, paintings, and prints in commemorative or festive events. Here I turn to anti-mafia photography that, thanks to photography's capacity of representing reality on the ground (Dubois 1990), was a useful medium for giving evidence of the existence and nature of the mafia. Anti-mafia photography was useful not only to disseminate objective information about the mafia but also to spread an interpretation of it that gradually became dominant. Previous works examined the subversive and critical power of aesthetic practices, including the practice of photographing the mafia, now considered as a form of art (Virmani 2016). In this chapter I focus on the indexical power of anti-mafia photography—when this practice began in the late 1970s as a form of committed journalism—that aimed at pointing out what the mafia *is*. A new aesthetic of violence was introduced in two ways: one, through the production and circulation of photographs of the devastation caused by the mafia; and two, through a new form of inquiry (Zecchin 2016) that, parallel to the investigations of the prosecuting authorities, aimed for a visual representation of the causal relationships between mafia crimes and other "social ills" of the everyday life. The concept of "cognitive mapping" (Jameson 1991) can be useful here to define the photography as a cognitive act that modified the social and political perception of the mafia phenomenon by creating a semantic network of logical connections.

Classical works in anthropology have explored the methodology of photography and its role in the analysis of ethnographic material. From Margaret Mead and Gregory Bateson (1942) to Howard S. Becker (1981), photography has been conceived as a powerful instrument to explore society. Mafiacraft has a different purpose. I do not take photographs as a source to explore the mafia world but rather focus on how the photographers, through these images, tried to understand and explain the enigmatic word "mafia." Their witnessing was based on the capacity of their photography to reproduce something that *was there*, in front of the camera lens (Barthes 1980), thus testifying not only that the mafia existed but also how it could create havoc for people in every area of society and especially for the underprivileged. Conceived as an anthropology of *traces*, or of the "secretions" (Zempleni 1996) left by this secret phenomenon, Mafiacraft looks at the category of "signs" supposed to have a "physical connection" (Pierce 1978: 86) with what they indicate or represent. Some anti-mafia activists exploited the photography's "power of designation" (Piette 1992) as a finger pointing out mafia responsibility. Through the sense of sight alone, photography activates a process of thinking, interpreting, and speaking about the mafia during the photographic performances organized by the engaged photographs. Rather than approaching anti-mafia photography as an archive reconstructing memory (Salvio 2014), this chapter analyzes the contexts in which this monumental work was produced and circulated with the aim not only of *telling the truth* but also of enlarging the field of vision and perception (Conord 2007: 21) of what was commonly referred to as the "mafia."

It is necessary to return to the genesis of this photographic activity, which is, at one and the same time, a political and a cognitive act. During the 1970s, the anti-mafia movement was considered subversive and was delegitimized and made illegal by the ruling powers. The collusion between the mafia and the local authorities was so strong that anti-mafia activity was, to say the least, not encouraged from within the state institutions. In fact, anti-mafia activists were often suspected of conspiracy against the state (see chapter 8) and were forced to do their work undercover. The strength of the mafia lies in its ambiguity, in its capacity to avoid any clear definition of what it is. The competing interpretations of this phenomenon cancel each other out, producing an effect of silence.

Breaking the silence for anti-mafia activists entailed not only speaking about the mafia but also communicating assertively and efficiently, giving this word a precise meaning. Photography could help in this task by drawing on the indexical power of images.

To engage in the anti-mafia fight meant for activists to reject the common understanding of the mafia as a mere cultural code and to demonstrate with all their means that it was rather a criminal alliance that brought harm to society: through corruption, environmental degradation, poverty, violence, underdevelopment. Identifying the mafia in this manner meant that citizens could no longer pretend that the "mafia was not their concern": by catching their eye, the photographs forced them to take a clear stand toward it and assume responsibility for the position they took. Exploiting the power of images to force such a face-to-face confrontation was the main task of anti-mafia photography. With the images, photographers provided citizens not only with information but also with an interpretative framework that allowed them to see to a much larger extent the role of the mafia in their midst. Photography thus became a tool by which anti-mafia activists forced state institutions to become concerned about the fight against the mafia, and citizens to be committed to that same cause.

Two photographers invented this working method in the late 1970s: Franco Zecchin and Battaglia.[1] Arguing that the media, colluding with political power, routinely converted information on mafia deeds and violence into counter-information, they saw it as their professional "duty to report" these facts honestly and directly (Battaglia and Zecchin 2006). In an effort to counter the distortion of reality by most journalists working for newspapers of the parties in government during this period, they accepted positions as reporters at the left-wing daily *L'Ora*.[2] Here they paid particular attention of how sub-editors and editors captioned their photographs of mafia killings as these texts often altered the sense of their images. But their activity was not limited to reporting on reality; by photographing the mafia, they also began to construct a framework for seeing the world differently. By composing different kind of images, by capturing different aspects of reality in their pictures, they showed that it was not only violent crimes that needed to be attributed to Cosa Nostra but that there were other, much wider social injustices that were directly connected to the mafia as a broader system of governance.

---

1. Franco Zecchin, interview with author, Paris, April 2005; Letizia Battaglia, interview with author, Paris, April 2005.
2. On *L'Ora*, see Nisticò (2001, 2004).

Figure 1: Exhibition "Mafia & territory," 1978: Impastato, center. (Source: Photo Archive, Centro Siciliano di Documentazione Giuseppe Impastato. Photographs displayed on the poster by Letizia Battaglia.)

From the late 1970s the two photographers began to display their work across Sicily as part of travelling exhibitions. In 1978, shortly before his murder, an extreme leftwing leader organized an exhibition called *Mafia e territorio* (Mafia and territory). The photographs exposed, accompanied by descriptions written in capital letters, the wide range of damages that had been caused to the environment by the collusion between mafiosi and the local political authorities in the little town of Cinisi near Palermo (see Figure 1). The murder of the exhibition organizer, anti-mafia activist Giuseppe Impastato, on May 9, 1978, only a few days after its opening, did not deter the organizing of other anti-mafia exhibitions with photos on poverty, environmental degradation, violence, social inequality, squalor, neighborhoods in ruin, and killings. One of the most famous of these exhibitions, called *Mafia Oggi* (Mafia today), opened on May 9, 1979, just one year after Impastato's murder (Figure 2). It was organized by the Centro Siciliano di Documentazione,[3] with

---

3. The Centro Siciliano di Documentazione was founded in 1977 by Umberto Santino and Anna Puglisi.

Figure 2: Cover of the catalogue of the *Mafia Oggi* (Mafia Today) exhibition. (Source: Photograph by Franco Zecchin.)

the active involvement of Battaglia and Zecchin. A national demonstration against the mafia provided an ideal context for exhibiting these images (see Figure 3).[4]

The exhibitions organized elsewhere in Sicily by Battaglia and Zecchin took the form of installations for which string was strung across the main square of the towns and villages, to which the photographs were pegged. The mafia was the common denominator for the images: it was the theme that framed the installations. The aim of the exhibitions

---

4.   See Battaglia and Zecchin (1989, 2006) and Battaglia (1999) for collections of these photographs. These volumes are today considered art books. See also https://francozecchin.com/mafia/.

Figure 3: National demonstration against the mafia. (Source: Photographs displayed on the poster by Letizia Battaglia.)

was to deconstruct the image of the mafia as a Sicilian way of being, which many connected to positive values such as pride, courage, solidarity, friendship, commitment to the family and group, honor, and even piety, and to replace it with its other, negative face. For this, the exhibitions wanted to make visible the mafia's negative side and to provoke at least a reaction in the viewers if not lead them to ask more critical questions. These photographic installations can be viewed as a provocation, challenging the cultural practice of turning a blind eye toward the mafia, a phenomenological condition that allowed the maintenance of *omertà*: if you had not seen anything, you could not speak about it. The photographers countered this practice by using a visual device that forced the viewer to come face to face with images depicting the violence and destruction caused by the mafia—by photographs that were in the way, that created an obstruction in public spaces—thus forcing the viewer to confront this reality and make sense of it (see Figure 4). This posture of engagement directly challenged the haziness that existed around what the mafia is: the mafia acquired a concrete meaning, one that was visible, tangible, and intelligible.

By conveying new ways of seeing the social world, the anti-mafia photography provided innovative categories of thinking. The critical

Figure 4: Posters bringing people face to face with the mafia. (Source: Photo archive Centro Siciliano di Documentazione Giuseppe Impastato.)

power of these images depended on their contextualization. In their exhibitions, Battaglia and Zecchin replaced the media's routine chronological order of daily crimes and murders with the new logical order they created with the sequence they gave to their exhibits. In this way they provided continuity for what was considered discontinuous: poverty, degradation, corruption, and mafia violence. For this, they employed the heuristic device of the photomontage (Didi-Huberman 2009) to push forward a new visual order: bringing the mafia into an order of visibility and thus increasingly drawing it out of its *invisibility*. More than that, the montages embedded the mafia in a narrative, suggested a way of reading the images, and pointed out the hidden that should not be ignored. As a pedagogical tool, such a montage not only had to show that the mafia existed but also to tell the viewer what it *was*. The "duty to report," as the photographers described their task many years later (Battaglia and Zecchin 2006), was connected with the citizen's right to know. But, prior to this, it was connected to the citizen's need to know how to see, how to read, and how to interpret the pictures—of killings, attacks, poverty, corruption—in order to recognize the links between them, to reveal their common underlying basis, to expose the unseen relationships.

Georges Didi-Huberman considers the montage as an art of war: a method of knowledge and a formal procedure acknowledging the world's disorder, endeavoring to compose a new order of things. The way in which these photographic images also reported the attacks that had taken place against state officials showed how Sicily and Italy were, in fact, at war and how the mafia was becoming increasingly similar to some terrorist threat. Images documenting the havoc caused by mafia attacks could be used as evidence to demonstrate the "terrorist" nature of the mafia. When the most representative and most protected of anti-mafia judges, Falcone and Borsellino, were made the target of these attacks, the scale of the destruction unleashed by the mafia crushed "any hope of any honest Sicilian," to remember the words a citizen wrote on the street where General Dalla Chiesa and his wife had been murdered in 1982. The possibility of even imagining fighting mafia crime, including through photography, seemed to have become utterly pointless. In 1992, Zecchin and Battaglia stopped photographing the mafia: "There was nothing more to photograph," explained Battaglia.

The ground zero of 1992

Returning to the dramatic September 11, 2001, terrorist attacks in the United States, Belgian philosopher Laurent de Sutter (2016) hypothesized that—despite the fact that the expression "ground zero" to refer to the exact location of the disaster was borrowed from the language of war—this conflagration was less a matter of conflict between civilizations or religions than a matter of images. More relevant than the act of killing people, for the Islamist terrorists, was the flash provoked by the crashing planes that led to an escalation of shocking pictures. This provocative hypothesis can retrospectively be applied to the mafia bombings of 1992. After the Capaci massacre and the Via D'Amelio bombing, the mafia was recognized not only as a criminal association but also as a terrorist organization by the media, the Italian people, and the state. Spontaneous shrines set up in New York after the attack on the Twin Towers (Fraenkel 2002) were in all aspects similar to the Albero Falcone memorial site (see chapter 5). Islamic terrorists and mafiosi share the same prohibition of depictions or a relationship to images that is, at the very least, ambiguous and problematic.[5] In 1992 Cosa Nostra created a ground zero: it entered into a new visual order by putting on a pyrotechnical show of its capacity to inflict damage. The aim was no longer to remain invisible but to become visible by razing everything around to the ground, blinding everyone with a flash. These terrorist acts spoke for themselves, giving a frightening answer to the question, "what is the mafia?" "It is all over," commented Judge Antonino Caponnetto, father of the anti-mafia pool, in July 1992, amid the rubble caused by the car bomb that had just killed Judge Borsellino and his five bodyguards,[6] echoing Battaglia's words. The images produced by Cosa Nostra with the flash of an explosion of superhuman power triumphed over all other images. Widely relayed by the media, they were somewhat unreal. In one of the first times that the mafia presented an icon of itself, it placed itself under the regime of the unpresentable: one could only look away from the appalling violence of the images of the massacre. The magnitude of the disaster spoke for itself; one did not need to report, list, or number. As mafia violence was incommensurable, it was now (again) un-(re)presentable.

In 1992, the Court of Cassation convicted the leadership of Cosa Nostra, which confirmed the mafia as a centralized criminal organization. The Cosa Nostra reaction to this verdict paradoxically confirmed the Buscetta theorem, providing clear and resounding evidence of the mafia's existence, thereby affirming in a thunderous voice that it was more prevailing than ever before.

The banalization of the mafia

After the bloody 1980s and its culmination in this terrorist wave of the early 1990s under the leadership of the bloodthirsty Salvatore Riina, Cosa Nostra turned back to keeping a low profile under the subsequent leadership of Bernardo Provenzano in order to survive repression by the state. Once again the most notorious of secret organizations became invisible.

---

5. See Puccio-Den (2009) for an examination of the relationship between the mafia and iconoclasm.
6. For the failed interview with Judge Caponnetto where he uses these words, see "Antonio Caponnetto–E' finito tutto," YouTube video, uploaded by Giacomo Torricelli, no date, 0:26 min, https://youtu.be/1WMLdc1a7hQ.

During this period, the only trace of its resilient existence were the *pizzini* (little pieces, or short letters) that Provenzano, as the new head of the Cosa Nostra, exchanged with its members (see chapter 10). In January 1993, when Riina was arrested, a new era began under the leadership of his right-hand man, Provenzano, who understood that, to pacify the organization, weakened by a "civil war" after the rise to power of the Corleonese clan, to rebuild the consensus lost during its terrorist period, the mafia needed to be quietly powerful and pervasive. The organization thus went back to secretly infiltrating Italian society. Some lawyers and magistrates tried to create a set of legal categories (such as "external complicity with the mafia association" or the offense of "voting in return of mafia favors") capable of grasping the invisible forms of participating in mafia crimes. A growing proportion of the population, however, wanted to recover from the long state of emergency created, first, by the terrorist threat and, second, by the explosion of mafia violence, and return to "normal life" (an indigenous paradigm, considering that a certain dose of mafia in Italian society is somewhat normal). Generally speaking, the second half of the 1990s was a period where the mafia fell out of view. The 1992 bombings were events that marked and changed the lives of many Italians (see chapter 4). So too it was for Battaglia and Zecchin: the latter left Palermo, attempting to escape being identified solely as "the photographer of the mafia," whom he had been for twenty years; the former entered politics by joining the Palermo city council under Orlando. Both photographers decided to archive their work: Battaglia collected more than 6,000 photos (Salvio 2014) and Zecchin constituted his personal archive as a place of remembrance that would keep the memory of the mafia phenomenon alive, especially the period of the "second war of the mafia" (1981–1982) when the Corleonese family's rise to power led to more than a thousand victims (Zecchin 2016). The mafia under Provenzano, in turn, went back to its normal practice of making insidious and invisible the everyday injuries it inflicted, the corruption it engaged in, the harm it caused. By returning to the order of invisibility, the mafia was again out of the limelight, and the lens of the camera could not grasp it anymore.

If Zecchin and Battaglia attempted to photograph something that cannot be named, that does not exist, and that evades definition, then a new, relative tolerance toward the mafia in the second half of the 1990s (as long as this became, in outward appearance, less violent again) allowed mafiosi to appear in public much more brazenly than before. For this we can turn to the photographs produced by Sicilian photographer

Figure 5: Camorristi, masked as witches, preparing lines of coke. (Source: Photograph by Mauro D'Agati.)

Figure 6: Kids, one of them holding a weapon, play games in a rundown neighborhood of Naples. (Source: Photograph by Mauro D'Agati.)

Figure 7: Tattoos on skin and rocks. (Source: Photograph by Mauro D'Agati.)

Mauro D'Agati, published in *Napule Shot* (D'Agati 2010), on his experience sharing everyday life with a Camorra group. The artist did not conceive of his work as a political act or civic duty.[7] He photographed the Camorra *from the inside*, taking pictures of its members engaging in daily activities: eating, playing games, performing music, holding festivals, manufacturing cocaine, marrying, engaging in street skirmishes with the police, being arrested. Environmental degradation is still there as the backdrop. But the aesthetic code has changed. It is not the black and white of the Zecchin and Battaglia images anymore, but the use of bright colors, showing happy and relaxed faces and people in nonchalant poses: men wearing witches' masks and preparing cocaine (Figure 5), boys playing football or handling a weapon (Figure 6). The dramatic tension is gone. The images show that the Camorrists do not want to hide but to showcase themselves, as when they expose their tattooed bodies to the sun, blending in with the stones that are covered with graffiti (Figure 7). Their lives are not concealed but openly displayed. The images show a mafia that is integrated into its environment, where there is no stigma attached to it, where it is not seen as a plague. Being illegal is presented as an ordinary way of living. The images suggest that

---

7. Mauro D'Agati, interview with author, Palermo, August 2015.

the changing visibility of the mafia is linked to a deeper and ongoing transformation of its mode of presence. But we must retake it from the beginning if we want to understand the claims of people who placed obstacles in the path of seeing the mafia as an inevitable counterpart to the "normal physiology" of the modern state.

CHAPTER 4

Bearing witness

Pilgrimage to the Falcone Tree

After Falcone's murder in 1992, activists began to note a perplexing practice taking hold at the Falcone Tree: "I saw a bride getting out of her car and donating her bouquet....I saw two young girls kneeling down: they prayed in silence and, before leaving, offered up their jewelry: a gold chain and a ring containing a precious stone," notes Sandra Amurri (1992: 16), journalist for *l'Unità*, the Italian Communist Party daily.[1] Acts like these, triggered by a shocking incident or an extraordinary event, are consistent with the Catholic devotional repertoire and recall in particular the cult practices in honor of Saint Rosalia of Palermo: her reliquary is festooned with jewels, and the walls of her sanctuary are covered in ex-voto offerings and letters placed there by the believers.[2] While Palermitans pilgrimaging to Monte Pellegrino, Saint Rosalia's hermitage, place their written notes on the walls of the cave where she had lived as a hermit, people who visit the Falcone Tree attach their written messages to the trunk of the tree standing before the apartment

---

1. *L'Unità* was founded by Antonio Gramsci in 1922 and was the mouthpiece of the Italian Communist Party until 1991, when it was disbanded.
2. Written forms of communication with the saints are witnessed all over Catholic Europe. On votive writings to the Black Madonna of La Daurade (Toulouse, France) and in the chapel dedicated to St. Rita in the Parisian district of Pigalle, see Albert-Llorca (1993).

where the two murdered judges, Giovanni Falcone and his wife Francesca Morvillo, spent their solitary and isolated life (Puccio 2007). For each, these gifts of writing increase in number on the anniversary of their deaths: September 4 for the patron saint and May 23 for Judge Falcone.[3] In the same way that the Saint Rosalia cult is administered by a congregation, Falcone's memory is nurtured by the Fondazione Giovanni e Francesca Falcone (see chapter 5).[4] On the anniversary of Falcone's death, the written offerings are celebrated in a commemorative ceremony. Those who attend this ceremony consider the visit as a pilgrimage.

The Capaci massacre was an attack of unprecedented violence. As Judge Falcone was driving from the airport to Palermo, the man of honor Giovanni Brusca, from the Corleonese clan, sat on a hill overlooking the expressway and by remote control triggered a bomb—more than one ton of explosives previously placed under the tarmac—as the car passed over it. The car with the three bodyguards exploded and they were killed immediately. Falcone's car collided with the shock wave; he and his wife Judge Morvillo, who was sitting next to him, died a few hours later as a result of the accident. The official driver of the car, who was sitting in the back seat, miraculously survived.

One consequence of the Capaci massacre was that it destabilized engrained perceptions of mafia actions and ways of reacting to them. Unlike other spontaneous and ephemeral shrines raised after mafia murders in Palermo and its surroundings, the Falcone Tree was subjected to an enduring wave of writing that did not break off, even after the first upsurge of emotion after Falcone's attack had passed. Leaving written messages, drawings, flowers, and photographs at the Falcone Tree has become a persisting practice. For almost thirty years now, the citizens

---

3. We may notice that only Falcone has become an object of veneration. Paula Salvio (2012: 397) has analyzed "the absence of Morvillo's memory in the public imaginary specifically and the implications this absence has for imagining a feminist antimafia consciousness attached to ideals of self-sacrifice and martyrdom more generally."

4. The foundation is now called the Fondazione Falcone. Francesca Morvillo's family disaffiliated itself from the foundation in April 2017, due to the fact that Falcone's memorialization overshadowed the memory of Morvillo, a fellow magistrate, united with him in the fight against the mafia, in life and in death. The foundation is an NGO recognized by the United Nations and funded by the region of Sicily.

of Palermo and elsewhere have continued to offer expressions of anger, bitterness, hope, and sorrow at the tree in the form of letters, poems, and drawings, in black and white or color, on the widest range of materials and media. These gestures detach the writing from the intimate sphere and inscribe it into the public arena, forcing it into the register of action. As a result, this writing becomes a possible object of study for the social sciences. This chapter views these writings as a vehicle for political expression and argues that these humble acts of writing and drawing on these small pieces of paper and the minimal actions of placing these at the tree have contributed widely to establishing the anti-mafia movement as a national cause. I look at how, and attempt to explain why, this organization is modeled on religious groups of Christian origin. The chapter considers how each pilgrim, as a witness to martyrdom, is caught in an evidential process in which writings hold a central position. This is why I have attached such importance to the tiny pieces of paper attached to the Falcone Tree.

The secretary of the foundation, who acts as minister of the Falcone Tree cult, has since 1992 collected these transient testimonies, often already faded by exposure to the elements, in an effort to keep the judges' memory alive. I was able to draw on this monumental collection and on Sandra Amurri's book *L'Albero Falcone* that published messages from 1992. Some of them are reproduced there as transcriptions, while others, even more interesting for the ethnographer, are depicted in their original form, in particular when the creations combined drawing, photography, and/or newspaper cuttings with the writing. Many of them are signed and dated, often allowing one to determine the age and origin of their authors and the time when they were placed under the tree. These writings and images suggest that the practices devoted to Judge Falcone have taken on the form of a cult, thus shifting them into the religious sphere. When all letters from 1992 are considered, it becomes apparent how this collective form of creativity has emulated certain iconographic models specific to Christianity. A recurring motif in Christian iconography is the use of the tree to symbolize the foundation of a religious community (Donadieu-Rigaut 2005). By reframing the Capaci massacre as an *event*—that "strange fold [in time] from which point nothing was ever the same again" (Bensa and Fassin 2002: 11)—embedded in Christian symbolism, the founding act of the new Christian era, namely the death of Christ, is called to mind (Agamben 2000).

The tree

Why did the magnolia tree situated in front of Falcone's house become the rallying point for anti-mafia activists immediately after his death, and what are the consequences of its adoption as symbol for the anti-mafia cause?

We must go back in time to understand the political context in which the Capaci massacre was perpetrated. When Orlando was elected mayor for the first time in 1989, he tried an experiment that was totally new to Italy: a coalition between Christian Democracy and the Italian Communist Party. This political alliance—the Palermo Spring—was as seasonal as its name suggests. In 1990, under pressure from Christian Democracy, the municipal government fell. The mayor resigned and established his own movement, called La Rete (the network). In his program, Orlando used the symbolism of spring to talk about the regeneration necessary in the political system. For his anti-mafia party, the Falcone Tree, nurtured with the blood of the judge, was a place where it could symbolically root its efforts, and the location thus became a focal point for its legitimacy and continuation. The perennial leaves of this magnolia tree represented the continuation of the "dreams" the two judges had believed in: "Justice, state, duty to the point of sacrifice" (Amurri 1992: 13). Those leaving messages at the tree pledged to take their task forward: "We shall fulfill your dreams!" wrote Loredana, a young woman of eighteen (Amurri 1992: 71). Orlando too tried to hook into this language—echoing Martin Luther King's "I have a dream" speech—with his own dream of becoming mayor of Palermo. His party, which covered a broad political spectrum, brought Orlando back to head the municipal government in 1993, when he was reelected mayor of Palermo with 75% of the votes.[5] With the Falcone Tree, the Palermo Spring was reinforced, institutionalized, and firmly implanted in the very heart of the city or, as captured in the words of Simon in his note on the tree: "You can crush a flower but you can't prevent spring" (Amurri 1992: 46). Regenerated by the judge's sacrifice, the tree would give rise to a new Palermo spring. Demonstrations, meetings, committees, associations, foundations, and the exploration of new forms of protest—like the unusual form used by women, who hung white sheets into the windows during the mourning ceremony after the Capaci massacre—announced this new political season.

---

5. Orlando was reelected as mayor in 2012, a position he still holds.

Based on these two powerful metaphors—the tree and the net—and structured along the lines of the first Christian groups, the anti-mafia movement seemed destined for limitless expansion. The Falcone Tree filled the gaping hole left by the Capaci bombing. And it countered the explosion of the mafia bombs with a counter-explosion: "Here [by the tree], you have left your miracle. Would you like to know what that is? The desire to defeat the mafia has exploded," wrote Rino (Amurri 1992: 76). The anti-mafia cause imitated the religious expansionism of the early Christians. Orlando's network and web of people continued to extend the branches of this "anti-mafia tree." The sacrificial death of the judges and their bodyguards added not only a political dimension to the Palermo spring—weaving the anti-mafia web to rebuild the social fabric after the catastrophe, and ensnare the mafia's tentacles—but also an eschatological one. As Anna's message confirmed: "With you, now, we speak more than before/and there will not be a night when/through you, a prayer does not rise up/to God, so we can bring the longed-for Spring to our land" (Amurri 1992: 51).[6]

Those who first assembled at the tree, those who witnessed the murder of the two judges and their bodyguards, people from the left and far-left who declared themselves as atheists, all used religious grammar, and not just any such grammar. In Christianity, the death of Christ is the founding point of a community whose expansion throughout the world, with a view to spreading the word of the Lord, finds a special significance in the tree. The group assembled around the Falcone Tree recalled spiritual families—trees—that featured in Christian history. In the Middle Ages, the tree-order that springs forth from the intestines of the founder of the monastic order represents religious communities and their attachment to the source as well as their capacity for expansion.[7] By associating the memory of Judge Falcone to the symbol of the tree, anti-mafia supporters placed him on the same register as that rooted in the Passion of Christ and applied to saints, martyrs, and the founders of monastic orders (Donadieu-Rigaut 2005: 205). This assimilation can easily occur in a society like Sicily where even non-believers are profoundly influenced by Christianity because the wider culture and society is deeply rooted in Catholicism.

---

6. I have kept the spelling and rhythm of the original messages.
7. A rich corpus of images of the tree-order is shown in Donadieu-Rigaut (2005).

In other forms of writing than that which spontaneously emerged at the Falcone Tree, Christian symbolism was even more explicit. The suffering of Falcone in an unjust land is a thread that runs through a biography written about him posthumously (La Licata 2002). His "sacrificial" death following "betrayal" by friends, to use the biographer's terms, reverberates closely with the Christly theme that emerged at the Falcone Tree. Indeed, in drawings and photographs, the tree often resembles a cross, with its perpendicular branches directing the gaze of anti-mafia supporters upwards, as captured in an image by Zecchin.[8] Like Christ, the judge never fully died: in death he seems to have attained a new life. "Falcone lives" (La Licata 2002: 43), students declare when they gather, like apostles, at the feet of the Falcone Tree. And so, like Christ, the judge seems to be instantiated at a place different from where he is buried. Honoring him elsewhere than at his grave indicates a desire to remove him from the usual mourning procedures. In the final resting place of the Falcone Tree that his followers have assigned him, the judge is not alone:

> In this strong, thriving trunk, which reaches up into the sky, everyone continues to see Giovanni and Francesca, as in the legend of Philemon and Baucis where Ovid recounts that the gods allowed this husband and wife, who loved one another dearly, to die together, turning into a single tree: united in death as in life. (La Licata 2002: 16)

In the same way, Falcone and his wife Morvillo became a legend. Like members of a religious community who reproduce themselves by means that are not carnal, they decided not to have children of their own: "We didn't want to create orphans," Falcone explained in an interview. After their assassination, they became the imaginary ancestors of a community that chose them: "You didn't want any children. I would like you to be my dad," Luisa from Naples wrote to Falcone.[9] These blood

---

8. This photograph is reproduced in Puccio-Den (2009: 281), a book that examines the links between politics and religion in Southern European reconciliation processes after civil wars (Spain, Sicily).

9. In April 2017, Falcone's remains were moved into Palermo's San Domenico church, the pantheon of all prominent Sicilian personalities. Morvillo's remains were not moved, however, thus creating a hierarchy between the two murdered judges and provoking the disaffiliation of Morvillo's family from the Falcone Foundation.

relationships created by writing will be borrowed by Provenzano, Cosa Nostra's new head, in an attempt to restructure the relationships of trust among the mafiosi (see chapter 10).[10]

The theme of the tree is omnipresent in posters and drawings produced in schools as part of an educational program run by the Falcone Foundation to promote a culture of lawfulness. Many schoolchildren draw the tree, with the judge as the trunk and the branches as links to other "mafia victims," a category that could be created when the Capaci massacre and Via D'Amelio bombing linked the mafia with terrorism (see chapter 8). In these posters, the Falcone Tree has become a kind of anti-mafia family tree, suggesting a genealogical theme: Falcone is displayed as ancestor in a line that includes all those who have been murdered by mafiosi (regardless of their true dates of death): ranging from trade unionist Salvatore Carnevale (d. 1955) to far-left activist Impastato (d. 1978) and carabiniere Captain Emanuele Basile (d. 1980) to General Dalla Chiesa (d. 1982). Falcone's death marks the beginning of a retrospective genealogy that starts with his sacrifice, like monastic families literally taking root in the innards of their dead founder (Donadieu-Rigaut 2005: 239).[11] These religious communities existed (and exist) only to spread the word of their founder, conceived of as a martyr and a witness who died to affirm the absolute value of his religion. Let us examine whether the same can be said of the anti-mafia movement.

Pilgrimage as bearing witness

On July 7, 1992, not even two months after the slaying of Falcone, Judge Borsellino, who had taken over from him, became the next high-status victim of a mafia attack when he was killed in a car bombing that took place in the Via d'Amelio, together with five police agents who were escorting him. Both killings heralded a new era for the anti-mafia movement, projecting it far beyond Sicily as numerous Italians began to realize that they could no longer remain indifferent toward aggression on

10. About blood relationships shaped by texts, see also Puccio-Den (2009: Chap. 1).
11. For a discussion of the prototype of these representations, Jesse's tree, which depicts the lineage of Christ and designates him as a new David, see Donadieu-Rigaut (2005: 245).

this scale.[12] With these two sacrificial figures for the public good, the state took on an absolute value, in a country and particularly in a region from which it had been absent until then. Far from undermining the judges's aura, revealing their weaknesses, or exposing their failures, this attack on their physical bodies made them martyrs for the country. The nation, a nation without heroes, tarnished by the experience of fascism, was by now considered sacred.

Falcone and Borsellino were martyrs primarily in terms of the word's Greek etymology of being a "witness (of God)," thus someone who experiences in the flesh the ordeal of a Christly sacrifice. Bearing witness means affirming the value of something through one's actions and words. The two anti-mafia judges faced an ordeal of fire, cutting short a life dedicated to promoting justice. The following statement by Falcone has become his moral testimony: "To this city [Palermo], I would like to say: men perish; ideas endure. What endures are their moral ideals which continue to walk on the legs of other men" (Amurri 1992: 30). This declaration is often seen on banners paraded at the numerous public demonstrations triggered by the deaths of the two judges. Demonstrating is a commonly accepted form of bearing witness. As the demonstrators marched, they brandished life-size photos of the smiling faces and upper bodies of Falcone and Borsellino. The banners bore the words: *le vostre idee camminano sulle nostre gambe* (your ideas walk on our legs). If, as Paul Ricœur (2000: 201–208) stated, "the event, in its most primitive sense, is that about which one bears witness," the thousands of people who came from all corners of Italy to attend Falcone's funeral became witnesses to his martyrdom. This opens the question of whether the messages they left at the Falcone Tree at the time would not thus have become a kind of evidence for the existence of the mafia.

The need to leave one's mark is a distinguishing characteristic of a pilgrimage. It can be seen in very old practices, such as the way pilgrims in the Middle Ages traced their hands and footprints on the walls of the churches they visited (Spera 1977: 238). The new pilgrims of the 1990s also seemed very keen to leave a mark of their visit to the Falcone Tree. This explains the importance they attributed to attaching their signatures to their messages, despite their informal nature, drawing on a signature's power to "serve as a sign of validation" (Fraenkel 1992: 18). "Thank you,

---

12. From this moment onwards we find the mafia referred to as a plague, pointing to how it cannot be contained and isolated from wider society (see chapter 2).

judges FALCONE and/BORSELLINO for having/taught us that simple and honest/men can defeat the/mafia and for having encouraged us to/carry out a lifetime pilgrimage of hope and ACTION," wrote Vincenza, who came to Palermo from the town of Cosenza in Calabria to pin her small note to the Falcone Tree (Amurri 1992: 117). But why have the youth who participated in the Falcone Foundation's educational tours, inspired by a culture of lawfulness, been called pilgrims? It does not point to the religious nature of their visits but to the political dimension of this experience, which implies a personal commitment in a validation process that authenticates a saintly life through a personal ordeal (Puccio 2007). The writing of the youth is endowed with additional powers: it commits the individual to a collective action, through a written and signed contract that forms a counterpart to the bloody signature with which the initiation of a "man of honor is signed (see chapter 10), and brings writing out of the intimate sphere into the public. As Giuseppe wrote:

> Falcone:
> Today, nearly one month since the
> Capaci massacre, I find myself in
> Palermo, you know, I felt the need to write these few lines
> and to pin them to the tree below
> your home, to testify that
> your memory, and that of your wife
> and bodyguards, is still alive in me. (Amurri 1992: 120)

For this activist, Falcone's testimony is a memorial and his body a war memorial. Through these messages, their abundance and the reiteration of their content, the judge's memory is now indestructible, despite the transient nature of the media on which the letters are written. The Capaci massacre creates an event, after which the old order can no longer be restored. Falcone's sudden physical absence[13] due to his murder formed a break and introduced a new time, the timeless time of memory, guaranteed by the messenger-writers who act as witnesses to the past. Rising up like a tombstone, decorated—as grave markers are in the Italy's south (Faeta 1993)—with photographs of the slain judges and their bodyguards, the magnolia displays the classic signs of a funeral monument: "In eternal memory of all those who have died in the struggle against the mafia" (Amurri 1992: 28). The writing becomes an epitaph aimed at

---

13. On the place of the absent body in Christianity, see de Certeau (1982).

communicating with the deceased. It attracts the gaze of passers-by, encourages meditation, strives to move them, and, above all, reminds them of the victims' tragic fate. These fluttering bits of paper that, at first sight, appear so fragile sum up two essential functions of public writing: making people think and making them remember (Corbier 2006).

Some of these letters are read out loud at various events of remembrance, and some writers base their letters on this knowledge. Thus Angelo, who implicitly identifies the tree as the judge's grave, addresses his note to Falcone's sister in the hope that she will read his letter out loud at the grave: "I wrote you this poem with all my heart and I hope that, when you bring flowers to your brother, you will read it to him" (Amurri 1992: 33). We must interpret these texts within the framework of the ritual conditions of their performativity. The tree has thus become a place of praying to the judge, and the letters a means for doing so. Every year, the anniversary of Falcone's murder on May 23 presents an opportunity to perform these acts collectively, thereby renewing the vow to remember. "Not to forget" is an obligation for Falcone's heirs, the anti-mafia supporters, a community of remembrance based on writing. The intrinsic characteristic of bearing witness is that something is passed on, hence the common Italian expression *passare il testimone* (passing on the baton, with *testimone* meaning both "witness" or "testimony") (Di Lorenzo 2000: 85). For these pilgrims, witnesses, and potential martyrs, this involves following the indicated path: "I will never have peace/until the work that you have started/and which it is our duty to continue/is accomplished," writes Giuseppe, whose signature is preceded by the words "WITH DUTY" (Amurri 1992: 120).

A duty to remember, a duty to pursue justice, and duty as the ideal proclaimed by the murdered judge during his life. The death of the two judges led to a pact with the people, encouraging new vocations to the profession of the judge. Gaetano Paci,[14] the deputy prosecutor for the Anti-mafia District of Palermo, wore his robe for the first time on the day he carried his teacher's coffin to its grave. So did Antonino Di Matteo, Antonio Balsamo and other anti-mafia judges. Many law students from cities all over Italy and Sicily came to Palermo for this state funeral, showing that they were willing to step into the shoes of the assassinated judge. The messages they left around the Falcone Tree reveal that these future judges identified with the model of professional excellence he had expected: "I'm studying law in Florence with the intention of carrying out my future

---

14. Gaetano Paci, interview with author, Palermo, October 2006.

profession as judge or lawyer as you did," wrote L. (Amurri 1992: 24). The pledges of emulation elicited by the murders of Falcone and Borsellino extended far beyond this profession: "I want to fight, GIOVANNI, for you and for PAOLO…Your example has made me a better person. You didn't die for nothing, because you have won, you have defeated the cowardice that is part of man, the fear of being alone in death," wrote Cristiana (Amurri 1992: 126) who declared without further ado: "Now, you are heroes for me." Between hero and saint, there is but one small step.

An arbitrator of justice while he was alive, in death Falcone became a figure of intercession between heaven and earth, like Saint Rosalia, the "advocate of Palermo" since the seventeenth century. The tree, which spreads its branches heavenwards and sinks its roots into the earth, is the vector of this two-way communication, as inferred by a letter deposited at the tree and addressed to Falcone's sister: "Your brother is looking down at us from above, he urges us on, smiles at us and encourages us" (Amurri 1992: 33). Mariangela's letter directly elevates Falcone to the realm of the saints and invokes him as a channel of communication between heaven and earth: "Now, I think of you in peace and very close to the heavenly throne, from which God's smile came down and, thanks to you, touched us poor mortals too. You are my saint. Pray for us!" (Amurri 1992: 65). The step has been taken. The letters that citizens continue to place at the foot of the tree or to send to the address "Falcone Tree, Palermo," as though the judge could read them from up in heaven, demonstrates the persistence of this symbolism linking this martyr for justice to the prototype of all Christian martyrs, the Passion of Christ.

Imago Christi

The similarity between Falcone and Jesus Christ is created by melding the judge's body with the magnolia, like the Son of God is inseparable from the cross—a cross that, as all Christians know, is made of wood.[15] Whether written, whispered, or thought, the prayers addressed to the judge were prompted by the Falcone Tree, as invocations of Christ are inspired by the sight of the crucifix: "I am here, in front of your tree, which makes me think more and more of your honesty and courage," wrote Roberta (Amurri 1992: 33). Verses from the Bible were often quoted in

---

15. On the cult connotations of wood in the Middle Ages, see Pastoureau (1993).

the letters: "Happy are the persecuted for the cause of justice: for they shall enter the kingdom of heaven!" (Amurri 1992: 33). Did God abandon Falcone on the fateful day of May 23, 1992, like he delivered his son Jesus to his fate on the day of his crucifixion? "And you, merciful God, where were you?" asked Germana (Amurri 1992: 110). A child's drawing shows the three crosses on Golgotha: one of them is Christ, his heart bleeding, and at his feet the two martyrs Falcone and carabinieri Captain Basile. The prayer on the back of the paper, torn from a school exercise book, is addressed to the mafiosi: Ezia, a 5th grader attending elementary school, calls on them to think about their sins (Amurri 1992: 138–139).

The theme of sin and forgiveness is present in other messages: "SEE YOU IN HEAVEN!/Maybe if your assassins repent/through the divine purifying blood of our/SAVIOR JESUS CHRIST, they will be there too!!/I'm sure that you would forgive them/with a handshake" (Amurri 1992: 113). Just like Christ, Falcone forgives his persecutors. In Alba's prayer, Justice is the Word of the judge: "I hope that, from where you are/in heaven, you will make these people understand/that they are men and not/animals, try to make them understand/that the justice you wanted may be/their word of life now too/I believe in your word 'JUSTICE'" (Amurri 1992: 115). Amurri's book L'Albero Falcone itself ends on an appeal intended to be affixed to the tree and read by visitors. It is an appeal to Man, the definition of which remains closely tied to that of the Christian: "Man: Why do you create discord? Why do you like violence? Why do you not see in others your brother? Man-God who forgives from the Cross: 'Father, forgive them for they know not what they do'" (Amurri 1992: 106). To understand these texts, one must go back not only to the practices that drive them but also to the context in which they were produced: the transformation of the anti-mafia struggle into a religious battle.

During the celebration of mass for the murdered judges and their bodyguards in the cathedral of Palermo, one of the widows took the microphone to ask the mafiosi who were present to repent:

I, Rosaria Costa, widow of agent Vito Schifani, baptized *in the name of the Father and of the Son and of the Holy Spirit*, on behalf of all those who have given their lives for the State...the State...I ask first of all that justice be done.

Now, addressing the men of the Mafia...—because they are here inside...but not, they are certainly not Christians—I want you to know that for you too there is a possibility of forgiveness.

I forgive you, but you have to get on your knees, if you have the courage to change...—But they do not change, they do not want to change [repeated several times]—...to radically change your plans, the mortal plans you have. Go back to being Christians!

That's why we pray in the name of the Lord who said in the name of the cross: "Father, forgive them, for they know not what they do."

That's why we ask you for the city of Palermo, that you have made a city of blood, too much blood, to work for peace, justice, hope, and love for all. But there is no love here, there is no love, there is no love at all....[16]

She cried, with a voice interspersed with tears, before being moved by the crowd like one of the Three Maries in the Passion.

Some mafia members declared that they were deeply touched by these words and that they decided to break their silence as a result of this plea. It bears recalling that *pentitismo* (repentance) by individual mafiosi—thus cooperation with the law, in which Falcone played a major role—is very often described as an act of conversion by those who disclose their deeds. This is how Leonardo Vitale, the first Cosa Nostra pentito, ended his confession, after having equated the mafia with a "social illness": "These are the ills I have been victim to, I, Leonardo Vitale, resurrected in the true faith of God" (Lupo 1999: 312). His words, pronounced on May 30, 1973, became audible only twenty years later. On May 9, 1993, Pope John Paul II called on mafiosi to "convert" during his homily at the Valle dei Templi in Agrigento, another Sicilian town where a judge had been murdered, by using words echoing the plea by Schifani's widow:

Let there be concord, this concord, this peace to which every people and every human being aspires, and every family. After so many times of suffering, you finally have a right to live in peace. And those who are guilty of disturbing this peace, those who carry on their

---

16. I attach particular importance to this plea because it played a crucial role in the anti-mafia struggle, a struggle shaped by political emotions. See the plea in "Io vi perdono, però vi dovete mettere in ginocchio," YouTube video, uploaded by ergrillodermarchese, May 22, 2012, 2:26 min, https://www.youtube.com/watch?v=ff0wgrgkCBM. Translation by author.

consciences so many human victims must understand that it is not permitted to kill innocents. God once said: "Do not kill!" Man, any man, any human agglomeration, or mafia, cannot change and trample on this most holy law of God.

Pointing at the life-sized crucifix he was standing next to, he loudly declared: "In the name of this crucified and risen Christ, of this Christ who is the way, the truth and the life, I say to those responsible: Convert! Once will come the judgment of God!"[17] This marked a huge change in attitude by the Catholic church toward the mafia as the links between the two had been deeper and longer than one would imagine possible seeing the criminal nature of the latter (see chapter 10). The mafioso is known for being a practicing Catholic (Dino 2008): he goes to church, is often a member of a religious brotherhood, partakes of all sacraments, and goes to confession. This faithful behavior could be considered as one—though not the only—explanation for the church's tolerant attitude toward the organization and the practice, where possible, of turning a blind eye toward its evil deeds. Indeed, the church only began to change its stance when the wider global context—the fall of the Berlin Wall, the end of the Cold War with the decreased fear of communism within the Catholic universe—changed, and when the moral and spiritual revolution initiated by anti-mafia activism in Italy conquered Catholic audiences.

Called upon in the 1980s to reform society, to set it right, and to amend its morals, the judges became the representatives of a humanist credo that encouraged people to turn away from egotism. Cosa Nostra, which means "our business" ("Our Thing"), is just the criminal version of attitudes considered as quite "normal" in southern Italy, called "amoral familism" by Edward Banfield (1958). But anti-mafia judges, who were also Sicilians, seem to contradict this assumption, devoting themselves to others, in the name of Justice, this higher, transcendent principle. It is useful to compare the unpretentious, apparently disparate writing in the letters on the Falcone Tree to a different literary genre that flourished in the 1990s and that continues to bear fruit: the biography of anti-mafia protagonists. This literature focuses on the theme of sacrificing one's private life for the sake of the public good,

---

17. The homily can be viewed at "Giovanni Paolo II contro la mafia—Agrigento, 9 maggio 1993," YouTube video, uploaded by Veritatem facientes in Caritate, no date, 4:41 min, https://www.youtube.com/watch?v=rFTZglCS78M.

highlighting the exceptional resolution of the anti-mafia people in the face of the mortal danger this exposed them to on a daily basis. Their extraordinary courage set them apart from ordinary mortals. They led solitary, if not hermitic, lives. Their conduct surpassed human limits. This effacement of the self, the power to withstand an unbearable pace of work, the ability of subduing one's physical needs of food and sleep, the capacity of cutting oneself off from the world all made the judges heroic figures. When their sacrifice was sealed by death, these heroes turned into martyrs.

The theme of martyrdom creeps surreptitiously into the biography of Falcone by Francesco La Licata. A journalist for the center-left daily *La Stampa*, La Licata still cannot avoid mentioning that, on the day the judge was born, "the calendar showed the feast day of St. Venanzio the martyr." Similarly Falcone's sister Maria referred to symbolism of martyrdom when putting together a commemorative work on him: "When Giovanni was born, a white dove entered the house. It came in through the window and didn't want to leave. It wasn't wounded. It stayed in the room and we fed it: it never flew away, even though the window remained open all the time." In the Christian tradition that was very present in Falcone's pious parental family, the dove represents the Holy Spirit. Its appearance at his birth—a time when, in Mediterranean societies, omens are predicted—clearly announced his fate as a sacrificial Christ. In the same biography, this vocation to sacrifice seems to be a legacy from his mother, as Falcone's sister remembers::

> I remember Mum, when she spoke of her dead brother....He died at eighteen on the Carso,[18] where he had gone to fight as a volunteer. He was a model for my mother, this hero brother whose memory she celebrated unceasingly....The memory and example of her brother never left her. So much so that when her son Giovanni was born, she was happy and gave him the second name of Salvatore. (Amurri 1992: 26)

With the name of Salvatore (savior), which recalls Christ once more, Falcone received as gift and heritage the fate of a heroic and sacrificial death. But more than his death, it is the judge's life that, in its ascetic austerity, recalled that of a saint. "The capacity to suffer, to endure much

---

18. The Carso was one of the frontlines during the First World War.

more than others, without ever giving up" (Amurri 1992: 19) is one of the principal qualities Falcone is acknowledged to have had. "At night, he slept on the floor to prevent himself from falling into a deep sleep and lowering his vigilance" (Amurri 1992: 113). This iconography immediately reminds the Palermitan reader of Saint Rosalia and the restless nights she experienced, lying on the ground in her cave alert to all dangers (wild beasts, snakes, the temptations of the devil) that might assail her.

Saint Rosalia is an imago Christi, a human made in the image of Christ. As the judge's life neared its end, it became a way of the cross. His biographer tells the story of his last evening out, a story into which he created strong parallels between the suffering and death of Falcone and that of Christ. La Licata spoke about the event as a "farewell drinks party," suggesting with this implication of Christ's Last Supper that Falcone knew what was going to happen. During this event, the judge gave a speech in which he spoke of the difficulty of his struggle, his professional solitude, and the gap he felt had widened between himself and others. As he was leaving, one of his colleagues came to say goodbye and with this act, in the description of La Licata, betrayed him: "And he, Giammanco, without batting an eyelid, slapped him on the shoulder and kissed him twice on the cheeks: like Judas" (La Licata 2002: 126). He was not the only one who mentioned Judases in relation to the anti-mafia judges. In a speech shortly before Falcone's assassination, Minister of the Interior Claudio Martelli spoke of the Judases who, out of jealousy, obstructed Falcone's projects (La Licata 2002: 179). In his speech, Martelli addressed the matter in this way, according to his biographer: "What saddened Falcone the most was the hostility of those he had felt, ideologically and politically, to be the closest to him" (La Licata 2002: 155). And yet, for Falcone the bottom line was: "One must do one's duty to the end, no matter what the sacrifice to be endured" (La Licata 2002: 20). Only a short while later, this sacrifice took its most extreme and literal form.

It must be remembered that an anti-mafia iconography, modeled on the Passion, had arisen well before the publication and distribution of these hagiographic biographies. Two examples are photographers Battaglia and Zecchin and their photography between 1978 and 1992. Battaglia's *Passion, Justice, Liberté* (1999) and their co-authored *Chroniques siciliennes* (1989) intersperse photographs of the murdered judges with scenes from Holy Week processions in Sicily. Zecchin's *La Conta*, a black book of mafia victims, was written at the time of Judge Costa's murder in 1980 (reprinted as Zecchin 1993)[19] and shows on its cover the assassinated judge in the pose of the dead Christ taken down from the cross (see also figure 2).

Martyrs as witnesses

To complete the picture and understand the devotional practices surrounding judge Falcone in a wider context, we must now take into account a new category. In its broad sense, this category takes to the extreme the heroization of those who are prepared to sacrifice their lives for an ideal of justice. But in a narrow sense, this term refers to martyrs recognized by the Catholic church through a process of beatification. During the religious Saint Rosalia celebration in Palermo on July 15, 1997, after a procession had carried the saint's urn through the streets, Cardinal Salvatore di Giorgi announced the start of a *super martyrium* process for Father Puglisi, the priest who had been assassinated by mafiosi on September 15, 1993, in Brancaccio, the district of Palermo where the priest had been born and, later, had preached. The cardinal described it as "the first step in order for the supreme authority of the Church to recognize the martyrdom of this servant of God killed by the mafia."[20] Father Puglisi was beatified on May 25, 2013.

The cardinal's announcement marked a historic reversal toward the mafia that had begun in the Catholic church. Members of the mafia traditionally formed the backbone of Christian Democracy's power in Sicily, the Catholic bulwark against the Communists. After the fall of the Berlin Wall, a whole new range of possibilities opened up. In his homily in May 1993 during his visit to Sicily, Pope John Paul II spoke about Judge Livatino, killed by the mafia in 1990, and described him as "a martyr of the law and, indirectly, also of the faith," considering him to have been among those who "assert[ed] the ideals of justice and legality, paid with their lives the struggle they led against the violent forces of Evil" (Di Lorenzo 2000: 87). The pope's speech marked the start of Livatino's beatification process—thus one of the very first public signs that the church was changing its approach to the mafia—with the bishop

---

19. The title of this book refers to a children's game which takes on a macabre twist here: Who's next?
20. I was present at this homily. This sentence is taken from the recording I made of it.

of Agrigento, Carmelo Ferraro, initiating investigative proceedings and a commission of enquiry. On December 20, 2020, Pope Francis recognized the fact of Judge Livatino's martyrdom.

Livatino is the first magistrate in the history of the church to be beatified. A beatification process is no more than a trial and, as for any other trial, it has to be based on evidence and testimonies. As in the case of Father Puglisi, a crucial testimony in Livatino's process of beatification was that of one of his murderers, Gaetano Puzzangaro. Nowadays a pentito (just as Salvatore Grigoli, Father Puglisi's killer), Puzzangaro (who is still serving his prison sentence) states that he was converted by Livatino, the judge he considers a "saint." Since the start of Livatino's beatification process, numerous biographies have been written on this "judge who believed in the religion of duty and in the law" (Di Lorenzo 2000: 87). These biographies must be regarded as forming an integral part of the process of beatification, which involves an investigation to discern the signs of holiness in the lifetime of the candidate. It was through witnesses certifying that he led a saintly life, inspired by the Gospel, that the judge's sacrifice for the city was accepted as an edifying example worthy of beatification. Bishop Ferraro entrusted Ida Abate, a secondary schoolteacher who had taught Livatino as teenager, with the task of collecting the testimonies for Livatino's *super martyrium* process. Just as Livatino continued Christ's mission as "witness to the faith," Abate's witnessing is intended to *passare il testimone* (pass the baton) to others. The journey the teacher undertook in Italy in order to make her former student's experience known is described as an "extraordinary, moving pilgrimage" (Di Lorenzo 2000: 85), affirming its continuity with the semantics of the "pilgrimaging" to the Falcone Tree as an act of witnessing. Furthermore, the testimonies Abate collected describe Livatino as "reserved...allergic to the limelight," connecting him with the genealogy of the other solitary anti-mafia heroes who found in the "pilgrim Saint Rosalia" their illustrious predecessor.

The acts performed by the persons convinced or "converted" by Abate to become witnesses of Livatino's holiness are the same as those performed by Falcone's "pilgrims." In Canicattì, Livatino's friends, relatives, and acquaintances began their pilgrimage immediately after his death (Di Lorenzo 2000: 81). First they met at his house or gathered around his grave. The gestures that took place at his gravestone closely resemble the pious acts carried out at the Falcone Tree, so characteristic of Catholic devotion to the saints. The expression used is once more that of the eyewitness, which embodies and authenticates past experience with a performative uttenance ("I was there...I saw everything"), creating the witness as well as the community of his or her interlocutors (Dulong 1998): "I saw many strangers from all over Italy, kneeling in front of his grave and praying. I saw a mother lift up her child so that he could kiss the young judge" (Di Lorenzo 2000: 90). On what is nearly a funeral shrine, we once again find written offerings: "Among the flowers, there are many messages and letters: short, moving testimonies written mainly by young people. They are the ones who mostly go on pilgrimage to his grave....From this grave, [Livatino] is still able to speak to the conscience and hearts of the men and women of the Third Millennium," declares the assassinated judge's biographer (Di Lorenzo 2000: 90–91).

But not without difficulties. Only few months after Livatino's murder, his tomb was desecrated, an act which was interpreted as intimidation against the prosecutor who pursuing his anti-mafia inquiries in Canicatti. Only two months later, it was the president of Italy, Francesco Cossiga, who attacked the judge's memory characterizing him as a young and irresponsible judge ("giudice ragazzino")—though he subsequently retracted this statement. The funeral stele erected by Livatino's family at the site of his murder was also vandalized, on July 18, 1997, a date that coincided with the commemoration of the Via D'Amelio bombing. There is more than a point of coincidence between the two anti-mafia judges and heroes. Several church dignitaries have called for opening a beatification process for Paolo Borsellino, in light of the faith with which he exercised his profession of judge and his vocation to sacrifice.

If so much praise was written about them after their death, one might ask how the judges reflected on their experience while they were alive. In a speech given on April 7, 1984, entitled "The Role of the Judge in a Changing Society," Livatino spoke of the relationship between action in the public and private spheres: "The claim whereby...the judge can do what he wants in his private life, just like any other citizen, must be dismissed....A judge's independence lies in his morality, in the transparency of his moral conduct including outside the office....Only if a judge fulfills these conditions himself can society accept that he has such great power over its members" (Abate 1997: 61–74). In other words, to judge men, one must be above society, and to be above society, one must be outside of it. In the daily exercise of a profession that is unlike all others, for the personal, bodily sacrifice it requires, this is therefore what links justice and religion. In the rich corpus of writings and images about the patron saint of Palermo, which was republished in a monumental work at the time of the Palermo Spring (Gerbino 1991), the hagiographic and iconographic model of an ascetic, solitary life clearly emerges, informing the way in which anti-mafia judges were transformed into saints.

The writers of the messages at the Falcone Tree, playing on the homonymy between the judge's surname and the *falcone* (falcon), often refer to the judge having the same piercing vision as Saint Rosalia who, in paintings and engravings, looks down on Palermo from the top of Monte Pellegrino: "Like a large falcon, Falcone peers down from on high" (Gerbino 1991: 128). In certain paintings, Saint Rosalia is one with "the sacred mountain" (Giunta 1991: 21) that guards her remains and owes its name—Pellegrino (pilgrim)—to the isolated position it occupies among the other mountains in the Gulf of Palermo. Falcone, isolated from all the others, as he is depicted by his biographers,[21] found himself in the same solitary position as the patron saint overlooking the city from the top of this mountain (Gerbino 1991: 128). In one of the drawings pinned to the Falcone Tree, the judge's head replaces the body of Saint Rosalia as she is posed in classical Rosalian iconography, between the mountain and the city (Puccio-Den 2009: 283-284). From the masters of the seventeenth century to this modest drawing by a schoolchild from the twenty-first century, the same structure is involved. But what new things has this "event" constructed?

Saint Rosalia's hermetic experience was the very condition that enabled her to intervene in public affairs. This beneficial intercession transformed her into the advocate of Palermo and enabled her, according to the hagiographic legend, to free the city from the plague that struck in 1624. Livatino, Falcone, Borsellino, and Rosalia Sinibaldi (to use Saint Rosalia's secular name), are sacrificial figures for the city. In order to implement their salutary project, the saint and the judges must live an ascetic life. Their commitment to the world requires them to be detached from it, to renounce worldly goods. Ascetic and public-spirited aspects coexist, revealing the intrinsically religious nature of the administration of justice. This explains why eminently religious practices, like pilgrimages, are directed at the judges.

The martyr judge, a paradigmatic figure of the complex ties that the law maintains with religion, makes the pilgrimage the emblematic

---

21. Elsewhere in Sicily, "Falcone" is the name given to the highest summits in a chain of mountains. Monte Falcone, to take but one example, is the highest mountain in Marettimo, the island forming part of the Egadi archipelago, off the coast of Trapani.

Bearing witness

experience of personal trial and sacrifice. This sacrifice must be experienced by everybody and form part of everyone's life so that they, in turn, may become witnesses. From this moment on, they testify to a cause and form the framework of a community that is situated, like the pilgrimage for which they are the medium, at the crossroads between the individual and the collective. This anti-mafia community is perhaps the most enduring fruit of the Falcone Tree and its transient writings.

Every murder of an anti-mafia judge is an attempt to silence the truths he holds about the mafia, its existence, its very nature, its functioning, and its relationship to politics. But we have seen how the murders of anti-mafia magistrates in the early 1990s had the opposite effect, namely that of building and structuring a community of witnesses. These anti-mafia pilgrims came and visited the scenes of the massacres not so much to bear witness to the faith in God of these murdered judges—as their beatification processes *super martyrium* would lead one to believe—but rather to call God as witness for the defense of their truths about the mundane world. Could their statements, fraily and ephemerally embodied by witnesses, be stabilized on lasting supports? Could they be set in stone? Could they build a collective, historic memory of what the mafia is?

CHAPTER 5

The unnamable mafia

Crafting the anti-mafia (silenced) memory

This chapter examines the future of the Falcone Tree now that the assassinated judge's remembrance has taken on a more institutionalized form, in particular through the activity of the Falcone Foundation. While focusing on the writings, drawings, and other graphic objects[1] left at the Falcone Tree, I here also take into consideration the physicality of the writing media employed (Petrucci 1980: 1995). I question whether the use of paper rather than marble enables the emotional system—characterizing the time when the "spontaneous shrines" (Haney, Leimer, and Lowery 1997; J. Santino 2006; Margry and Sánchez-Carretero 2007) were created—to be distinguished from the remembrance system, whose instruments are monuments or archives. Can the unsettled and shifting forms of the Capaci massacre commemoration stabilize, and possibly become fixed, through the institutionalizing processes initiated by the Falcone Foundation? This chapter therefore analyzes the tension between institutionalized forms and non-institutionalized forms of remembrance. Can we speak of a process of institutionalization of the anti-mafia memory over the length of time that has elapsed since the massacre?

---

1. I borrow the term "graphic objects," which refers to objects of great visual power that combine written and figurative signs, from Fraenkel (1992, 2002, 2007).

The starting point of this chapter is the event of May 23, 1992. I first question the appropriateness of the local, emic use of the term "event" that induced a change in the way Palermitans grasped the mafia and the tools to fight against it. I then explore the heuristic dimension of this term, exploring its semantic weight in the social sciences (Bensa and Fassin 2002). The analytical notion of an event shifts our attention toward the act of "witnessing." Where chapter 4 analyzed witnessing in terms of the development of anti-mafia activism, this chapter takes witnessing to the institutional level and analyzes how the Falcone Foundation constructed and managed the remembrance of the assassinated judge. It takes a broader look at the ways in which anti-mafia remembrance is inscribed in Palermo's topography. Starting from the special characteristics of this remembrance—the difficulty in commemorating the judge by naming public roads or structures after him and the controversies this still triggers—I examine the contradictions that underlie the anti-mafia remembrance due to its problematic relationship with power and the state. In the framework of the failings of official remembrance, the forms of grassroots memorialization take over.

The "event"

What happened on 23 May 1992 is an incredible event because Palermitans behaved uncharacteristically, doing things they would never have done before. For the first time, our entire city, the whole of Palermo, expressed its indignation and a need for justice and freedom from mafia violence.[2]

With these words the secretary of the Falcone Foundation described the reaction to the Capaci murders. The massacre led to reactions similar to those engendered by the September 11, 2001, terrorist attacks in New York (Fraenkel 2002; Zeitlin 2006) and those on March 11, 2004, in Madrid (Sánchez-Carretero 2006): gatherings, the collective building of makeshift shrines, and the frenetic use of writing as the final means of communication between the living and the dead and a way of forging a bond between those who considered themselves survivors. What was it that created these parallels?

---

2. Secretary of the Falcone Foundation, interview with author, Palermo, October 2007.

The Falcone Tree stood at the center of the initial, spontaneous reaction many in Palermo had to the murder: "I was barely twenty at the time. I remember I was going somewhere on my moped. When I heard that Falcone was dead, I turned around and drove to his home, just like that, inexplicably," the secretary remembered. The spontaneity of this tribute to the assassinated judge contrasts with the official acts (lying in state of all five coffins of the Capaci bombing victims in a Catholic chapel and a state funeral) instituted by the government, which was strongly suspected of mafia collusion. The link between the ruling parties (essentially Christian Democracy and the Italian Socialist Party) and the mafia association Cosa Nostra had been outlined in several anti-mafia investigations and widely reported in the media. Only one year later the First Republic was to collapse in the upheaval generated by the *Mani pulite* political scandal, and the Andreotti trial began in Palermo. In this context, the Falcone Tree provided an alternative to the official mourning process. Writing and placing messages under the Falcone Tree seemed to be the last resort for outraged, frightened, and lost Palermitans: "I was overcome, profoundly overcome, by the Falcone massacre. I must protect my country, and the only weapon I have is to write to you," wrote Patrizia (Amurri 1992: 138). The Falcone Tree became a rallying point for anti-mafia supporters and a catalyst for the emotions people were experiencing: "It was a day of untold violence. The violence in the air, and the rage in people, were palpable," recalled the foundation's secretary .

The instruments of protest, the flags and posters the activists had made, were left at the tree, which was also the location where the mourners started human chains that wove their way through the town and where anti-mafia demonstrations ended. By being linked in this way with the protests, the tree allowed the messages tagged to it to come out of the private sphere and assume a political sense. Does writing enable a shift to take place from the intense and visceral emotional reaction of individuals to the moral shock triggered by a violent event (Traïni 2008: 23) to forms of communal protest and expression of grievance that might even stir Palermitans to political action?

One of the most striking aspects of the letters attached to the Falcone Tree was the origin of their authors. The Capaci massacre elicited intense emotion throughout Italy: it was clear that the mafia was going to become a national issue. Many Italians who until then had felt that the anti-mafia fight was of little or no concern to them were touched and traveled to Palermo to pay their last respects to the five victims. Some of them also left messages at the Falcone Tree:

We want you to know that, now more than ever, the will and strength to continue the fight bravely, as you did, lives on in us, the youth from all over Italy. This is not only a voice that comes from the Sicilian people, it is something greater that also concerns us, the youth from the North. The "Youth of Milan."

I came from Treviso to Palermo today to be close to Sicily and the Sicilians, people I know to have wonderful hearts, determination, talent, and feelings....Long live Sicily. Long live Italy! Mario. (Amurri 1992: 142, 105)

Inspired by the figure of this judge who died for the state, many Italians acquired a national conscience, a sense of belonging to a nation under attack, and wished to defend their country against members of the mafia who had devolved into attackers or foreigners. A change occurred in the way that mafia members were perceived: suddenly they were no longer considered as people who required protection by *omertà* (silence)—the way in which one would help relatives and close friends with regard to a foreign state. Instead, people shifted their positions and began to side with the state, seeing members of the mafia as enemies who needed to be denounced. In Sicily, the very act of accusing the mafia, in black and white, on a piece of paper displayed in a public space is an "event" in itself, an act that certifies this break with the past. Falcone's death tested the capacity of Sicilians to modify atavistic behavior: "I pray to the Palermitans that they will do you justice, by climbing the wall of *omertà* that they have built all these years," wrote Corrado from Milan; or "May the bombs, massacres, and violence not crush people, but rather destroy the silence that has been engulfing us for too long," prayed Tiziana, a Sicilian (Amurri 1992: 136, 141). During these dramatic days, many other Palermitans sent letters to the magistrate's court with information that might help the investigators identify those responsible for the massacre—magistrates I interviewed were unanimous that this was the first time this had happened. It seems that the Capaci massacre changed not just the behavior of people but their capacity for critical analysis, entailing a transformation in the moral stance and attitude taken toward the state, the nation.

One must remember that Italy is a relatively young nation: it unified only in 1861. It was discredited by fascist nationalism in the first half of the twentieth century, and never rewarded its Second World War resistance heroes, sidelined in post-war political arrangements built to achieve a balance between parties. In these arrangements Christian Democracy came to play a pivotal role with the help of local power groups and the mafia. It was therefore a nation without heroes, until redeemed by the "sacrifice" of government representatives, starting with General Dalla Chiesa, murdered in September 1982, and culminating ten years later with Falcone and Borsellino. These sacrifices affirmed the intrinsic value of the state, and some of these victims were turned into heroes or martyrs. From its beginnings as a space of transient writing, the Falcone Tree gradually became the place for inscribing the memory of a national event. For the first time in Italy's recent history, individual experiences were seen to merge in the collective experience of a national drama:

> Wherever you go in Italy, there is not a single person who doesn't remember what they were doing at 5:58 p.m. on May 23. Everybody remembers extremely accurately and every day I meet people who start telling me what they were doing at the very moment the judge was assassinated. (Secretary of the Falcone Foundation)

The tree has become a place where memories are crystallized in space because many of the people who were in Palermo on May 23, 1992, decided to set in writing their memories of that day and the thoughts and feelings experienced. Writing, then, led to a shift from an emotional system of bearing witness to a memorial one.

The term "event" is an emic category mobilized by the parties involved. Here I explore another sense of this word: a heuristic tool proposed by social scientists and, in particular, the French historians and epistemologists working on issues of memory. For them, an event is specifically "that about which somebody bears witness" (Ricœur 2000: 229). "In order for there to be an event," writes Pierre Nora, "it needs to be known" (Ricœur 2000: 212). When one examines the messages placed at the Falcone Tree, one is surprised by the uniformity of this writing. This observation is not specific to our case study but common to many other scenes of spontaneous writing in the wake of disaster, as in the scenes studied by French anthropologist Béatrice Fraenkel (2002) in New York after the September 11, 2001, attack. The similarity of content highlights the importance given to the act of writing itself, of being on the scene, and of leaving proof of one's presence. Those who gathered around the Falcone Tree describe themselves as "witnesses": "They were people who freely decided to... who felt the need to bear witness," explained the secretary of the Falcone Foundation. Aside from often only slight variations, the letters placed under the tree all contained the witness's implied performative utterance: "I was here" (Dulong 1998: 167). Here writing serves as bearing witness of the mafia, leaving *here* a real, visible, and tangible piece of evidence. Unlike the memory of the event, which is recounted by a speaker to an attendant audience, the writing left at the Falcone Tree speaks to any subsequent visitors, communicating the basic message that "I came here to bear witness to the event of Giovanni Falcone's death by the mafia." It is the presence of the witnesses at the scene, as proven in their writings, that institutes the Capaci massacre as an event.

The journeys to Palermo that many anti-mafia activists made in the weeks and months following the attack kept alive the memory of the judge and his fellow victims. With this we have shifted from an emotional system to a remembrance system, one that was quickly appropriated by the Falcone Foundation.

Institutionalizing remembrance

The concept of remembrance contains two ideas: the duty to learn lessons from the past, and the duty to commemorate victims (Gensburger and Lavabre 2005). The Falcone Foundation takes care of both of these tasks, the first through educational programs extending from Palermo to the whole of Italy and the second through commemorative actions carried out on the anniversary of the judge's death. These two aspects are linked, the commemorative ceremony being the culminating point of a course offered at schools participating in the foundation's projects on a culture of lawfulness.[3] Through these commemorative practices, the memory of this traumatic event is collectively reprocessed.

Between two and five thousand students come to Palermo every year on the anniversary of the assassination. Their socialization begins on the "lawfulness train." This vehicle, chartered for the occasion, travels through the country, filling up with students as it makes its way southwards toward Sicily. When it gets to Palermo, the youths are supervised by the foundation's organizing body. The mobile commemorative train travels to the two key sites that mark Falcone's life and death, the bunker

3. Maria Falcone, the judge's sister and the foundation's chair, explained that the Falcone Foundation does not wish to define itself negatively, as what it is against, but prefers to describe itself positively as what it fights for, namely a culture of lawfulness.

room and the Falcone Tree. It is in the bunker, built near the Ucciardone prison to house the Maxi Trial undertaken by Falcone, that the young people present the academic work they prepared over the year leading up to this trip. A committee is charged with awarding prizes to the best works. The judge's story is then relived, brought up to date, and commemorated through readings, songs, films, videos, plays, and musical performances. In this manner each school, each young person, contributes to the writing and rewriting of a national story whose celebration turns it into legend. This is the effect initiated, for example, by the play *Storia di Giovannuzzu beddicchiu* (The story of handsome little Giovanni), which used the formal structure of the *cunto* (an epic form used for accounts of Charlemagne's knights fighting the infidels) to narrate the story of the judge's life.[4] The ultimate aim, the foundation secretary explains, is the following:

> We tell young people that Falcone's life was not easy. Through us, they therefore no longer see Giovanni Falcone as a victorious hero, in the traditional sense of the word. Giovanni Falcone did not win his battle. Giovanni Falcone lost, but he never gave up fighting. This is what we try to impress upon young people's minds: Giovanni Falcone's commitment as well as the adversities he encountered along the way.

Since 1992, there has been a slow shift from the immediacy of the event to the eternal present of the myth, a myth whose hero is a loser. While the students fill the bunker, the works of art (posters, paintings, etc.) they created and brought along with them are put on display outside. Inside the bunker a huge white sheet is suspended onto an inside wall for the students to write messages: "It is a time for them to write, a spontaneous time that we have created," explained the foundation's secretary. Her words aptly capture the contradiction and tension inherent in these activities, one between allowing freedom of expression and overseeing remembrance. The sheet bears an inscription in black: "Dear Giovanni...," an encouragement, the secretary continued, to "express one's own thoughts about the event, remembrance, Judge Falcone's values, etc." Signing one's message is essential, she emphasizes, even though at the end there are so many messages that they merge with each other

---

4. This theme refers back to our discussion in chapter 2 of the new perception of mafia members as infidels.

and authorship becomes difficult to identify. The foundation archives artifacts like this, undertaking a major task of writing and bearing witness. Outside, after each student has presented their work to the jury, all merge into a single procession, regardless of age, gender, or place of origin: "We identify with each other as a group because, on May 23, we speak a common language, irrespective of our differences," said the secretary of the Falcone Foundation. The youth then proceed from the bunker through the streets of Palermo, carrying the banners and placards they have made and signed collectively in the name of their schools.

About two kilometers on, the students reach the Falcone Tree, the end point of the procession, where they place their banners and placards. Here a "secular communion" of great emotional intensity takes place: "This is the real commemorative moment. For us, the commemoration occurs at this point, when we meet [under the Falcone Tree]," the secretary of the Falcone Foundation, the master of ceremonies, explains. A requiem mass completes the commemorative event, held at a church able to accommodate all participants. "The force of Judge Falcone is impossible to contain. We do our work but it is his memory, being so powerful, that draws people," the secretary states. This magnetic, captivating force holds the participants truly riveted at the moment of remembrance of the murdered judges under the Falcone Tree. The time of the attack is marked by a police trumpet call, and then, as the secretary captures,

> there is absolute silence. Not a sound is to be heard for a long, long time. The silence goes on and on; it is one of the most incredible silences I have ever heard in my life. It's as if, suddenly, everyone had disappeared.

The Falcone Tree, standing upright like a stela and decorated by the visitors not only with their letters but also with photos of Falcone, Borsellino, and their bodyguards,[5] displays a plaque with the standard expressions of a memorial to the dead, as captured in the words on one letter: "In eternal memory of all those who have died in the struggle against the mafia" (Amurri 1992: 28). Among the images deployed in every commemorative ceremony, we can find the photograph of the smiling Falcone and Borsellino, portraying the bond that had existed between them. This has become the archetypal image to represent the anti-mafia movement. Another shows Falcone with his wife, both smiling. This smile is

---

5. These photos are archived by the Falcone Foundation.

presented as the sign of triumph over death. If the silence that resounds after the trumpet call is also a secular form of prayer resembling the funeral rites and commemorative ceremonies for soldiers fallen in the First World War (Prost 1984: 209), the Falcone Tree, this spontaneous shrine in memory of the victims of the mafia, takes the place of a war memorial.

The foundation's secretary distinguishes between the functions of the Falcone Tree and those of the Falcone Foundation, presenting the latter as a driving force for "real change, which has nothing or little to do with emotionalism." Must we accept this distinction between the emotional system and the remembrance system as given? Indeed, emotion is what revives this memorial site; without it, it would be as static and lifeless as the memorial built by the state in memory of the victims of the Capaci massacre.

Remembrance on paper, remembrance in stone

The memorialization process is conventionally linked to the place where the death occurred. Indeed, the secretary of the Falcone Foundation describes the spot on the expressway where Falcone was attacked as the only place that truly recalls the judge's death. An official monument has been erected there, a set of stone pillars engraved with the victims' names. On the hill above, where the perpetrator had pressed the remote control, is a white hut painted with blue letters to read "NO MAFIA." All of this is part of the monument project initiated by the government. And yet this official monument, solemnly decorated with wreaths on every anniversary, is disregarded by anti-mafia activists and mostly ignored by pilgrims and tourists: "Every now and then," the foundation's secretary noted, "somebody places a flower there; but it is not the Falcone Tree!" People rarely stop on this section of the expressway, despite the fact that the road has been widened to allow for it. The local authorities have also designated other spots to commemorate the Falcone and Morvillo, yet in vain. At a garden in the heart of Palermo that is dedicated to them, the commemorative plaque is weather-beaten and some of the iron letters dislodged, making the names illegible. In this manner the Falcone Tree is the real monument that commemorates the victims of the Capaci massacre, even if reduced to its basic function as a writing medium, a "document."[6] Palermitans

---

6. On the monument as document, see Petrucci (1995).

and visitors, both Italian and from further afield, continue to keep this spot alive, through their offerings, practices, and, above all, their writing, which continues to accumulate on the tree trunk. However, the fact that this unconventional and messy monument—where everyone comes to make their thoughts public under their own names—has not been replaced by a memorial with an officially approved engravement perhaps also indicates the difficulty in settling disputes of memory about Falcone, this undisputed "hero of our times" who was so disputed during his lifetime.

Memorializing the death and, through it, celebrating the life of Judge Falcone is also achieved through writings that have a wider reach than the messages on the Falcone Tree. Many books have been written about Judge Falcone, as they have about other "mafia victims," in a new genre of biography of anti-mafia protagonists.[7] These writings can be controversial and clearly identify the political barriers the judges encountered in their work that reveal the highly compromising relationship between part of the Italian ruling class and Cosa Nostra.

Francesco La Licata, author of Falcone's authorized biography (La Licata 2002) and for which he was allowed to interview Falcone's family members, decries the hostility of some of the judge's colleagues and superiors (see chapter 4). In *Storia di Giovanni Falcone* he tells how the anti-mafia judge's enemies increased in number as his fame spread, winning him public support within and beyond the Italian borders. La Licata argues that it was Falcone's own colleagues who betrayed him to the mafia. Betraying someone is to leave him alone in the fight against the mafia, exposing him to the hatred and violence of the mafiosi. Some of his colleagues held him responsible for the repression that the government instituted against members of the mafia. The traitors, therefore, were enemies on the inside, installed in what was known as the "Poison Palace" courthouse in Palermo. Alexander Stille levels the same accusation in *Nella terra degli infedeli* (1995), a work in which we can see parallels with Sciascia's famous novel *Dalle parti degli Infedeli* (Sciascia 1993) that deals with the persecution of a Sicilian village priest by the highest echelons of the Vatican for having "allowed" the Italian Communist Party to win the municipal elections. Stille suggests that the "infidels" that Falcone and Borsellino were fighting were not only members of Cosa Nostra but also people they viewed as their

---

7. This bibliography is huge and would be impossible to list here. I have extensively studied the biographical works on Livatino, Puglisi, and Impastato.

natural allies within the state institutions, colleagues who decided to betray the anti-mafia cause. For this La Licata often gives the example of Falcone's superior, public prosecutor Pietro Giammanco, who is said to have hindered judicial investigations, particularly those involving ties between the mafia and politicians. In these books, the veneer of official memory begins to wear off, revealing the dark side of the story. This "true story" is silenced during the official commemoration day.

Under the shade of the magnolia, those participating in May 23 ceremonies hear the orthodox version of the life and death of Falcone, transformed into a national hero, accompanied by the authorities who have progressively integrated the commemorative process. This explains the modifications that this originally dissenting performance, a ritual space created in order to allow the public expression of dissent, had to undergo, shifting from an angry, raw protest register to a smooth, complacent celebratory register. Does this mean this spot has now lost the power specific to *lieux de mémoire* (places of remembrance) to generate "a new story" (Ricœur 2000: 528), so that the protest function has to take up other forms of writing and can no longer be expressed by the letters attached to the Falcone Tree?

Unlike other anti-mafia organizations, the Falcone Foundation is not an organ for criticizing the state. Although it does consider that the state partly betrayed Falcone, it does not use the commemoration to express critique. As one of the rare anti-mafia organizations to be recognized and funded by the regional government (even though it is well known that politicians involved with the mafia served in this government), it regularly invites institutional representatives to the commemorative ceremony. To understand the complex relationship that the Falcone Foundation maintains with state institutions, we should perhaps recall Falcone's words when asked whether he was prepared to sacrifice himself for this state: "Do you know any others?" he answered, pointing, somewhat sarcastically, at the pragmatic nature of the state, as opposed to its idealistic one. This state, such a (corrupted) state, is not the one for which sacrifice is worthwhile, but it is the only one which exists. However, since the judge's assassination, we do need to ask to what extent the memorial policies instituted by the city of Palermo can meet the need to recall the wounds inflicted by the mafia on individuals and society, and, through complicity or indifference, by certain elements of government and society on other elements of the same government and society, a situation that may justify the emic concept of "civil war" used to depict the anti-mafia fight.

Politics of remembrance, poetics of remembrance

In his book *Cultural Intimacy: Social Poetics in the Nation-State*, Michael Herzfeld (1997) uses the concept of social poetics to outline the boundaries of cultural identity, by exploring the differences between official models of national culture and the experiences of ordinary citizens. We have examined the various ways in which the populace constructs memory. The concept of the "duty to remember" is also political. Although it can be defined as a wish to remember victims, this memory is also maintained through officially assigned place names determined by what municipalities chose to define as history and how they decide to deal with it. Inscribing the memory of the Capaci massacre in the city of Palermo would be one way to ensure that this traumatic event is not forgotten. And yet, as the secretary of the Falcone Foundation pointed out, this was not taking place in Palermo:

> Far from Palermo, you will find as many Falcone streets as you like. In Palermo, they fight over where a [single] Falcone street should be placed. Every now and then they talk about it and then, for reasons unknown, the problem is not resolved. They talk about it but nothing gets done. On the other hand, if you look at city maps in Italy, you'll find a Falcone street in practically all Italian cities and villages, in the most unlikely places....Because he is without doubt a national figure!

When challenged on the matter, city administrators retort that their initiatives are hindered by practicalities. One is the argument that, as there are no new roads in Palermo city, there are none that could be named after anti-mafia fighters; only roads in new suburbs could be allocated to his name. Another is the allegation that proposals to rename secondary roads after these figures are dismissed by their families who consider the roads not important enough to carry the names of someone who played such a significant role in Italy's history. The refusal by the Falcone family to have a minor road named after the famous judge is a case in point: "On the one hand, you have the city and its inhabitants, who would like an appropriate place; on the other, we have the practical problem of finding a place that meets these needs," said architect Salamone,[8] who was in charge for the allocation of place names in Palermo, in an attempt to justify himself. Salamone was also involved in

---

8. Michelangelo Salamone, interview with author, Palermo, July 2007.

the anti-mafia cause. He had joined the anti-mafia struggle in the late 1970s and was secretary to Jesuit priest Ennio Pintacuda whose activism to remove the mafia from its power-making role in Sicilian politics was threatening the position that Christian Democracy had held in the country since the Second World War. His interpretation is worthwhile to consider, namely that "the Falcone Tree is an informal place of remembrance that the city has appropriated…and which has already been integrated into customs and the collective imagination." He concluded that it is better for the families to see their heroic assassinated relatives honored in this spontaneous memorial than have them reduced to the rank of minor figures.

While most public spaces belong to the state, which lays down the rules for the display of written communication by stipulating what type of graphic objects could be used and how they should address their target audience (Petrucci 1980), the users of these spaces nonetheless manage to appropriate them in unintended ways. They leave their mark on them and manipulate their meaning, never allowing themselves to be reduced to mere spectators or passive readers. The authorities' tolerance of this form of spontaneous shrines is also due to their discomfort with the competing memories of the anti-mafia. According to architect Salamone:

> Our administration has allowed citizens the possibility to express themselves through these physical signs within the territory.…There is an official plaque where Boris Giuliano, the head of the Brigata Mobile [mobile brigade], was assassinated; but there is a little shrine where Judge Terranova was killed. This was not erected by the administration but by his family. It is a place where you can put a plant, leave some flowers. There's a plaque.…It's a little shrine, you can call it that.…And there are many others spread throughout the city. Where the administration has not met citizens' needs, where it has failed or been remiss, this void has been filled by family, friends, and relatives.

Such a situation may also reveal the failings of city administrators and their negligence with regard to "mafia victims." Umberto Santino—a scholar who, with his wife and fellow scholar Anna Puglisi, led a long fight against the local authorities before founding the first anti-mafia memory museum in Palermo, the No Mafia Memorial—proposes the phrase *la memoria difficile* (difficult remembrance) for it. He coined this phrase in relation to the memorialization of Impastato, the young activist murdered by the mafia on May, 9, 1978 (see chapter 8).

But the same question arises with respect to Falcone: can we expect more of local authorities that are partly in league with Cosa Nostra? Other examples illustrate this contradiction, one the memorial erected in honor of Padre Puglisi in Brancaccio, the Palermo neighborhood where he was killed. The monument is shaped like an enormous, transparent leaf, on which each participant at its unveiling wrote a sentence and which was then sealed under a layer of plastic, thus immortalizing these messages. Several of the authorities who took part were suspected to have links to the mafia, in particular Salvatore Cuffaro, the former regional president who was indicted for aiding Cosa Nostra members escape investigation and prosecution (see chapter 9). Not long afterwards, the memorial site was abandoned and then profaned. To return to the example of the commemoration of Impastato, the difficulties his family and comrades experienced in having a main street named after him, followed by vandalism of a plaque erected in his memory on the seafront in the town of Cinisi, show that these commemorative undertakings are more easily committed to paper rather than to stone: their controversial nature prevents them from being inscribed in a more lasting manner. The difficulty in assigning the names of mafia victims to enduring media reveals how contentious these commemorative undertakings still are.

The Falcone Tree has never been subjected to violence, profanation, or acts of mafia aggression. During the months after Falcone's assassination, it was under twenty-four-hour armed military surveillance as it was considered a possible target for the mafia; but the mafia never did attack the memorial. Possibly the mafiosi did not fear the dead judge, but they feared the living who gathered around his powerful memory. When examining why people write about or to the dead, historian and epigraphist Armando Petrucci (1995) observed that it is not intended so much for the deceased as for the living. Commemorative acts create a far stronger link between the living than they do between the living and the dead. But this link is complex and challenging to estimate, opening the question as to whether the disparity shown in the messages left behind at sites erected in memory of mafia victims would not mean that the anti-mafia movement is not a unified one. After all, the writing does not emanate from a distinct and institutionalized source that could enforce uniformity, such as the state, but from separate individuals. And in this absence of a mutually agreed-upon truth, each writer signs their statement in their own name. However, if the idea or ideal of a mutually agreed-upon commemoration contradicts the very nature of remembrance as an individual action (Gensburger and Lavabre 2005),[9] how can we postulate a consensual way of remembering when the events commemorated took place in the context of a "civil war" (Puccio 2009: 270-275)? Indeed, many Sicilians regard the struggle that took place between the mafia and the anti-mafia during the 1980s and culminated in the Capaci bombing as a "civil war." In contrast with the "duty to memory" of memorialization processes, French historian Nicole Loraux (1997) coined the phrase "duty to forget," using Athens as case-study but referring much more broadly to societies that have experienced civil war. It is a concept that could be very useful for defining what is at stake in the conflicting memory of the anti-mafia.

The permanence of the emotional system and the difficult access to remembrance indicate the reversibility of all commemorative undertakings that are related to the anti-mafia struggle. Literature that points out how institutional representatives hindered those who are now viewed as heroes reveals that the "true story" (Montanaro and Ruotolo 1995) of the anti-mafia movement is, perhaps, impossible to write given the diversity of conflicting memories.[10] The question remains open, like a gaping, silent hole that cannot be filled by the calm and reassuring writing of a bygone past. Given the impossibility of this story, all the possibilities of remembrance are deployed, including these transient forms of writing that one could be tempted to view as an intermediary phase, before memory becomes fixed, but that we must now consider permanent, perpetuating the difficult remembrance of the anti-mafia movement.

However, this embarrassment when it comes to naming victims and culprits is not only related to a political configuration of collusion between mafia and the state, responsible for the institutional processes of attributing responsibilities. It is rooted in the nature of the mafia phenomenon, which is *ontologically* as well as *semantically* uncertain.[11] This

---

9. Gensburger and Lavabre (2005) consider remembrance a controversial space par excellence. While it is possible to create a universal history, it is impossible to remove this controversial aspect from remembrance.

10. This is also shown by the difficulties that Santino, Puglisi, and the Impastato Documentation Center encountered in setting up a museographic project for a mafia memorial, now installed as the No Mafia Memorial, an institution which has foregone public financing to exercize its freedom to remember.

11. On the role played by institutions in fixing the semantics of social reality, see Boltanski (2009: 117).

chapter completes the first stage of our journey by interpreting the performative politics of commemoration of the assassinated judges as a fight to confront the deadly silence of the mafia. Part I underscores the power of naming: to call a thing, a person, or an entity by its name is a critical step toward appropriating it and thus disempowering silence of its terrifying force. This first part of Mafiacraft describes this process (or *work*) of naming the mafia and its limitations. Part II now provides a careful description of the *work* of anti-mafia activism as a mode of knowledge in areas of judicial and political interventions.

PART II: JUDGING THE SILENCE

CHAPTER 6

The Falcone method

Investigating the Sicilian mafia

"Investigating the mafia is like crossing a minefield," said Falcone in an interview with Marcelle Padovani (Falcone and Padovani 1997: 45). These were sadly prophetic words, portending his own death by bombing in 1992. Falcone was born in Palermo in 1939 into a conservative bourgeois family. He passed the entrance exam for the Italian magistrature in 1964 and was first appointed judge at the Lentini district court in south Catania, before working as prosecuting attorney in Trapani in 1967. In 1979, he was appointed examining magistrate at the Court of Palermo, where he put together the most dramatic proceedings ever brought against the mafia, the Maxi Trial. This "minefield" is a particularly revealing case for studying the similarities between ethnographic and legal investigations and showing how an anthropological approach of the mafia phenomenon has allowed a response to the question "What is the mafia?" grounded on evidence supplied by internal "informants." It is thanks to the work of examining magistrates that we now have access to an abundance of information on Cosa Nostra, its way of operating, its internal rules, and its code of honor. The manner in which the examining magistrates reconstructed the truth by way of clues, essential when dealing with a world protected by silence, invites a comparison with the epistemological model that has underpinned the social sciences since the nineteenth century (Ginzburg 1989b). But the use of informants from

Cosa Nostra, the pentiti, establishes an even more direct parallel with ethnographic methods (Puccio 2001).

An analysis of the process that established the legal principle of the mafia as a criminal organization cannot be dissociated from the study of the historical conditions that produced a change in the mafia's image. Until the early 1970s, anyone who spoke of the mafia as a criminal organization was reduced to silence. On September 16, 1970, Mauro de Mauro, a Palermitan journalist who regularly published the findings of his anti-mafia investigations in the communist newspaper *L'Ora*, mysteriously disappeared. Despite an increasing number of assassination attempts and murders that pointed to the responsibility of the mafia, folklorist Pitrè's theory of it continued to prevail: criminality is criminality and should not be confused with the mafia, which is simply a way of being, feeling, or behaving, a psychological attitude or temperament linked to "Sicilian-ness." Sciascia, the most famous Sicilian writer and engaged intellectual, similarly questioned seeing the mafia as criminal organization, but arguing from a very different ideological position. In writings halfway between literary fiction and essays, he suggested that the mafia was intimately linked to the governing power and the product of a general, inevitable, incurable state of corruption. Consequently, he did not believe that Cosa Nostra could really be extracted from Sicilian society, identified, examined, and judged. For this very reason, and not for the purpose of defending Sicilian culture as was the case for Pitrè, he showed strong opposition to the anti-mafia front at the Maxi Trial (Renda 1997: 248, 304–305). Nevertheless, Pitrè and Sciascia share a key understanding: both consider the mafia to be a form of behavior and not a structured, unitary organization. Their culturalist argument was definitively dismissed by testimony given at the Maxi Trial in the pentiti confessions, which may be summarized as follows:

> That the mafia exists, that one enters it by an oath, that as part of this ritual the new member declares his willingness to pursue the organization's ends and to submit to a series of behavioral rules of which the most fundamental are absolute obedience to the bosses, secrecy, and omertà. (U. Santino 1994: 105)

Before we get to the heart of the historical and social process that led to the disclosures about Cosa Nostra, I first examine several examples of "cultures" exposed by "detective" methods.

The ethnographer and the inquisitor

Marcel Griaule likens the heuristic processes of ethnography to a pre-trial investigation. In *Méthode de l'ethnographie* (1957), he associates ethnographic investigation with a legal cross-examination. Just as the investigating magistrate gathers evidence and compares the different versions of events reported by witnesses to discover the truth, ethnographers check what they are told by the indigenous people whose culture they are interrogating by using all the information available to them, confronting informants with divergent versions obtained in other interviews, and attempting to provoke them to reveal truths they had not intended to divulge (Griaule 1957: 51, 60). Griaule's disconcerting and provocative description exposes—though it does not denounce—the violence inherent in ethnographic practices, a violence that is irreducible within a power relationship. Griaule saw fieldwork as the continuation of a long tradition of adventure and exploration. Indeed, his Dakar-Djibouti mission, during which he travelled across Africa in twenty-one months in the early 1930s, was an enterprise both of knowledge discovery and of "colonization" (Clifford 1996: 61). His aggressive attitude to ethnography reminds us of other forms of proto-ethnography enacted in a context of colonization and cultural domination.

Conquistadores provided an abundant literature on the beliefs and customs of the New World. These were carefully recorded as part of the Spaniards' repressive strategy to eradicate these practices. These seventeenth-century Mexican extirpators left us "dates, places, portraits of the culprits, narratives of their existence, and detailed descriptions of their practices" to substantiate their accusations and interpretations (Bernand and Gruzinski 1988: 148). Similar attention to detail captured observations of Andean "idolatry": in the Cajatambo region of Peru, "repentant" caciques and sorcerers were used to trace the genealogy of the period's "pagan" ministers. In Mexico, the "art of confession" was employed to force those who refused to talk to disclose the names of their accomplices. The "hunters of idolatry" used all tricks of the trade to make natives reveal what they were hiding, including pretending to know more than they did and playing on contradictions to confuse the "guilty" (Bernand and Gruzinski 1988: 150, 171).

In their case, the acquisition of knowledge was intrinsically linked to the exercise of power. Observation of the customs and practices of inhabitants of New Spain was, in fact, motivated by the goal of dominating the recently conquered peoples living there. Although the urge to identify "idolatries" cannot be dissociated from a thirst for knowledge, the extirpators' efforts to gather knowledge were aimed at setting up and legitimating the massive repression of the indigenous populations. This undertaking of political and cultural uniformization built on a project that had begun in Europe two centuries earlier. In the fourteenth century, Jacques Fournier, bishop of Pamiers in France from 1317 to 1326, scrupulously interrogated the peasants of the counties of Foix and Haute Ariège in an effort to track down any Cathar heresy among them, or any other deviation from the official Catholic norm (Le Roy Ladurie 1975: 10). The volumes in which the records of the procedures and interrogations against 114 implicated people are collected reveal an attitude somewhere between detective interest and ethnographic curiosity that goes largely beyond the strict bounds of inquisitorial prosecutions against heterodox tendencies. Indeed, the inquisitor was obsessed with detail and recorded information on everyday life in the "guilty" village that went far beyond a simple chronicle of deviance, and provided Emmanuel Le Roy Ladurie with the material for his monograph.

Similarly, Carlo Ginzburg reconstructed the "mentality," "religious behaviors," and "popular beliefs" linked with witchcraft in the rural society of Friuli using the records of trials against the *benandanti*, custodians of a fertility cult, in this northeastern Italian region where Germanic and Slavic traditions met. In a classic of Italian historiography or *microstoria*, Ginzburg (1983) strives to show how, between the late sixteenth and mid-seventeenth centuries, a metamorphosis was enacted, turning these "defenders of the harvest" into "witches" and transforming their "nightly battles," which aimed to secure the fertility of the fields, into a diabolical Sabbath. The Spanish colonizers imprisoned the cultures they came across in the Americas in a series of religious categories centered on the notion of "idolatry," in a legacy of both ancient paganism and medieval scholasticism (Bernand and Gruzinski 1988: 6). In the same way, the judges of the Friuli trials tirelessly superposed their interpretive scheme of witchcraft (pacts with the devil, Sabbath, desecration of the sacraments, etc.), developed by theologians and inquisitors from the mid-twelfth to the mid-thirteenth centuries, onto the beliefs and "superstitions" glimpsed during their interrogations. Under pressure from the investigators, which ranged from various levels of violence to outright torture, the accused ended up admitting the judges' version. Critically, however, the records of the early trials give view of the *benandantis'* resistance to being defined as witches and thus bring a level of genuinely popular belief within reach.

Other archival documents that Ginzburg studied indicate an increase in inquisitorial trials in the Italian diocese of Modena between the late fifteenth and mid-sixteenth centuries. The feverish activity of the Modenese inquisition is related to the presence of fra' Bartolomeo of Pisa, who was as meticulous as the bishop of Pamiers and led all witchcraft trials personally. The accounts of the accused provided the monk with precious material for developing his treaties of demonology, revealing a link between the practice of repression, theoretical reflection, and doctrinal elaboration. Once again, the historian notes the aggressive techniques of the interrogations. The judge would skillfully lead the defendant on a predetermined path, implicitly suggesting the answers to be given, and striving to make the confession of the accused coincide with a truth he already possessed. There was nothing for the defendant to do but to give up meekly, ask for forgiveness, "repent," and accept the penance imposed by the inquisitor (Ginzburg 1989a: 1–15).

When Ginzburg switches his focus to the contemporary era, it is the terrorism trials against the Italian Left in the 1980s that interest him, as he detects in them the same mechanisms that he saw in the trials of the Inquisition. Reexamining the records of proceedings instituted against Adriano Sofri—a leader in the extreme left organization Lotta Continua, accused by pentito Leonardo Marino of having ordered the 1969 murder of carabinieri Commissioner Luigi Calabresi—the historian likens the attitude of the president of the court to that of the inquisitors who used their powers to persuade witnesses to share their point of view (Ginzburg 2002: 94). Admittedly, the examining magistrate claims to have been guided in his investigation by a "specific purpose," "a problem to solve," and "a working hypothesis to test" (Ginzburg 2002: 31). Yet any research aiming to establish truth must question the quality of the hypotheses used and these must be modified and abandoned if contradicted by facts. In Sofri's case, however, instead of testing the pentito's confession against objective data available, the investigation treated it as an authoritative source with which to assess or even dismiss eyewitness accounts (Ginzburg 2002: 21). Several clues suggest that Marino's confessions were manipulated, or even "made up," with the consent of the carabinieri (Ginzburg 2002: 36). The fight against the mafia used the same devices and concepts as the fight against terrorism that preceded it (such as a pool of prosecutors, categories of collective responsibility, maxi trials). It is therefore easy to extend this parallelism and to consider that the mafiosi, like the terrorists before them, became the new "sorcerers to hunt," with the help of pentiti testimonies. This was exactly the argument used by Sciascia (2002) in his criticism of the Maxi Trial against the Cosa Nostra. I think, on the contrary, that the relationship between "facts" and "law" is inverted in relation to witchcraft—hence the need to create another interpretative paradigm, Mafiacraft. Far from assuming a reality from their mental schemas, anti-mafia magistrates have created new conceptual categories and repressive forms on the basis of elements that emerged during a judicial investigation based on the ethnographic method.

In looking at the Sofri trial, Ginzburg intended to explore the intricate and ambiguous connections between the profession of the judge and that of the historian. For it, he compared the systems of validation specific to the legal world with those employed in the study of history. Like legal argument, historical analysis uses clues and traces to build evidence and establish a truth. Ginzburg called the epistemological model on which the social sciences have been based since the nineteenth century the "evidential paradigm." I now turn to an analysis of this model before returning to the Falcone method in order to point out the differences between Mafiacraft and witchcraft.

The evidential paradigm

In his essay "Clues: Roots for an Evidential Paradigm," Carlo Ginzburg (1989b) uses the "Morellian method," a system for attributing old paintings, as basis for illustrating an epistemological model that combines medical symptomatology, physiognomy, jurisprudence, the detective novel, and artwork identification skills. Giovanni Morelli maintained that in order to identify a painting's true creator, an examination should be based not on its most prominent characteristics, as was common in the nineteenth century, but rather on its most negligible details: earlobes, nails, the shape of fingers and toes, and so on. "Any art gallery studied by Morelli begins to resemble a rogue's gallery," Edgar Wind (cited by Ginzburg 1986: 159) described the visual outcome. Enrico Castelnuovo likens Morelli's presumptive method to the one ascribed to Sherlock Holmes by his creator, Conan Doyle, in about the same period. The art connoisseur resembles the detective who discovers the perpetrator of a crime (or the creator of a painting) on the basis of clues that, to most people, are almost imperceptible. Examples of Holmes's shrewdness in the interpretation of clues abound.

Ginzburg draws a parallel between the ability to trace experimental data of a seemingly trivial nature back to a complex reality that cannot be directly experienced and the knowledge of a hunter who reconstructs the shape and movements of invisible prey from tracks left in the mud, broken tree branches, feathers clinging to bushes, and clumps of fur and droppings left on the ground. "Deciphering" and "reading" animal tracks are metaphors that refer to the inaugural act of writing's invention (Ginzburg 1989b). Chinese tradition ascribes this to a senior civil servant who observed the tracks of a bird imprinted on a riverbank. Umberto Eco classifies "tracks" (in the sense intended by hunters), "symptoms" (in a medical sense), and "clues" (as in objects left by a criminal at the scene of the crime) under the heading of "recognition" (cited by Caisson 1995: 120). The model of medical semiotics—a discipline that enables the diagnosis of diseases inaccessible to direct observation on the basis of symptoms imperceptible to the layman—can also be glimpsed in the evidential paradigm. Indeed, the epistemological model that became dominant in the social sciences in the 1870s is itself centered on semiotics (Ginzburg 1989b).

Can ethnology be counted among the sciences that use this model? Claude Lévi-Strauss highlighted the importance of seemingly insignificant details in the work of Marcel Mauss, who advised his students never to neglect anything and even, or perhaps especially, to focus on what appears to be rubbish, waste, or "leftovers." Indeed, Lévi-Strauss defined the discipline of ethnology as a "science whose object is made up of things that academics in other social sciences have let slip off their tables" (cited in Caisson 1995: 115). It is with these leftovers that ethnology "cobbles together" its meaningful world. The debris of other views, when reassembled in a different order, reveals to the ethnologist a meaning that was originally hidden (Caisson 1995: 115–116). There is a clear affinity between the art of interpreting signs and the hermeneutic process of ethnology. The *bricolage* (cobbling together) that Lévi-Strauss speaks of in *The Savage Mind* (1962) is also the translation of one cultural system to another. "What I mean by the term *pensée sauvage* is the system of postulates and axioms required to establish a code which allows the least unfaithful translation possible of 'the other's' into 'ours' and vice versa," he explained to Paul Ricœur (cited by Caisson 1995: 116). Ethnologists use indigenous informants or "translators," whose role as mediators between one culture and the other is comparable to that of witnesses or informants used by the justice system, seen as snitches and "spies" by the group to which they belong. Having recourse to these intermediaries is

all the more important in certain "minefields" where participant observation is particularly difficult or practically impossible. This justifies the
parallel made between methods of building ethnological knowledge and
the investigation techniques of magistrate Falcone, which are based, on
the one hand, on the word of informants (and, more specifically, on the
"confessions" of one specific informant, Buscetta) and, on the other hand,
on the meticulous interpretation of clues.

Heuristics of silence

Morelli had studied medicine. Conan Doyle was a doctor before dedi-
cating himself to literature. And, on a side note, the Holmes-Watson
partnership—the detective and the doctor—was based on the dual personality of a real person, one of Conan Doyle's professors known for his
extraordinary diagnostic skills. For his part, Falcone vacillated between
a legal and a medical career before the law eventually won him over.
While he used medical language to describe his profession, speaking of
the "diagnosis" of criminal acts subject to his "examination" (Falcone and
Padovani 1997: 119), it was the Morellian method that proved essential
in his processes of verification, not so much for identifying the perpetrator of the crime as for authenticating the picture painted by his witness.

> In the early 1980s, he sent an official from the Guardia di Finanza
> to São Paulo in Brazil to check if, in a certain place, he could see the
> iron bench opposite a joiner's workshop that Tommaso Buscetta had
> spoken of in his confessions. Not for the love of incidental detail, but
> to assure himself of the credibility of the famous "pentito's" testimony
> as a whole. (Falcone and Padovani 1997: 5–6)

Like an ethnologist, the magistrate could not overlook a single detail, especially as "in the world of Cosa Nostra, every detail has a precise
meaning, and is related to another detail in a logical pattern" (Falcone
and Padovani 1997: 16–17). When it comes to unlocking the secrets of
a society whose sense of belonging was based on the law of silence, an
investigation could only begin with the interpretation of signs.

The first investigation into the mafia led by Falcone was the Spatola
investigation. "Contained in the Spatola trial documents was a complex
reality to decipher," he said a few years later (Stille 1995: 33). Although
the reality was opaque, there were certainly clues with which it could be

discovered. Defying the official theory that the impossibility of breaking the barrier of *omertà* would mean that no investigation into Cosa Nostra could ever succeed, Falcone endeavored to reconstruct the dense networks of connivance between the Sicilian "families" and the Gambino family of New York, using minute clues such as bank statements, airplane tickets, photographs, and fingerprints. Financial investigations, which follow the traces left by checks and money transfers in banks all around the world are one of this examining magistrate's greatest inventions. Another technique he used to track down the perpetrators of a murder was the examination of weapons. In a society where the obligation to secrecy forbids both talking and writing (see chapter 10), criminals may choose to leave behind a weapon at the crime scene to serve as a signature. Mafiosi generally prefer to leave behind no traces—with victims, for example, dissolved in acid to eliminate all traces[1]—unless they *want* to sign a murder and, in an interplay of signs specific to the mafia world, be recognized as the perpetrator of an act of violence against an influential figure. The method of execution can also point to the motive of the murder.

> Singer Pino Marchese was found with his genitals in his mouth: he had had an affair with the wife of a man of honor. Pietro Inzerillo was discovered in New York, in the boot of a car, with banknotes stuffed in his mouth and around his genitals. Message: "you ate too much money and look where it got you!" (Falcone and Padovani 1997: 27–28)

Such messages, which are also warnings, reestablish the unwritten rules that apply within the mafia world and the morality these rules underpin. "No one will ever find a list of members of Cosa Nostra, or receipts for dues paid. That doesn't mean that the rules of the organization aren't ironclad and that they aren't recognized by everybody," said Buscetta (Falcone and Padovani 1997: 101).

"Everything is a message, everything is full of meaning in the world of Cosa Nostra," was Falcone's evaluation (Falcone and Padovani 1997: 51). Yet to interpret these messages, a code is needed: "Our work as magistrates also includes mastering a key for interpreting signs. For me, a Palermitan, this is only natural" (Falcone and Padovani 1997: 51). For

---

1. This action is called *lupara bianca*, literally white lupara from the name of the sawn-off shotgun used by mafiosi.

any ethnologist entering a foreign society, learning the language in its broadest sense is a necessary experience; the Palermitan magistrate took this for granted. To be able to understand a culture that is nothing less than "a heightened attachment to typically Sicilian values and behaviors" (Falcone and Padovani 1997: 61), one must have "breathed the air of the mafia with every breath" (Falcone and Padovani 1997: 68). The fact that the magistrate had, in his childhood, lived in the same world as the men of honor created the conditions for a hitherto impossible level of communication. "I collaborated with Falcone because he is a man of honor," pentito Calderone told the newspapers (Falcone and Padovani 1997: 17). "Why did these men of honor trust me?…I was born in the same neighborhood as many of them. I know the Sicilian spirit well. I can understand much more from an inflexion in the voice or a wink of the eye than from a long statement" (Falcone and Padovani 1997: 17). "Every so often during the interrogation of Michele Greco, a Palermo mafia boss, we would say to each other, 'Look me in the eye!' because we both knew the importance of the look that goes with a certain kind of statement" (Falcone and Padovani 1997: 16). The magistrate went on to list the blunders committed by earlier magistrates who had failed to "break the wall of *omertà*" behind which the mafiosi were hiding. It is on the basis of this relationship of complicity and mutual respect that, in July 1984, Buscetta began to collaborate. Here Falcone indicates the indirect manner in which Buscetta expressed this willingness:

> [Buscetta] "Your Honor, to answer such a question even the entire night would not be enough time." I [Falcone] turned to the Italian magistrate who had accompanied me and said, "I am sure that this man is going to collaborate with us." What he had just said to me was, in fact, a clear signal of peace and openness. (Falcone and Padovani 1997: 51)

On initiation

There were two phases to Falcone's investigation: before and after Buscetta. "Before him, I had—we had—only a superficial idea of the mafia. With him we began to look inside" (Falcone and Padovani 1997: 40). Griaule's research was similarly marked by the involvement of a key mediator: Dogon Ogotemmêli's involvement marked a watershed, first, because it provided "the opportunity to completely renew the perspective of his investigation" (Griaule 1966: 7) and, second, because, by implicitly acknowledging the authority of his informants, it marked a change in the epistemological foundation of his research (Clifford 1996: 87). It began when, in October 1946, a blind old hunter—Ogotemmêli—called for Griaule with the message that he wished to reveal to him Dogon thought, a vast philosophical construction to which access was strictly controlled. Although at the outset Ogotemmêli was in the position of the "patient," the "accused," or the "candidate," patiently answering the questions of the "doctor," the "magistrate," or the "examiner" (Griaule 1952: 542), as Griaule's knowledge of the Dogons grew, the informant took on an increasingly active role, not only in the transmission of factual details but also in the interpretation of his own culture (Rodeghiero 1998: 32). What, then, was Buscetta's contribution to the Maxi Trial investigation?

> He gave us an essential key for interpretation, a language, a code. For us, he was like a language teacher who makes it possible for you to go to Turkey without needing to speak with gestures....Other pentiti have perhaps had greater importance than Buscetta in terms of the content of their revelations. But he was the only one who taught us a method....This method can be summed up in a few concepts: we must resign ourselves to conducting very large investigations, to gathering as much information—whether directly relevant or indirectly—as possible...so that once we have all the pieces of the puzzle, we can develop a strategy. (Falcone and Padovani 1997: 41–42)

In order to achieve a high revelatory power, the legal files that had until then been divided by province had to be assembled into one investigation into the mafia in Sicily. Falcone considered teamwork an effective means of addressing mafia crime and the key to producing a fully documented dossier on a multitude of cases. For this reason, following the assassination of Chinnici, the head of the examining office and inventor of the anti-mafia pool (Zingales 2006), in the summer of 1983, Falcone decided to join the team gathered by Judge Caponnetto. The anti-mafia pool, which brought together the four prosecutors Falcone, Borsellino, Di Lello, and Caponnetto, was based on the principle that each prosecuting judge would share investigatory results with the team, since individual details might not make sense by themselves but could acquire deeper significance when seen as part of the larger picture. This was based on the basic assumption that the island's crimes, controlled if not executed by Cosa Nostra, were connected by imperceptible links. The meaning of one event could thus be clarified through information gathered on another. As investigations deepened, networks emerged, structures took shape, and, from one relationship to the next, the "unified nature of Cosa Nostra" became clear. This was the essence of the "Buscetta theorem." By reconstructing the culture "from the inside," which is the aspiration of any ethnologist, Falcone was able to organize the data already collected into a coherent system. The pentito's collaboration allowed him to take a qualitative leap forward. Falcone crossed the same threshold as the one that separates the ethnographer, a patient collector of material, from the anthropologist, who develops theories and methods that serve to apprehend, organize, and interpret. Ogotemmêli's contribution to Griaule's investigation was no less important: "Here too, a comprehensive set of myths provided the key to institutions and customs, and there were many clues to suggest that under the varied appearance of their rites and behavior, the diverse black populations of these regions hid the outline of a single religion, of a shared way of thinking about the organization of people and the world" (Griaule 1966: 219).

Yet Griaule was criticized for the excessive trust he showed toward his preferred translators and informants. One may wonder to what extent Ogotemmêli's interpretation directed the course of the research and to what extent he was representative of his culture (Clifford 1996: 50–51). The same reservations were voiced with regard to Falcone's investigative work, seen as too dependent on the subjective, self-interested viewpoint of one ex-mafioso who was using the state apparatus to pursue a personal vendetta (Sciascia 2002: 109). In fact, however, the building of evidence on the basis of directly verifiable clues remained a source of information quite independent from the oral collaboration with Buscetta and created favorable conditions in which to provoke, control, and verify his confessions. Furthermore, the judicial proceedings of the Maxi Trial were not based solely on Buscetta's deposition. By crosschecking the testimony of several informants, Falcone was able to "outline a fairly comprehensive panorama of Cosa Nostra from all possible perspectives" (Falcone and Padovani 1997: 63). Falcone, thus, shared with the ethnologist a scrupulous concern for "optimizing the relevance of information by confronting the statements of the various individuals involved" (Bonnain and Fanch'Elegoët 1978: 352), for checking the information collected from different informants through comparison, and for taking only corroborated testimony to make evidence-based decisions.

There was another reason why it was so essential to crosscheck all testimony in the Falcone investigation, namely the very nature of the world being explored, as Buscetta explained:

> One of the most important rules is to split up information. Cosa Nostra is not only secret to the outside...but also within itself: it discourages full knowledge of the facts and creates obstacles to the circulation of information....Cosa Nostra is the realm of incomplete speech. It should therefore be no surprise if, today, revelations of facts unknown even to the men of honor who have been at the top of Cosa Nostra come to light. (Arlacchi 1994: 85–87)

Yet behind these strategies of concealment lies an even more essential truth, one which Buscetta sensed: "Once I had entered the secret society, I realized that behind the circumspect ways of the men of honor there was nothing particularly important" (Arlacchi 1994: 46). While an examination of the secret knowledge that Ogotemmêli revealed to Griaule showed that its significance has been systematically exaggerated (Clifford 1996: 65), it becomes similarly clear that, upon closer inspection, the importance of mafia secrecy, just like insider secrecy, "lies less in what it hides than in what it affirms: membership of a class or a status" (Jamin 1977: 13). The two phases of Griaule's career are joined by the notion of secrecy, as the documentary and initiatory paradigms are linked to the idea that culture is structured as something to be revealed. James Clifford (1996: 88) suggests replacing the view of truth as a "revelation" by a conception of ethnography as a "dialogical enterprise" (Tedlock and Mannheim 1995). Similarly, it could be suggested that in Falcone's investigation it was not the mere transmission of secrets from the former man of honor to the representative of the state but rather the productive dialog established between this particular magistrate and this particular informant that was so effective.

The failure of the performance of a Cosa Nostra member who can be considered as the first pentito suggests as much. On May 30, 1973, mafioso Vitale, racked by deep religious torment, presented himself to the mobile brigade, a carabinieri unit responsible for public security, and confessed. After having told of his initiation and revealing the names of dozens of members of the Palermo families, he lost himself in endless "waffling":

Mental illness=psychological ill; mafia=social ill; corrupt authorities=social ill; prostitution=social ill; syphilis, warts=physical ill that has affected my mind, which has been sick since my childhood; religious crises=psychological ill that stems from these ills. These are the ills I have been victim to, I, Leonardo Vitale, resurrected in the true faith of God.[2]

Vitale was judged insane and locked up in a correctional psychiatric hospital before being killed by the mafia after his release, in December 1984. Five years later, another Cosa Nostra member, Giuseppe di Cristina, invited the carabinieri to an abandoned country house where he provided them with an organizational chart of the Corleonese family. He identified two of its influential members, Provenzano and Riina, a Corleonese nicknamed the "Beast." Let free by the carabinieri, he was murdered in a Palermo street in May 1978 (Lodato 1994: 21–27). Neither of these two pentiti (even if this term was not yet available when these mafiosi decided to speak) was likely to be listened to. Breaking the silence could not be a unilateral act. The conditions of listening to such testimony are just as important as the willingness by the perpetrators to break the silence. Again, was an encounter between a magistrate of Falcone's caliber and a pentito of Buscetta's intelligence required to expose the reality of the mafia?

The novelty of the Maxi Trial lies in the fact that the mafiosi spoke in court so that what had up to then taken place in the form of a necessarily ambiguous personal relationship between mafia and police became institutionalized and legalized (Lupo 1999: 307). Even so, this trial alone would never have had an impact on society if it had not occurred along with other, more profound changes. Pino Arlacchi speaks of a "cultural revolution…that consists in no longer considering the mafia as essential to Sicilian society or as a sort of fate specific to the island and, consequently, in believing in the ethical superiority of the state of law and its representatives" (Chinnici et al. 1992: 56). I will now try to pinpoint where and by which means the mafia was transformed, from incorporating the intrinsic character of the island to representing a "social evil" and a "disease afflicting Sicily."

2. *Ordinanza Sentenza contro Michele Greco + 18*, vol. 8, p. 1219, Office for the Investigation of Penal and Civil Trials, High Court of Palermo, 1991.

Constructing the other

"When Buscetta, to justify his confession, told me that his pals had broken the most basic rules of Cosa Nostra and that they were going to ruin the organization through their behavior, I felt it was a great moment, a historic occasion," said Falcone (Falcone and Padovani 1997: 39). What Falcone was pointing to was that Buscetta was promising to reveal the internal functioning of the mafia families exactly because these were no longer keeping to their own unwritten rules, they were not being true mafiosi anymore. Buscetta was, in fact, suggesting that Cosa Nostra's internal system was breaking apart, imploding. The mafioso began talking at a point when the Corleonese family, known for its brutality, had taken hold of Cosa Nostra and the organization seemed to be going wild. He said that "the families were tearing each other apart and suspicions of betrayal and double-dealing wormed their way through everything" (Arlacchi 1994: 140). He described an apocalyptic scenario with himself as a "witness to a vanishing world," a "general in a ghost army" (Arlacchi 1994: 222). It was exactly because he considered that Cosa Nostra was in its death throes, and with it the whole world he had believed in, that he did not consider his collaboration with the police a "betrayal." Instead, as Falcone recounted, Buscetta "claimed to be the real man of honor, while the Corleonesi and their allies were the dregs of Cosa Nostra, since they had not respected its rules" (Falcone and Padovani 1997: 60). It is at this very point that the magistrate was present, pen in hand, the feverish chronicler of this crumbling world that must be captured in writing to save it from the danger of evanescence to which societies "without writing" are exposed.

The merit of the examining magistrates in the Maxi Trial was to have enabled confessions that they alone were in a position to record. Once again, these magistrates recall the Spanish conquistadores who hurriedly set down in writing the rites and customs of the peoples they encountered (Bernand and Gruzinski 1988: 27). By describing in careful detail the mafia's initiation rituals, festive practices, leisure activities, appointment system, family structure, killing techniques, and ethical code, the magistrates helped us discover a world at the very same time as they did everything in their power to destroy it. Like the information gathering of the extirpators of idolatry, the magistrates' endeavor for knowledge had to lead to a struggle against "evil." The fight waged against the mafia took on the quality of a crusade. "Falcone seemed to be motivated...by a desire to free Sicily from the plague of the mafia" (Stille 1995: 36). It is at this point that the terrorist methods used by the Corleonesi no longer generated a consensus, as in the past, one that denied its engagement of violence and affirmed its membership of Sicilian society, but rather generated alarm and protest across Sicily and Italy more widely. The romantic image of the mafia was being undermined and the image of the "man of honor" began to turn and increasingly conform to the stereotype of an outsider, marked by a primitive barbarism and associated with sickness and plague. Were not idolaters too shown in the guise of the plague-stricken, and idolatry likened to an "illness" whose "contagion" we must fear (Bernand and Gruzinski 1988: 163–164)?

The association between the mafia and the plague took root over a long period. It first appeared following the proclamation of the unification of Italy in 1871. When the unified state looked toward Mezzogiorno, a distressing social picture emerged. In Sicily, the misery of the working classes, illiteracy, and a land monopoly controlled by a few large landowners were perpetuated by violence enacted by the *gabelloti*, the "violent peasant entrepreneurs" identified by Blok (1974) as the "mafiosi" who served as intermediaries between landowners and peasants. An investigation in 1876 into the social conditions of Sicily (by Tuscan intellectuals Leopoldo Franchetti and Sidney Sonnino) is an example of the paternalism with which the newborn Italian state confronted the "Southern question." Sicilian society was identified as an "illness" that needed "to be treated." "Emaciated, starving, covered with sores," Sicilians bore the scars of physical and social harm and it was up to the "educated class of central and Northern Italy...to the exclusion of all Sicilians or, at least, almost all Sicilians" to cure this condition as quickly as possible, "because the wounds were gangrenous and threatened to infect Italy" (Renda 1997: 105). In an article published in January 1900, social critic Alfredo Oriani painted the whole of Sicily as "a cancer at the foot of Italy, as a province in which neither custom nor civil laws were possible" (quoted in Renda 1997: 156). In 1910, public prosecutor Salvatore Pagliano denounced "the region's endemic social infirmity" (Renda 1997: 175). Sicilians themselves, especially those from the chief town of Palermo, shared this grim view of the island. A reporter for the Palermo newspaper *L'Ora*, who visited the village of Santo Stefano di Quisquina in Agrigento province in May 1911 to cover the umpteenth murder, described the area as a "land ruled by barbaric and primitive customs." He portrayed the funeral he attended as "the ceremonial of a wild tribe's archaic and incomprehensible rites" (Renda 1997: 189). It took folklorist

Pitrè to take on the role of spokesperson and present an "apology of the mafia" in defense of Sicily.

So, in the early decades of the twentieth century, debate on the mafia focused the north-south antagonism. Once the republican state was established in 1945, the conflict turned political. In the late 1950s, there was an intense mobilization for the south's renaissance. Attempts at land reform intended to build on the "healthy forces of Sicily," while the peasant movement took on the aura of a "regenerative movement" (Renda 1997: 308–309). A number of ethnographic investigations were born in this climate of cultural and political effervescence, published in the 1950s and 1960s. In 1955, Carlo Levi published *Le Parole sono pietre*, which concludes with the biography of militant unionist Salvatore Carnevale, who was murdered on March 6, 1955, by the Sciara mafia of Sicily. Sociologist Danilo Dolci's investigations in Sicily were motivated by social projects aiming to revive the fishing and peasant villages of the bay of Castellammare, which were fighting against mafia bosses and large landowners. For his studies, he collected biographies that told of the peasants' ongoing struggle to have the law enforced, and recorded the clashes between the *gabelloti* mafia and the police. A new literary genre was born: the anti-mafia biography. The history of Sicily and the mafia is told through the narrative framework of the life stories of those who fought against (or tried to survive) this form of social and human degradation and violence. Two decades later, in 1976, a parliamentary inquiry into the Sicilian mafia led to the collation of the first biographies of mafia figures. In the 1980s the magistrates of the anti-mafia pool in Palermo made use of the vast amount of information collected by this parliamentary commission, which, in turn, led to a season of biographies on pentiti. In this manner, they took over from social researchers like Anton Blok (1974) who continued to use the biographical method to probe the mafia phenomenon. They had come full circle.

In the 1980s, the pentiti's declarations, recomposed and reorganized in written legal records by anti-mafia magistrates, produced new knowledge, opened up unexpected perspectives, and enabled researchers with an interest in the mafia to make significant theoretical advances. Nowadays, acknowledged mafia specialists may obtain special authorization to interview the pentiti in jail, thereby stepping into the magistrates' shoes. One such academic is sociologist Pino Arlacchi, who has written books recounting the confessions of pentiti Calderone and Buscetta (Arlacchi 1992, 1994). For their part, some magistrates publish articles in specialist journals. Scarpinato, the magistrate who continued Falcone's investigation after the latter's murder, exposing the links between Sicilian mafia and political power, suggests that the mafia, with its ranks and its roles, offers an identificatory path to individuals who do not want to remain *nuddu miscatu a nenti* (a person mixed with nothing), to use an expression often employed by the pentiti. The attempts by a few magistrates to elucidate the deeper motives of the men of honor have parallels with sociological studies of violence in criminal gangs. Sociologist Alain Ehrenberg, for example, strove to show, on the basis of interviews and the perusal of legal records, that hooligans "are not gangs of lunatics, degenerates, or animals…[they are not] a pure social monstrosity because they lack, it is thought, all sense" (Ehrenberg 1991: 46). Similarly, in Falcone's social and professional experience, the desire to crack down on the mafia went hand in hand with an effort to understand them and, in turn, to understand ourselves.

Returning to the self

To begin with, the mafia—a world of violence which seemed to lack all reason—had aroused feelings of repulsion and strangeness in Falcone the law student. "I saw Cosa Nostra as the seven-headed Hydra: something magmatic, omnipresent, and invincible, responsible for all of the world's ills…In the face of the brutality, the murders, and the assaults, I was overcome with horror" (Falcone and Padovani 1997: 39). Then, as his knowledge increased, a greater understanding of the internal rules governing this world brought about a more comprehensive insight.

> The things that horrify us in the event of a violent death, as magistrates or ordinary citizens—a man eliminated by his best friend, a brother strangled by his own brother's hand—do not produce the same reactions in men of honor…It is a strange interpretation of the concept of honor that dictates that you must never delegate the task of killing someone of your own blood! (Falcone and Padovani 1997: 30–31)

In order to understand the mafia, Falcone employed a comparativist approach, comparing men of honor with what were considered outlandish societies. One comparison was made with the Sioux, for example, who also hold a sentiment of being the only "Men," recalling that the word *omertà* is claimed to derive from the Sicilian *omu* (man). But Falcone never yielded to exoticism. He used comparisons to gain a better grasp of the internal logic of mafia behavior, whether it was by understanding the elimination of the weakest individuals as a strategy for group survival (as among the Inuit) or recognizing the symbolic benefits of murdering a prestigious boss (as among Native Americans). "The more bloody, merciless, and cruel the execution seems to us ordinary citizens, the prouder of it the man of honor can be," he explained; and that "the most loathsome retaliations,…those that to the honest citizen seem needlessly cruel, are never executed lightheartedly but with a sense of duty" (Falcone and Padovani 1997: 31, 32). Once he had discovered the "rationality of the rules on which the mafia was based," this "Sicilian of the Enlightenment," as he has been defined, took pleasure in sweeping away all the "myths" that surrounded it:

> I would like to do away with another widespread platitude, which is even glorified by a certain type of literature: that of the so-called murder rituals.…Many stories have been told about *incaprettamento*. [3]…Any killing technique is legitimate as long as it works and it does not cause too many problems. (Falcone and Padovani 1997: 27)

Falcone overlaid the image conveyed by the press of a "traditional" mafia, a "relic" of a bygone era, with that of a criminal organization that was adapting to modernity (Falcone and Padovani 1997: 78). With the mafia rid of its folklore, there was no room for the common representation of the bloodthirsty Sicilian belonging to an outdated world.

> Newspapers, books, and movies all dwell on the mafia's cruelty. It exists, of course, but it is never an end in itself…In the organization, violence and cruelty are never gratuitous. They always represent the final option, when all other forms of intimidation have proven ineffective or when the offense committed is so serious that it deserves only death. (Falcone and Padovani 1997: 28–31)

"Serious and perfectly organized," Cosa Nostra functions like a modern state, with specific control systems and mechanisms of repression.

---

3. The *incaprettamento* is a technique by which the victim's wrists and ankles are tied behind his back in such a way that the rope runs around the neck, so that any effort at freeing himself will result in self-strangulation. The term means "to tie up someone like a goat [*capra*]."

Cosa Nostra is, in its own way, like a legal society or organization, which requires effective penalty mechanisms in order for its regulations to be respected and applied. Given that inside the mafia state there are neither courts nor law enforcement agencies, it is essential for each of its "citizens" to know that punishment is inevitable, and the sentence will be executed immediately. Those who break the rules know they will pay with their lives. (Falcone and Padovani 1997: 37)

Paradoxically, it is within the mafia, "this mafia which, when you look closely, is essentially nothing other than a need for order and, therefore, a state," that Falcone finds his ideal of statehood. "This adventure has made my sense of the state even more authentic. By confronting the "mafia state," I realized just how much more functional and effective it is than *our* state" (Falcone and Padovani 1997: 71). This "adventure," as he called his experience in the mafia world, led him to look differently, critically, at his own society, and to question it at a profound level.

At times, these mafiosi seem the only rational beings in a world of lunatics....Men of honor are neither evil nor schizophrenic. They would not kill their father and mother for a few grams of heroin. They are men like us. The Western world, and Europe in particular, has tended to exorcize evil by projecting it onto ethnicities and behaviors that seem different from our own. But if we want to fight the mafia effectively, we must not turn it into a monster or think of it as the mob or a cancer. We must recognize that it is like us. (Falcone and Padovani 1997: 72, 82–83)

At the end of his path, the magistrate no longer saw Cosa Nostra as the "seven-headed Hydra." His original "horror" was replaced by a feeling of familiarity and the recognition of a shared humanity.

Knowing the mafia has had a profound influence on my relationship to others, and even on my convictions. I have learned to recognize the humanity in the worst of beings, to have a true rather than a merely formal respect for the opinions of others....Although it might seem strange, the mafia has taught me an important lesson in morality. (Falcone and Padovani 1997: 71)

For Falcone, investigating the mafia meant learning to understand people and to recognize them, over and above their differences. This learning about otherness, this recognition of what is the same in others, this lesson of tolerance, confers an anthropological significance on his investigation. The mafiosi are not sorcerers, lunatics, or savages—the categories into which "others" are usually locked. "They are men like us." On the far side of the mirror held up to him by a "different" culture, Falcone recognized himself, ourselves.

On January 30, 1992, the Appeal Court confirmed the conviction of the men of honor accused and found guilty in the Maxi Trial as well as the conception of Cosa Nostra put forward at the trial by Buscetta and codified by Falcone. The murders, a few months later, of magistrates Falcone and Borsellino were the immediate consequence of "the collapse of the judicial and cognitive taboo on the nature of the mafia, and of the break of a second taboo that prevented any in-depth investigation into the relationship between mafia and politics" (Arlacchi 1995: 12–13). After Falcone's death, Buscetta opened a new chapter in his confessions, spilling the beans on "the political complicity in the highest spheres that allowed Cosa Nostra to prosper undisturbed until the 1980s" (Arlacchi 1994: 206). With authorization by the Senate, as granted in May 1993, Scarpinato and the Palermo magistrates instituted proceedings on March 2, 1995, against Andreotti, the man who for forty years had been the most high-profile figure in Italian politics. "The time is now ripe to utter that name," stated Buscetta (Arlacchi 1994: 206). The politician was accused of participation in a mafia association—a charge changed to "external complicity with the mafia association Cosa Nostra" (*concorso esterno*) in 1994—on the basis of the declarations by Buscetta and eleven other pentiti. But on September 24, 1999, the Assizes Court of Perugia acquitted Andreotti and his co-defendants, including mafioso Tano Badalamenti (see chapter 8). The repudiation of the magistrates and the pentiti followed, commented on by Buscetta in these terms:

> Tano Badalamenti never repudiated me. He behaved like a defendant, and his only assertion was that he didn't even know what the mafia was. So those who claim that Badalamenti repudiated Buscetta, and that he was believed by the magistrates, if they want to be consistent they should also claim that Cosa Nostra does not exist, that it never existed. (Buscetta 1999: 168)

We were back to the starting point. Falcone's legal adventure, continued by the Palermitan magistrates, proved to be a tremendous endeavor for knowledge, but one that proved to have no significant impact on the transformation of the political realm. "The transformation of the

Andreottian movement into a sort of mask-appendix of the mafia" (Arlacchi 1995: 22) dragged us from concealment strategies implemented within a secret society to the ambiguity of political games. It also led to the discovery of a worrying anthropological truth: that very often, behind the mask of the "Other" is hiding "Our Own." Let us go back and analyze in more detail the translations, transactions, and transfers that occurred between the mafia and the state.

CHAPTER 7

The Buscetta theorem

On responsibility

—I would like to express a wish: I wish you peace, Your Honor. To all of you, I wish you peace, for peace is the tranquility and serenity of the soul and the conscience.

—That is what we also wish…

—…because, for the task ahead of you, if I may be so bold, Your Honor, serenity is the fundamental basis for exercising judgment. These are not my own words; these are the words of Our Lord, who advised Moses: "When you must judge, may you do so with complete serenity," which is the essential foundation on which judgment is built.

And I also wish, Your Honor, that this peace might stay with you for however long you have left to live.[1]

---

1. Speech by Michele Greco, head of Cosa Nostra, during the final session of the Maxi Trial against the mafia (see "Augurio di Michele Greco alla Corte," YouTube video, uploaded by Ninovox, no date, 1:02 min, http://www.youtube.com/watch?v=PIleRcE9wzY).

Palermo, November 11, 1987. The last of the 349 sessions of the Maxi Trial draws to a close, a trial brought against Cosa Nostra, its 485 members, and its bosses as instigators of several hundred murders committed in Sicily during the Second Mafia War of the early 1980s. The judges and jurors prepare to leave the dais in the bunker-courthouse where they have sat for almost two years, to withdraw to the Council Chamber—they would deliberate there for thirty-five days before giving their judgment. At this point Michele Greco asks for permission to speak. He is the boss of Cosa Nostra, known by the nickname "the Pope." It is under him that the Commission made a clearly observable shift from ordinary mafia violence to "terror." The court grants him this right. And it is now that a spectacular reversal of roles takes place: the accused impresses on the judges the difficulty of the task of judging and the responsibility they carry when attributing responsibility. His words imply that there are several sources of authority, and that divine law, embodied by Moses, takes precedence over human law. A death threat, barely concealed by the "gentleness" of his words, concludes his speech.

This is how responsibility, a legal concept, can become a research topic for the ethnologist. It can become perceptible in scenes where different normative orders come into conflict: moments of uncertainty in which the source of authority, that which attributes responsibility, can falter or fail. It can also appear through scenes in which the function of a third party, guaranteed by certain bodies as the judiciary, can be challenged by other bodies, as the mafia pretend to be, whether they have greater or lesser force; or through scenes where the extent of responsibility is called into question, and this is all the more significant when the party to whom responsibility is attributed is a collective entity—in this case Cosa Nostra—with unclear boundaries. Finally, it can appear through scenes where words are used that carry connotations that are quite contrary to what the words actually denote and that thus require interpretation.

Anthropologists have addressed the relations that connect people, collectively and individually, with social norms, moral values, laws, customs, and institutions. A number of recent publications indicate a new interest in the concept of responsibility among anthropologists. James Laidlaw has moved his attention from the analysis of the *quality of action* in rituals, where the *actors* are not necessarily the authors of their acts (Humphrey and Laidlaw 1994), to the study of responsibility (Laidlaw 2014). Other anthropologists have analyzed the different forms or processes of "responsibilization" at the heart of the political preoccupation with and challenge to the neoliberal era, with its multiple interplay of conflicting normativities, various commitments, and decomposition and recomposition of collectivities based on emotions, intentions, or convictions (Trnka and Trundle 2017). Such anthropological approaches make it possible to free the issue of responsibility from the domain of law (or morality), to which it had been limited, and to demonstrate its action in society: its power to alter the statuses of individuals and groups, or to establish ontological boundaries (Puccio-Den 2017a). Why should we not, then, "take responsibility seriously" as an object of anthropological study in itself?

Responsibility is a legal notion, a philosophical concept, and a domain within the field of morality, but it is also a practice that aims to establish a link between an individual and acts that are attributed to him, and for which the individual must, if necessary, answer before the law. It is precisely the nature of this link that we must investigate by means of an analysis of the *processes of attributing responsibility*. Let us assume that this link is in no way self-evident or natural, but that it is historically constructed, that it manifests itself in different ways in different cultures, and that it tends to produce controversies within a given society or within the law itself, whether criminal or civil law, or national or international law. This chapter has undertaken to follow, step by step, the social and cognitive operations by which blame or liability for the mafia was attributed both to individuals (mafiosi) and to collective entities (Cosa Nostra).

It is, of course, obvious that the type of imputation of responsibility varies considerably depending on whether the accusation is directed at an easily identifiable individual or at a collective entity whose boundaries are difficult to define, and which are often defined during the course of the trial or process of attributing responsibility, which therefore has an ontological effect on the entity that it defines. The individualist conception of blame and punishment is, if not entirely called into question, then at least challenged by legal actions and social situations that blur the linear relationship between agent and action, as is the case in collective or organized crime. These situations offer a privileged vantage point, allowing a broader reflection on the place of the individual in relation to his group or groups of membership or belonging, but also allowing us to consider the ontological power of the law in our societies. Although the confrontation or co-existence of individualist and communitarian representations of society is played out, in part, through the judicial testing of legal concepts, these legal concepts in return play a determining role in the creation of "legal subjects" and, sometimes, in the ontological stabilization of the subjects and collectivities involved. This raises the following question: what transformations occur in a "moral economy" when members of a criminal association, who see their actions as collectively accomplished, come under the intense scrutiny of the judicial system and are forced to assume an individually conceived guilt?

Beginning with the legal concept of responsibility as an obligation to *respond* for one's harmful or criminal actions before the law (Ricœur 1995: 41), I analyze the conditions of this *speech act* (etymologically *respondere*, in Latin) for the mafioso, implying both a subject and the possibility of the latter enunciating his[2] actions in his own name. Such is the case of the "justice collaborator," as well as the "witnesses" who certify the truth through their presence in the related events. The statuses of "justice collaborator" and "justice witness" are very close, at least in terms of the legislation that governs their rights and duties, principally the right to protection of themselves and their families in exchange for the obligation to provide reliable testimony (D'Ambrosio 2002: 70–78). Both these positions imply a form of attestation that involves the assumption of the "I"—even though they are different from a moral point of view for, as the spokespeople for Italian witness associations assert, witnesses did nothing to "see" what they saw, and found themselves implicated, unwittingly, in a crime situation that changed their life and that of their family. As is the case for the witness,[3] I postulate for pentiti that their performative speech not only creates the attested event but also enables the emergence of the subject of the enunciator: in the assertion "I saw it…I was there," what is constituted and socially instituted is also the "I." We explored in chapter 1 the question of the legal and judicial construction of the mafia as a collective entity and the problems inherent in the imputation of offenses to a group or to a "mafia association." Here I approach the question of individual responsibility from this ontological perspective, as a legal performance where, by recognizing a certain number of crimes as his own before the state, the defendant implicitly admits, and ontologically establishes, the existence of him as a subject and author—something not at all evident for the members of a secret society who are

---

2. I use the male gender as generic since the people discussed here are all men, "men of honor."

3. On the social conditions of the "autobiographic certification" of the witness, see Dulong (1998).

"depersonalized," self-referential, and silent beings. Georg Simmel explicitly links the "depersonalization" affecting members of secret societies to the lack of responsibility stemming from the use of a "mask" (quoted in Dino 2002: 76). This depersonalization also emerges from the accounts of the pentiti, when they begin telling their criminal stories in a first-person speech act and realize the damages they caused by behaving like perfect automatons.[4]

As the opposite of responsibility, a locutionary regime centered on the individual, the mafia's honor is a normative system in which acts have meaning and value only in relation to the group. It remains to be discovered what authorities are legitimized to attribute a positive or negative value to actions, and thus honor or dishonor the agents involved. The same action may be honorable and dishonorable, depending on the collective in question: from the viewpoint of the mafia or from the viewpoint of the state that refers the individual to their own responsibilities. "A strange interpretation of the concept of honor, demanding that one does not delegate to someone else the task of killing an individual belonging to one's own blood," muses an astonished Falcone (Falcone and Padovani 1997: 31) in the face of crimes that seem to shake the moral categories of "modern" societies, forcing the judge to learn interpretative codes very different from those he had acquired from Western legal civilization (see chaper 6). I take up this question again in the name of an anthropology of honor nourished by the themes deployed by law and legal anthropology, exploring the mafia criminal practices in which this "strange concept" takes root and asking what it, in turn, as a symbolic and social system, helps found and justify. I do not concern myself with the question of knowing whether the "men of honor" are right to define themselves as such—which seems to be the main preoccupation of social researchers who have worked on the Sicilian mafia. I also leave aside an axiological point of view and rather adopt a pragmatic perspective, before taking up the question of responsibility as a *regime of action and speech*, which, at the opposite side of the spectrum of silent non-speech acts, reconfigures the relations between the individual and the state.

---

4. Interviews by the author with several pentiti, at the Servizio centrale di protezione dei testimoni e collaboratori di giustizia (Central service for the protection of witnesses and collaborators of justice), Rome, 2009 and 2010.

What does honor make and what is it made of?

Is it because we, anthropologists, consider honor as a "value" that we pronounce value judgments about those who claim to possess it? In an article devoted to the question of the "moral taxonomies" of Mediterranean societies, Herzfeld (1980: 340) urges us to situate "honor" and "shame" within the linguistic and social context of a localized region. This is what I attempt to do here, but by focusing on the *materiality* of honor rather than its "morality," following the trail of blood left by those who mobilize it in Sicily: the "men of honor."

Twenty-seven years after publishing his first monograph on the mafia in Sicily (1974), in a work entitled *Honor and Violence*, the anthropologist Anton Blok (2001b: 21) questioned the "respectability" of the brigands in the pay of the mafia, who claimed to act for the people while only protecting the relations of domination within a competitive context between elites in the young Italian state. The economist Clotilde Champeyrache (2007: 46–53) sees honor as no more and no less than a "myth" that researchers have the mission of "demolishing." In an essay named "Men of Respect," Raimondo Catanzaro (1992), for his part, links honor to the processes of modernization of the societies of southern Italy, marked by immobility, interpreting it as a code underlying forms of "instrumental friendship" that can be activated in local conflicts. But while associating it with change, the sociologist devalorizes this social resource by making it the expression of a "popular culture" or a "subculture" (Catanzaro 1992: 45–55). We can retain the idea that honor serves to preserve the "integrity" of a group and its property, provided that this notion encompasses—as I try to do later—representations of the person (which here includes the collective or "moral" person of the mafia in the legal sense of the term) and of the substances composing the latter. The question is thus one of knowing in which conceptions of the person honor and responsibility are inscribed, and which conceptions they help shape in return.

We shall see that the components of mafia honor—mobilized in the struggles to acquire it, capable of augmenting or diminishing it—are essentially bodily matter: blood, sperm, breath. To these we can add money, wherein the sociologist Pino Arlacchi (2007: 74–76) identifies a distinctive trait of the new entrepreneurial mafia but dissociates it from the honor for which it is a substitute as a good to be exploited in social rivalry—not to mention that its circulation and capitalization follow the same logic that makes all these substances erect boundaries to the outside world, while being shared inside the group.

In the Inchiesta Spatola, a legal inquiry into global drug trafficking from the United States to Sicily involving the Gambino and Inzerillo families, Falcone noted that:

> Inzerillo Franco does not have a personal account and this is quite strange if we consider that he has engaged in commercial and entrepreneurial activities: all this can only mean a substantial indistinction of the affairs between himself and his brother.[5]

Huge flows of money were crossing various European countries and the United States, but the Sicilian judge discovered that in Italy they were passing through the hands of just a single clan: the Spatola-Inzerillo. This family group was marked by a high level of endogamy, to the point of favoring marriage between first-degree cousins (Arlacchi 2007: 142). Women and wealth followed the same circuit, adhering to a logic of retention and accumulation rather than exchange and redistribution (Armao 2000: 18–19). The difficulty of the judge investigating the Spatola trial in the late 1970s consisted of surpassing this "substantial indistinction of the affairs" to determine the responsibilities of the individual people involved in the drug trafficking. This difficulty was exacerbated by the fact that the state's representative could not rely on an essential component of responsibility, speech, since it too was held within this dense network of economic and family solidarity.

Since the founding work of Pierre Bourdieu on Kabyle society in Algeria, honor has appeared as a traditional value that, associated with the clan, the patrilineage, and a particular group, opposes the universal values on which modern nations and states are built.[6] Whether at the level of gender—where the female ethos, centered on modesty and chastity, is opposed to the male ethos, centered on the courage and capacity to defend one's own—or at the level of classes, statuses, and social ranks—where honor is unequally distributed and serves only to nurture forms of distinction (Pitt-Rivers 1965: 42–45, 73)—its discriminatory effect is incompatible with the principle of democracy that pronounces the equality of all citizens. Charles Taylor (1989) sees honor as a kind of

---

5. *Sentenza instruttoria del processo contro Rosario Spatola + 119*: 656–660 (cited by Arlacchi 2007: 143).

6. "The ethos of honor is fundamentally opposed to a universal and formal morality which affirms the equality in dignity of all men and consequently the equality of their rights and duties" (Bourdieu 1965: 228).

premodern social relation where dignity itself is linked to a conception of the individual as a morally autonomous being (Mubi Brighenti 2008: 12). From a normative point of view, by imposing the exclusive defense of one's family, clients, or vassals, the "code of honor" diverges by nature from the human right to protection and security, which is applicable to all individuals as members of a common humanity (Smith 2006: 24–29). Here the borders of the human—not only those that divide, within the same species, *us from them* (Peristiany 1965: 173) but even more fundamentally those that separate the human from the animal, because this is where the decisive political conflict of Western modernity is played out (Agamben 2002: 82)—are restricted to the limits of the group.

In Sicily, this essentialist conception of the group is the point where, in indigenous thought, honor and *omertà* are articulated. Deriving from the Sicilian *omu* (man), *omertà* designates a quality that can be attributed to those human beings who can claim to be "real men." The mafiosi, in the glowing description by folklorist Pitrè, are the most illustrious bearers of this quality.[7] Remember that he notes that it is only after 1860—following Italy's unification—that the positive meanings associated with the word "mafia" (courage, pride, the capacity to assure protection of one's relatives without resorting to state justice) began to acquire negative connotations, gradually becoming the attribute of individuals living on the margins of the law, such as assassins, thugs, brigands (Pitrè [1889] 1944: 293–294). These remarks appear to anticipate the eventual fate of honor and the "men of honor" when the latter, and the value of which they made themselves the bearers, became subject to the judgment of the Italian state.

Almost a century after the unification of Italy, this gradation of humanity was revived by Sciascia who deployed it in the voice of one of the characters in his famous novel *Il Giorno della civetta* (The day of the owl, published in 1961), mafia boss Don Mariano Arena:

> I...have a certain experience of the world; and what we call humanity—all hot air that word—I divide into five categories: men, half-men, pygmies, assholes[8]—if you'll excuse the expression—and

---

7. This association between mafia, *omertà*, and honor is explicit in the case of the Calabrian mafia, the *'Ndrangheta*, a term that derives from the Greek *andragathia* (ἀνδραγαθία) referring to the virtues of the "true" men who make up this association.

8. The word that Sciascia used was *pigliainculo*, which means as much as "take it in the ass."

quackers. Men are very few indeed, half-men few; and I'd be content if humanity finished with them....But no, it sinks even lower, to the pygmies who're like children trying to be grown-ups, monkeys going through the motions of their elders....Then down even lower we go, to the assholes who're legion....And, finally, to the quackers; they ought to just exist, like ducks in a pond; their lives have no more point or meaning. (Sciascia 1990: 100)

This passage, perhaps the most commented on in all of Sciascia's work, is exemplary of the way in which the qualification of mankind, in a continuum descending to the animal (monkeys, ducks) via a degrading feminization of the asshole,[9] depend on the good or bad use of language. At the lowest level of humanity is the jabberer, the "quacker" *(quaquaraqua)*, someone who speaks too much, like Dibella the "snitch" in *Il Giorno della civetta*. When Captain Bellodi, the investigating officer, asks whether Dibella was a man, he receives the following answer:

—He was a quacker, Don Mariano replies contemptuously. He had let go and words aren't like dogs that one can whistle to make them come back.[10]

Ultimately it falls to the mafia boss to embody the ethics of this restrained speech that distinguishes man from beast, even if Sciascia confers this discriminating humanity also to the protagonist of his novel, Captain Bellodi from northern Italy, who dares to stand up to the mafia and heroically loses the fight: "Why am I a man, not a half-man or even a quacker? he asked with a toughness born of exasperation." A prophetic figure, a harbinger of a generation of police officers and judges recognized as "men" by the "men of honor" who, therefore, agree to establish a "man to man" communication with them.

Before we again get to the modalities of this encounter, let us try to comprehend what made it possible that some mafia members decided to let go of their secrets and loosen their tongues, like dogs kept on a leash their entire life and suddenly set free, thus infringing the rule subtly referred to by Don Mariano in Sciascia's novel. Falcone had certainly been

---

9. The sense of passive sexuality that is considered degrading for a "man" is implicit in the term.

10. These passages are discussed by Salvatore Sgroi (2014: 197) in a comparative study of translations of the term *quaquaraqua*.

imbued with this literature, as a Sicilian, and was versed in these meta-phors when he endeavored to persuade mafia boss Buscetta to "speak" when the latter, arrested by the Brazilian police, was handed over to the Italian authorities. The transactions between judge and prisoner lasted several months. But it is Buscetta who observed the judge, tested his ca-pacity to interpret his innuendos, his veiled, allegorical language, and his silences. And then, one day, he threw his investigator a line and Falcone was astute enough to recognize that the "man of honor" was ready to open up, to breach the seawalls of his silence and allow the words he had held back for so long to flow freely. Let us recall this decisive exchange, in Falcone's account:

> "Your Honor, an entire night would not be enough for me to answer such a question." I turned to the Italian judge who accompanied me and, eliciting an incredulous laugh, said to him: "I am sure that this man will collaborate with us." What he had said was, in fact, a clear signal of peace and openness. (Falcone and Padovani 1997: 51)

Let us return to Pitrè's ([1889] 1944: 296) description of a mafia member, par excellence a being of silence: "a simple movement of the eyes or lips, a half-word suffices to make himself understood." If, in Mediterranean societies, honor is a good to be won and defended, then "words also have their value as actions" (Pitt-Rivers 1965: 27), able to constitute an alternative or complement to the violent acts undertaken by groups of men. According to various anthropologists working on the concept of honor, women are generally excluded from this type of com-petition, limiting themselves to safeguarding the purity of the blood by preserving their body from potential male attacks, especially when the latter come from outside the group. This gender difference is identified as a primordial structuring element of Mediterranean societies (Gilmore 1987: 5–16). Research on the mafia has enabled a more nuanced inter-pretation of this strict partition of roles, leading to a re-evaluation of the place of women in the management of mafia crime, and thus of their criminal responsibility (Siebert 1994; Principato and Dino 1997; Puglisi 2005). Nonetheless, one of the main reasons why women are generally distrusted is their alleged incapacity to keep silent. Hence, the interdic-tion to speak with them. Thus, when we look at Sicily, we need to con-sider silence as a particular *regime of action and interaction* that structures the relationships between men and women at home, before structuring the relationships between mafiosi and the outside world.

154

Silence comprises, first of all, a modality of interaction with the state and its representatives whom the mafia counters with a tenacious silence, which is imposed by extension on all its entourage, by ordering them to keep silent under penalty of dishonor or death. Here resides the social meaning of honor and the essence of *omertà*: a social norm stigmatizing as dishonorable not only informers, those who denounce the misdeeds perpetrated by others, but also those who resort to the law to defend their own rights (Pitrè [1889] 1944: 296). Beyond the protective function that silence provides vis-à-vis the authorities likely to punish crimes committed by mafia members, we need to identify in it a "device of resistance" (Di Bella 2008: 76). Michel Foucault (1978: 27) persuades us to apprehend silences as "an integral part of the strategies that underlie and permeate discourses." A performative non-speech act, *omertà* seeks to weaken the state by refusing to recognize its legitimacy to know what happens in the territory over which it presumes to exercise its sovereignty.[11] Silence is a challenge, a proof of honor dishonorable for the state,[12] discredited by its own inhabitants who, by taunting it in this way, reveal its impotence to "enforce respect" for itself and its own laws. Hence, the law of silence is imposed by the very silence it imposes, ignoring all other laws, written and oral.

Because of its prohibition on leaving written traces of its activities, the mafia has been placed among the "societies without writing." Its code of honor forms part of its orality, though we will see in the last chapter of this book how this dogma can be called into question. We can anticipate that its law is signed—signed in blood and in the erasing out of all other laws. Anthropologist Julian Pitt-Rivers (1965: 34–35) had underlined "the importance of the oath in relation to honor," as well as the collective nature of the latter: "Social groups possess a collective honor in which their members participate." Mafia members also take an oath, precisely during the initiation ceremony: this rite turns a common man into a "man of honor," allowing him access to this "elite" of humanity, distinguished from animals by such a refined use of speech that it is reduced to

---

11. In this sense, "to keep silent" in Sicily is tantamount to "lying" in other Mediterranean societies, or "to lye is to deny the truth to someone who has the right to be told it and this right exists only where respect is due" (Pitt-Rivers 1965: 33).

12. In line with the analogy in the preceding note, we can also quote the statement by Julian Pitt-Rivers (1965: 33–34) that "to deceive a person intentionally is to humiliate him."

the essential, silence being the essence of purity (a question of aesthetics as much as ethics). Let us examine this more closely.

The ritual that "makes" the man of honor is a signature in blood. This is explicit in the literary prototype of the mafia initiation rite, *I Beati Paoli*. This novel by Luigi Natoli, on a secretive sect in sixteenth-century Sicily, was first published at the early twentieth century and republished in episodes during the 1970s, in the main Sicilian daily newspaper, *Giornale di Sicilia*. The mafiosi are entirely familiar with the work and refer to it as an origin myth of their organization, when they claim to have taken this sixteenth-century mythic sect as a model for their actions, with its mission to avenge victims, defend the weak, and punish injustice. In this narrative, the neophyte is led into an underground cave decorated like a sanctuary. The initiator makes a cross-shaped incision on the initiate's arm, dips a feather into it, and hands it to him, asking him to swear on the Gospel to keep the secret of the "venerable society":

> With a steady hand, Andrea draws a large cross at the bottom of the page shown to him and says: "I swear it; and may this cross written with my blood sign my condemnation should I ever shirk my obligations." (Natoli 1971: 123)

Henceforth, the signatory will be liable for his actions and will only have obligations to this society deemed worthy of veneration. The reference to a religious repertoire has persisted in the contemporary criminal rite. Below is a description of the ceremony marking entry into Cosa Nostra as made by the pentito Calderone in the early 1990s. When we compare his account with that of the "colaborators of justice" interrogated by the anti-mafia prosecutors,[13] we see that it still remains unchanged today:

> Uncle Peppino asks Calderone: "What hand do you use to shoot with?" and he pricked the index finger of the indicated hand with a pin so as to drip a few drops of his blood onto a small sacred image: the picture was of the Virgin of the Annunciation, the patron saint of Cosa Nostra....Uncle Peppino set fire to the image and Calderone had to hold it in his cupped hands, withstanding the searing pain until it had burned down to ashes. At the same time, he took his oath.

---

13. I was able to consult the transcriptions of the recordings made of the interrogations of several collaborators of justice by the anti-mafia prosecutors, particularly the ones of the collaborators that I succeeded to interview.

He swore to be ever faithful to the "commandments" of Cosa Nostra. If he betrayed them, he would burn like this sacred image. (Arlacchi 1992: 59)

The contamination of the Virgin with the initiate's blood establishes a transcendent order hierarchically superior to the existing political order. This absolute superiority is anchored in the pre-eminence accorded to "spiritual kinship" in Sicily (D'Onofrio 2004: 61–62), here created through the mediation of the Virgin Mary (a mother without any blood tie to her son) and in the presence of a "godfather."[14] The historian Luisa Accati (1998) identifies, in the privileged relation that men maintain with their mother in Catholic Italy, reflected in the iconography of the Virgin Mary, a "refusal of responsibilities," a niche that excludes the father, the founding figure of patriarchal authority. The result of this symbolic operation at the civic level is a side-lining of justice and ethics, replaced by aesthetics. If the figure of Joseph disappears from the iconography of the Virgin Mary—as in the scene of the Annunciation where the son "enters" directly into the lily, evoking the immaculate womb of the mother, without passing through the father, not even through God the Father (Accati 1998)—the Lord can literally become the target of the violence of the mafia "brothers," as in an early version of the mafia ritual:

The neophyte was led to a large room where a figure of Christ was hung. He was given a pistol and, without trembling, had to shoot him with a bullet to show that, just as he had shot the Lord, so he would have no trouble killing his brother or father, if the society wanted him to. After that the candidate became a *fratuzzo* [small brother]. (Gambetta 1993: 263).[15]

Deicide and the killing of the father bring about the order of the "brothers,"[16] while abolishing responsibility, obliterated at the same time as the limit is erased between symbolic death and the passage to the act

---

14. Here and in numerous other cases, the sponsor is the paternal uncle. For his role in securing family honor, see Jamous (1981: 149).

15. At the end of his work Diego Gambetta (1993) provides an anthology of descriptions of the initiation ceremony, the earliest dating back to 1884. The variant reported here dates from the final quarter of the nineteenth century.

16. On the importance of ritual and criminal bonds of "fraternity" in the mafia world, see Paoli (2000).

(Karsenti 2012: 153). This ritual also reaffirms the equivalence between "sign" and "shoot," which the other two versions of the initiatory scene, literary and real, had already suggested. Each murder reiterates the pricking of the finger that pulls the trigger in the initiatory scene, ratifying the initial commitment. This gesture is so important that it provides the name for the entire ritual, *punciuta* (to sting, prick, puncture). However, no specialist of the mafia phenomenon has ever analyzed it referring to "popular culture" and "superstitions," even though it refers precisely to criminal practices. Nonetheless, it is in this flow of blood enabling the "communing" of all those who "shoot"—namely, all Cosa Nostra's murderers—that we must distinguish the matrix of what the anti-mafia judges call a mafia theory of "collective responsibility" in murder (Scarpinato 1996: 78–79).

Initiation establishes *a community of murderers* by creating a blood tie between the shooters, united with and in the Virgin, signatories of the same pact, becoming "the same thing": Cosa Nostra. Each new spillage of blood revives this *communion* already prefigured by the Virgin of the Annunciation, the figure announcing Christ's sacrifice. The mafia attach great importance to "spilling the victim's blood together" (Dino 2008: 72): decided at a meeting of the Commission, the murders are carried out by a "group of fire" that acts in the name of Cosa Nostra and "signs" all the homicides by using a recognizable modus operandi or a specific weapon. This "signature," a language in its own right, is used both by men of honor—when they claim the glory of the homicide—and by the police and investigating judges—when they try to reconstruct the crime. The roles (shooting, taking the victim to the agreed murder site, keeping a lookout, driving the getaway vehicle) are allocated case by case. But who does what matters little since what counts is *fare un'azione di fuoco* (participating in a shooting).

We have seen that what is shared and consecrated by the initiation rite is also silence. From the moment of joining Cosa Nostra, the man of honor "opens his eyes"[17] to the ins and outs of criminal acts he will never be able to recount. If he is the initiate, this is because his silent apprenticeship has already begun, sometimes in the discretion he has to show when performing a first malicious act, often a murder he is asked to carry out even before being formally initiated. When successfully completed, this act is called a "baptism of fire" (Arlacchi 1994: 86). For the candidate to the Sicilian mafia it corresponds to his "true initiation," requiring he

---

17. Francesco Paolo Anzelmo, interview with author, Rome, December 2010. The expression is his.

accomplish the task without asking why (Falcone and Padovani 1997: 30). This is the basis of *assoggettamento* (subjugation) to the mafia: the man of honor applies his own law; he keeps quiet and does not say what he does or why he does it. The mafia's operational mode dissociates the orderer from the executor of the crime. We may see this dissociation as the outcome of a mechanism of "deresponsibilization" (Dino 2002: 78). In this silence, the perpetrator loses the sense of actions performed "for others" and, in this loss of intentionality, he also dissolves his own responsibility. The "combination" (*combinazione*)—another name for the initiation rite, depicting it as a kind of chemical process through which the individual becomes a member of Cosa Nostra by transforming his individual responsibility into collective honor—is the first operator of this *change of state*, taken as definitive.

Anthropologists have taught us to reinscribe the concepts and cognitive operations at the root of social practices in the materiality of the body (Héritier and Xantakhou 2004). This is what I attempt to do with responsibility and honor. In Sicily, the latter is presented as a normative system structured by rules—rules that have recently been written, following the evolution of the mafia and its modes of governance. Substituting an interdiction to write for an injunction to write, this "people" without state structures or their own territory chose to borrow the theocratic model of Jewish law (Karsenti 2012: 148) and, through the hand of its "legislator" bosses, write their "decalogue." Although the doxa on the mafia is that it has only "oral" rules, this list of ten commandments was found in a stash belonging to the man of honor Salvatore Lo Piccolo, in 2007, at the time of his arrest. With the decalogue this aspiring boss tried to replace Provenzano in his role as legislative boss and scribe of Cosa Nostra, as we will see in the last chapter. But for now, let us take a closer look at these rules.

At least three of the ten mafia commandments remind the initiate that affiliation to the mafia is not only a priority but incompatible with other forms of association: "3. Friendship pacts with police officers are not allowed; 4. Bars and gambling dens should not be frequented;…10. No affiliation for those who have a relative enrolled in the police forces." This principle is reinforced by the fifth commandment: "5. You must be available to Cosa Nostra at all times: even if your own wife is about to give birth." The blood that the murderer spills deliberately when he gives death is hierarchically superior to the blood his wife "sees" being spilled when she gives life (Héritier 1984: 20). But this blood, mafia blood in this case, is not individual, devoted solely to sustaining the glory of the hero

(Loraux 2010); it is collective. And this is a big difference, because it is the entire economy of honor and its relation to responsibility that becomes modified.

It should be immediately noted that the first flow of blood, the blood with which the initiate formalizes his contract of membership to Cosa Nostra, is accompanied by the promise to keep silent. During his initiation, the mafia member simultaneously "signs" his pledge to kill and his own death sentence: he knows that should he speak, he in turn will be killed; the blood will flow from his body if words flow from his mouth. But, according to the other mafia decalogue, this will also happen if he spills his sperm unnecessarily ("7. You must respect your wife") or even if a single glance escapes toward a woman not his own ("2. You must not look at the wives of friends [the men of honor]"). Salvatore D'Onofrio (2014) has shown the symbolic manipulation of bodily humors (particularly sperm) in the representations of honor in southern Italy and Sicily but without reference to the criminal practices of the mafia. Michel Masson (1999: 146) draws a parallel between "dispersing" sperm and "speaking thoughtlessly," two expressions that are both expressed by the Italian verb *sparare* (to shoot off). All these elements support the assumption that honor is neither a value nor a status, but a *shared substance*, a component of the (collective) person related to blood, sperm, speech, even money ("9. You cannot appropriate money that belongs to others or to other families").[18] All these matters are Cosa Nostra, *Our Thing*, and must remain within the group.

The man of honor is haunted by the fear of a loss (of blood, money, sperm, speech) that will result in a loss of honor, fracturing the entire Cosa Nostra system, quintessentially a closed system. He is called *omu di panza* (belly man) because he must be "capable of keeping secrets in his belly [*panza*, in Sicilian]" (Pantaleone 1970: 52). To do so, he must know how to close his mouth, close his eyes, block his nose: thus, how to make his body hermetically sealed.[19] Any infringement leaves an indelible

---

18. Again, the term "family" indicates the smallest mafia unit, not the biological family.

19. The ideal of an impermeable body is reflected in the Sicilian saying "*Cu è surdu, orbu e taci, campa cent'anni 'mpaci*" (He who is deaf, blind and silent will live a hundred years in peace) (Champeyrache 2007: 48). The sealing off of the mafia body is also manifested in the refusal of the man of honor to be fed by the state, which includes his refusal to be served food in prison (Stajano 2010: 79).

mark on the "face." In many societies beyond the Mediterranean, honor is concentrated on the "face" that can be "lost."[20] For members of this secret society, the name, an important site of honor and shame in the Mediterranean (Pitt-Rivers 2001), is less serious to attack than the face. This is why the name can be manipulated during trials, where some mafia members have claimed their innocence by invoking a miscarriage of justice based on a homonymy (as in the case of Michele Greco during the Maxi Trial). The face is the surface on which honor is rendered visible and can be measured: affronts and insults are the scratches and *sfregi* (scars) on it (Catanzaro 1992: 45).

Jeanne Favret-Saada (1980) defined the concept of "domain" apropos of sorcery attacks that may affect a family head, but equally his property, his wife, his children, or his animals. This notion is also relevant to redefining the mafia "territory." When someone ventures onto the "territory" of the man of honor—a notion that encompasses his body, but also the women from his lineage, his money, his house, his lands, his livestock[21]—invades him, penetrates him, attacks him by attacking one of the goods that constitutes his field of action and influence, by theft, rape, or an emasculating (and thus dishonoring) injury,[22] the victim strives to remedy the loss suffered by inflicting an equivalent loss on his adversary: thus the blood of the aggressor, or of the group to which he belongs, must be spilled not only to avenge a death but also to compensate for the dispersion of sperm (adultery, seduction of a virgin), an undue appropriation of money, or the revelation of a secret. The killing is finalized by a treatment of the corpse that involves plugging its orifices: a stone or plug is placed in the mouth of the "snitch" (Pantaleone 1970); the genitals of the seducer are cut off (the part culpable for the loss of sperm) and stuffed in his mouth; the mouth of the person greedy for money, and thus causing a hole in Cosa Nostra's "common fund," is filled with banknotes (Falcone and Padovani 1997: 27–28). If the body is the place where the code of honor is inscribed, it is in the mouth (or in the

---

20. On this point, see the games of social interaction described by Erving Goffman (1974).
21. These are the domains of the *haram* (what is banned) in the Moroccan Rif, where Raymond Jamous (1981: 77) studied the "systems of honor."
22. Nicole Loraux (2010) emphasized the feminizing character of the injury to the body of the Greek warrior, at the same time as the injured body was valorized and virilized. However, the mafia member is not a warrior but a murderer, and his body is only valuable if it remains intact.

throat, in the case of strangulation) that the punishment is located, as if all errors committed can be traced to an improper usage of this organ through which honor can seep away.

When the mafia punishes murder, infidelity, and robbery with the same severity, it is partially because, as Judge Falcone argued, "so long as inside the mafia state there exist no courts or forces of law and order, it is essential that each 'citizen' knows that punishment is inevitable and that the sentence will be executed immediately. Those who violate the rules know they will pay with their life" (Falcone and Padovani 1997: 37). But, significantly, it is also because these acts have the same gravity, are equivalent to each other insofar as they infringe honor as a *shared substance*, inscribed in a space whose limits are continually redefined (P. Schneider 1969) during and over the course of mafia interactions. If, in Mediterranean societies, "the emphasis is on the chastity and virginity of women" (J. Schneider 1971: 3), this is not because of a sense of "moralism," as is so often asserted by those who sustain the thesis of "amoral familism" (Dino 2008: 214–215; Banfield 1958), but rather because "the great danger to a man's honor comes from his women" (Pitt-Rivers 1991: 28). The female body, open by nature, is in effect a zone of vulnerability where honor can easily escape. Honor, therefore, in Sicily at least, is not defined differently for men and women, as Mediterranean anthropology has suggested (Gilmore 1987), but constituted as though it were one and the same substance that each person must defend, protect, and safeguard. Adultery committed by a man of honor with the wife of another man of honor is punished with death, because this action is likened to incest "of the second type," by which Françoise Héritier (1979: 219) denotes sexual intercourse between two consanguineal persons of the same sex who share the same sexual partner. This explains the punishment of death for the rape of a virgin belonging to a mafioso's family. This is the "strange interpretation of the concept of honor" which had awoken Judge Falcone's curiosity: blood, that of women as well as that of murderers, must remain within the group, because it is more than any other substance or component of honor "Our Thing," Cosa Nostra.

After this detour through the economy of the bodily humors linked to honor, looking to show their impact on the criminal practices of these men of honor, we can now determine the conditions for the transition of a number of them to another conceptual system—that of responsibility—grounded in other representations of the individual and social body. In effect, if the man of honor is so afraid of "losing" his honor, this is also because the limits between himself and the other men are porous, the frontiers labile. One can imagine that this is not true for "modern" indi-viduals: autonomous beings whose limits are constituted, well-defined, and consistent, the latter can exchange without fear with other people and with the state, accepting the loss necessary or inherent to all ex-change—so long as this does not involve a loss of their substance—and assuming responsibility for their actions, as emanations of their indi-vidual will. It is this conception that anchors a model of the responsible actor—or *author*—which mafiosi were obliged if not to conform to then, at least, to confront.

Analyzing this confrontation by making use of the conceptual cat-egory of "instrumentalization," as many social science researchers have done, showing that the pentiti have "utilized" state structures to "take revenge" and that the judges have in turn "utilized" them to construct an effective judicial model in the anti-mafia struggle, does not seem convincing enough for me. This notion—closer to common sense than the interpretative tools produced by researchers in social sciences—once again inserts the specialists of the mafia phenomenon in the debate on the mafia taking place in society, but more as actors than as producers of instruments of understanding.[23] Instead, I try to show what has ena-bled the changes and transmutations between two apparently incompat-ible normative systems, how this encounter, a true *test* in which the two sides compete, could have occurred, and what misunderstandings it has provoked.

Silence broken, truth recomposed

"I am not a pentito." This astonishing statement opens the "confessions" (Arlacchi 1994: 3) of Buscetta, still considered the most important of the pentiti to assist the Italian state. From the mid-1980s, a growing number of Cosa Nostra affiliates decided to collaborate with the jus-tice system. As we saw above, several transformations within the Italian judicial institution since the 1960s gradually made it possible to deal with the mafia as a criminal issue (Vauchez 2004; Briquet 2007). Never-theless, we cannot disregard the profound changes that occurred within Cosa Nostra, because they hold the key to understanding both the mafia *pentitismo* and the mutations of mafia honor.

---

23. I critique the catch-all concept of "instrumentalization" in the conclusion of Puccio-Den (2009: 275-279).

The pentiti were mostly members of the losing families in a war—the Second Mafia War, in the early 1980s—that represented the defeat of the Commission, the place where conflicts were traditionally solved without resorting to violence. It was a war that decimated the Sicilian mafia, killing almost a thousand people in the space of a few years, corresponding to 20% of mafia members, following an extermination plan conceived by Riina and the Corleonese clan to take control of Cosa Nostra. *Pentitismo*, interpreted as betrayal by mafia members and by a large part of Italian society, was justified by the justice collaborators as a gesture aimed at preserving the mafia's ancient order. My starting point, adopting a principle from pragmatic sociology (Boltanski and Thévenot 1991), is to "take seriously" these arguments, submitting them to the same critique, no more and no less, as any other indigenous discourse. This runs counter to an entire scholarly literature in the social sciences that encourages us to consider the declarations of the pentiti as "justificatory myths" and, on these grounds, to reject them as fallacious. The question of mafia justice as a "fiction" deserves more sophisticated analysis of the modalities of "saying," "silencing" and "believing" needed to *fit* the untenable ontological (im)posture of the mafia—as we will see in chapters 9 and 10. We must be aware that the justice collaborators had no reason to justify their criminal acts; it was (and is) enough for them to provide reliable information to obtain state protection for themselves and their families (D'Ambrosio 2002: 112). That is another reason why it does not make sense to reduce the dialogue between Falcone and Buscetta to a mutual "instrumentalization."

A very special communication was established between the pentito and the judge, "coded," as Falcone defined it—"I had the impression that our exchanges where always coded" (Falcone and Padovani 1997: 51)—or rather *encoded* by honor. Thus the chief merit of the judge was not, as he believed, to have known how to "break the wall of the *omertà*," but to have been able to *naturally* occupy the place of someone to whom the man of honor must tell the truth, as required by one of Cosa Nostra's commandments ("8. When someone [a hierarchical superior] asks you about a matter, you must tell the truth"). The man of law was able to take on the role of mafia boss by playing on the isomorphism between the mafia and the judiciary, two authorities dedicated to "doing justice." But he did much more than this: he allowed himself to be deeply impregnated by the morality of the other: "The categorical imperative of 'speaking the truth' has become one of the key principles of my personal ethics," the judge confessed (Falcone and Padovani 1997: 70).

According to Buscetta's reconstruction, confirmed by many other pentiti, this principle had been undermined when the Corleonesi took over the Commission, opening a season of lies, fraud, and betrayal (Arlacchi 1994: 12), giving rise to a world marked by uncertainty, fragility, ambivalence, and "tragedies," deliberately designed, making and unmaking the fates of men of honor. *Tragedia* in mafia language is a defamatory and false rumor that can be exploited as a pretext to eliminate an internal rival. Being a *tragediatore* (someone who arranges tragedies) is the worst thing a man of honor can "do." Thus, Brusca, Falcone's killer, after admitting to having killed hundreds of people, including his fifteen year-old godson, declared in his confessions: "I could do anything, except for the *tragediatore*" (quoted in Dino 2002: 184). We can listen to the pentito Calderone:

> If you don't know who killed whom, or if you have false information, then nobody is certain of anything anymore, not even their own life. And that is precisely the game played by the Corleonesi, evil and dishonest people: they lied about the homicides they were committing! (Arlacchi 1992: 24)

Calderone called them the "men of dishonor"; Buscetta, the "ruin of Cosa Nostra." After the Corleonesi took control of the organization, silence was no longer able to protect the truth, the supreme asset of honor: do Sicilians not say "word of honor" to mean a "true word"? It henceforth was up to the judges to restore this "thing" that circulated among mafia members like the blood in their veins, another precious substance they shared and that had been altered by the Corleonesi, restoring the truth by recomposing its fragments from the stories revealing the underside to all the murders committed during the mafia wars.

But this is not the only mission the pentiti entrusted to the judge. These ousted bosses also delegated their revenge to him, at the same time as they implicitly asked him to salvage their own honor,[24] after an internecine war that had deposed them from power:

> To defend myself, I could have killed one after the other...all the Corleonesi I blamed for the massacre of my relatives and other innocents. Instead, I chose to collaborate with the authorities....I have

---

24. The anthropology of honor teaches that "to leave an affront unavenged is to leave one's honor in a state of desecration" (Pitt-Rivers 1965: 26).

seen punished by written law people who I could have killed with my own hands. (Arlacchi 1994: 13)

This declaration became a position statement in a polemic that erupted between Sciascia and those he called the "anti-mafia professionals." This is what the Sicilian writer asserted in an article published in the *Corriere della Sera*, the main Italian daily newspaper at the time, on April 18, 1986, at the height of the Maxi Trial:

"Buscetta's mentality is perfectly mafia-like and his alliance with the law did not bother him: on the side of the law, he continues to do what he would have done within a 'family' still capable of doing something: he returns the blows received, he avenges himself." (Sciascia 2002: 109)[25]

But Falcone rises to the challenge:

The fact that, for the first time, the bosses of crime organizations, which have always considered it dishonorable to resort to the authority of the state, had decided to entrust to the state, implicitly recognizing its authority, the satisfaction of their thirst for revenge, far from causing a scandal, should be considered a positive phenomenon, a clear expression of the decline of the traditional *omertà*. (Falcone 1994: 49)

In *Manquer de parole: Omertà et denonciation en Sicile* (Breaking his word: *omertà* and denunciation in Sicily), anthropologist Maria Pia Di Bella (2008: 215) identifies the first "failure" of the system in the transgressions perpetrated by the Corleonesi:

The lack of respect for the "given word," inaugurated by the Corleonese "family," at least according to Tommaso Buscetta, provokes in turn vengeance in the form of denunciation. By importing "new" methods into the traditional association, the Corleonese gang gradually caused its members to lose the sense of bravery that translated *omertà*, the pillar of the Sicilian "personality."

---

25. First published in 1989, Sciascia's book *A futura memoria (se la memoria ha un futuro)* pulls together articles that previously appeared in the main national newspapers and played a crucial role in the debate about the limits of using force in a state governed by the rule of law.

My hypothesis is different: the pentiti did not rush into the breach opened up by the false denunciations of the Corleonesi in order to destroy Cosa Nostra but tried to recompose this world torn asunder by their lies by resorting to one of its normative bases: "You must speak the truth to your hierarchical superiors."

Falcone entered into this game. In the indictment to the Maxi Trial, which took place in Palermo from February 1986 to December 1987 and combined all crimes committed by Cosa Nostra in one and the same trial procedure, the investigating judge introduced pentito Salvatore Contorno as follows:[26]

> May I be allowed to state, with a serene conscience, that the accused [Contorno] has paradoxically shown his qualities as a man of honor precisely by his decision to collaborate. (quoted in Stajano 2010: 82)

Responsibility salvages honor and, vice versa, honor is placed in the service of responsibility. In effect, the judge granted the "word of honor" a probative value: "Within the organization, a single word is enough for one to be certain of a fact" (Stajano 2010: 86). And he assumed Cosa Nostra's internal rules, sacralized by the commandments, as the foundation of judicial truth:

> It has already been said, and we shall not tire of repeating it, that the demand for the information circulating among men of honor to be true is a fact essential to the very security of the organization, and that lies are punished by severe sanctions. Consequently, *if a man of honor learns, from another man of honor whom he knows, that a third party is a man of honor, this is the truth.* (quoted in Stajano 2010: 86–87, emphasis in original)

Here we can recognize a transposition from the first commandment that governs the rituals of presentation between men of honor. Falcone made use of mafia norms disciplining the use of speech and the exercise

---

26. The instruction (pre-trial investigative documentation) to the Maxi Trial is a 8,607-page document (*Ordinanza Sentenza contro Abbate Giovanni + 706,* Office for the Investigation of Penal Trials, High Court of Palermo, 1985). Excerpts from this writ, unique for its size in the country's legal history, written by the judges Giovanni Falcone and Paolo Borsellino, were republished by Corrado Stajano (2010).

of silence—norms that he manipulated to perfection—as a heuristic principle to shed light on the crimes committed in Sicily during the mafia wars:

> Knowledge of the patterns of behavior, and even the language employed by the members of Cosa Nostra, thus offers an important key to reading the mafia facts that, when utilized cautiously, can lead to remarkable advances in the investigations. (quoted in Stajano 2010: 87)

Falcone also reached the conclusion "that the leaders of this power group that gravitates around the Corleonesi, and that emerged victorious from the so-called mafia war, must be held responsible" (quoted in Stajano 2010: 400). The establishment of judicial responsibility is dependent, therefore, on the descriptions of the "inside" of the hierarchy and the decision-making structure of Cosa Nostra furnished by the pentiti. In a game of role swapping, the judge thus became the initiate and Buscetta his initiator, the one who, at the end of a period of "observation," had "opened his eyes" to the crimes and secrets of Cosa Nostra.

The conditions that allowed this "word of honor" to be transmitted according to the modalities of "collaboration with the justice system" were defined by the law, a law, in turn, that had to be reformulated to meet the requirements of penalizing a collective and secretive form of crime. The judges became the new depositories of mafia secrets (and honor), the ones now with the power to demand the truth from "men of honor." But for this to be possible and lawful, a legal framework had to be created: legislation regulating the rights and obligations of the pentiti—precisely what Judge Falcone was working on before his murder.[27] The contract with the state is a pact of speech that replaces the pact of silence sealed with Cosa Nostra. Signing it meant promising to speak—rather than keeping silent—and providing useful information, enough for the judges to be able to establish responsibility for mafia crimes. However, this information can only be provided within a legal framework, the *chiamata in correità* (acknowledgement of complicity): to denounce the crimes committed by others, the pentito first had to accuse himself (Falcone 1994: 48). This is what distinguishes the pentito from the informer, and

---

27. Falcone's proposals, implemented only after his murder, form the core of the current legislation on justice collaborators. They were collected and republished posthumously (Falcone 1994: 33–65).

simultaneously eliminates any "instrumental" reading of his "confession" (Puccio-Den 2019a). Contrary to the common opinion that the pentiti had everything to gain from their revelations to the courts—as shown by the responses to a questionnaire compiled by sociologist Alessandra Dino (2006), an opinion shared by some anthropologists (see Di Bella 2008: 214–220; Rakopoulos 2018)—and although the sentences of the justice collaborators were indeed reduced by one third, this happened at the cost of a self-accusation that led the pentiti to confess to facts, namely murders, that were sometimes entirely unknown to the judges and the police and for which they would otherwise never have been accused (Falcone 1994: 39–42).

This configuration—for which Falcone prescribed that the speech of the pentiti could have "a value in itself as a means of proof and independently found a judgement of responsibility" (Falcone 1994: 42)—led to the construction of "probative mosaics" where the offences of some merged with the offences of others. This probative framework formed the basis of the Maxi Trial pre-trial documentation: "When the facts are linked by indissoluble probative relations, any separation of procedures could only be arbitrary, and would certainly be detrimental to establishing the truth" (Falcone 1994: 50). It was through this minute and monumental work of verification that the "word of honor" became a powerful evidential tool, capable of supporting the proof of culpability of several hundred defendants, thus recuperating some of the strength it had lost. Honor was claimed by both the accusers and the accused, pentiti and these men of honor now called upon to answer publicly for their deeds.

Honor in the courtoom

"This is the case brought against the mafia association Cosa Nostra, a very dangerous crime organization, which, through violence and intimidation, has sown and still sows death and terror" (Stajano 2010: 27). This extraordinary statement opens the first hearing of the Maxi Trial that debuted on February 10, 1986. The trial immediately provoked criticisms, judged "monstrous" even within legal circles, at the same time as the investigating judge described any other form of proceedings not directed specifically at the entire organization as "legal barbarism…[and] the return to outdated forms of judgement" (Falcone 1994: 39) because it was inadequate in dealing with the collective and imbricated modalities of mafia criminal action. Indeed, unlike previous legal actions that had been brought against the mafiosi as agents of isolated criminal acts, this case involved prosecution of Cosa Nostra as a whole, pursuant to Article 416 *bis* of the Italian Penal Code that, from 1982 onwards, stipulates that belonging to a mafia-type organization is an "offence in itself." It is thus by collective accusation of participating in a mafia-type association that the 475 members of the organization were charged under this article, which penalizes "the mafia connection per se" (Turone 2008: 25). To circumvent the difficulty of constituting proof of this associative connection shrouded in secrecy, the jurist La Torre defined three "typical forms of behavior" identifying the mafia: intimidation, *omertà*, and subjugation (Turone 2008: 1–2). Thenceforth, "the proof, for the purposes of establishing responsibility, must relate not to the qualifications of the subjects (so-and-so is a 'man of honor') but to the behaviors that indicate the associative connection," insofar as they "presuppose prior conduct, characterized by an agreement of will intended to establish an associative connection for common unlawful purposes."[28]

It should be noted, first, that *omertà*, the pillar of honor, was now considered a *criminal* behavior, able to be charged as an offence and judged before a court. But I wish to focus on the third mafia method, subjugation, and its two forms, passive and active: the mafia member is an individual *subjugated* to an organization incompatible with the civic norms proper to modern democratic states (Falcone 1994: 83–86), who, in turn, *subjugates* his entourage by using his power of intimidation, namely his ability to frighten his peers by leaving death threats hovering over them, "implicit, allusive, immanent," based on a "common heritage"[29] (the memory of past violence), one that is able to operate "even in the absence of explicit words or gestures of intimidation" (Turone 2008: 20). In passing, we should note the extreme difficulty faced by the judges charged with demonstrating affiliation to the mafia association of providing proof of words that had not been spoken—*omertà*—or acts that had not been carried out—intimidation. What interests us here above all is this "condition of subjugation"—*assoggettamento*—that proceeds from the establishment of the mafia connection, a connection that implies renouncing one's own critical capacities (the mafia member must "obey" without questioning) and an atrophying of language, at least as a means

---

28. Palermo Court, Assizes Court, *Sentenza contro Abbate Giovanni + 459*, 1987, pp. 1111–1114 (quoted in Chinnici 1992: 104–105).

29. Palermo Court, Assizes Court, *Sentenza contro Abbate Giovanni + 459*, 1987, p. 1126 (quoted in Chinnici 1992: 107).

of expressing individual needs, fears, or desires (which, as we have seen, does not impede its collective usage for the needs of Cosa Nostra). The mafia subject is thus *de-subjectified*, deprived of the possibility of expressing himself in the first person (and not in the name of an impersonal authority like Cosa Nostra or Divine Providence), reduced to using words as code—as we will see in Chapter 10. For the judges involved in the Maxi Trial, therefore, preliminary work was necessary before attributing responsibility to members of the Sicilian mafia: the defendants needed to become accustomed to assume the "I" as the privileged point of view on their own actions.

This was not an easy task. For the pentiti, as we have seen, this assumption necessarily followed from the legal framework within which they had been induced to testify: the *chiamata in correità*. For the non-penitent mafiosi, this was carried out—or at least attempted—in court, during the hearings of the Maxi Trial and the interactions that took place there between judges and "men of honor," or between the latter and their accusers. While every trial sets up a scenographic space where conflicts are replayed according to the rules of judicial dramaturgy (Garapon 2010), this gigantic trial, followed by hundreds of journalists and transmitted by television news reports, was transformed—sometimes beyond the intentions of those who had initiated it—into a theatre of honor. This was then subjected to an even more formidable judgement: that of public opinion.[30] The analysis of some scenes shows how the "men of honor" exploited the potential of this platform to "dishonor" their adversaries, playing on the vast palette of mafia "dishonor," stigmatizing both the unbridled speech of their detractors and their "excessive" sexuality. The stakes were high since only the "word of honor" had value—including, as we have seen, for judges. It was thus a question of training the pentiti on this slippery terrain.

The dialogue between Buscetta and mafioso Pippo Calò is paradigmatic of this dynamic. After listening to the depositions against him for an entire week, Calò decided to challenge his accuser and demanded a confrontation with the pentito. The court granted his request, reserving the right to raise pertinent questions so that the accused could answer to the crime of mafia association. The head judge thus asked Buscetta

---

30. We can recall the words of Pitt-Rivers (1965: 27): "Public opinion therefore forms a tribunal before which the claims to honor are brought, 'the court of reputation,' as it has been called, and against its judgement there is no redress."

to revisit the topic of Calò's initiation: "But he remembers it very well! He can tell us in his own voice how I initiated him and why I initiated him. He can say it himself,"[31] Buscetta declared. The pentito thus replays his role of godfather and summons his godson, Calò, to "tell the truth," bringing into play the hierarchical relationship that bound them together within Cosa Nostra. But the man of honor Calò tried to play on another board—he brought the dispute back to the side of justice and its procedures:

> I kindly request the court to say to Mr Buscetta that everything that he must say, and everything he must accuse me of, that he limits himself to say what he is able to prove, to summon witnesses about these circumstances; that he not do as he has done thus far, when he said: "He told me" or: "I knew."...As I will do here, during this confrontation, providing documentation of everything I have to say, I would like him to do the same. He should not speak through hearsay and he should not say: "You told me that." He has no right to say that. He must provide evidence.

In reality, the mafia boss tries to devalue the pentito's word, not only in relation to the legal norms likely to validate or invalidate the testimonies of the collaborators (thus adding fuel to the polemic burning at this time in the legal fraternity),[32] but also in relation to the internal procedures of Cosa Nostra, insinuating to the judges that Buscetta had no first-hand information and that he thus had been *posato* (dismissed, literally "left aside"), discarded from the community within which truth is spoken and shared like a common good, "cosa nostra." Did the investigating judges of the Maxi Trial not specify in their indictment that "the *posato* man of honor cannot maintain relations with the other members of Cosa Nostra, who are obliged not to speak to him anymore" (Stajano 2010: 80)?

This trap appears elsewhere in the testimony when Calò cited the words of Buscetta's brother:

---

31. "Confronto fra Tommaso Buscetta e Pippo Calò," YouTube video, uploaded by Marco Lilli, April 27, 2018, 13:05 min, https://youtu.be/JJM_XnaFUbw.
32. On this point, see the texts written by Falcone (1994: 33–65) in response to criticisms raised against his use of the words from pentiti as evidential ground in the anti-mafia trials.

Look at Masino [short for Tommaso] what he did to me: he left again, leaving one of his sons in prison, the other a drug addict...he forced me to invite him to my home with his new wife, the last one: imagine the hell at my home at that moment for affording him that hospitality....Because his brother's wife was the sister of his wife, his first wife. That is what Mr. Masino Buscetta is capable of!

The conclusion Calò tried to insinuate: Buscetta was not a man of honor, because a man of honor would not behave like that to his wife (recall the seventh mafia commandment, "You must respect your wife") and, since he had been unable to restrain himself sexually, his word was worthless.[33] Calò called Buscetta a *bugiardo* (liar), knowing that the court would understand the consequences implied by this accusation within Cosa Nostra. In the instruction that formed the basis of the Maxi Trial, we can read that:

Anyone who does not tell the truth is called *tragediaturi* and is subject to severe sanctions ranging from expulsion (in which case the man of honor is said to have been 'left aside') to being sentenced to death. (Stajano 2010: 76)

Calò hinted that Buscetta could not be aware of the deeds and decisions taken by the Commission because he had been ousted from Cosa Nostra (even though this, by implication, admitted the existence of the Commission, the mafia decision-making body). When Buscetta defended himself, saying how "enraged" (*arrabbiato*) he was, Calò simply retorted: "Enraged? Dogs become enraged!" imbuing the pentito's words with a degrading animality, those of a man who does not know how to control himself, who speaks as though barking, driven by fury.

Buscetta may not have been, or may no longer have been, a man of honor, but Calò thus showed that he himself was one. His argument, typically mafia-like, convinced the court of the crime of association imputed to him, the basis for all the criminal acts attributed to him—not

---

33. This argument may not appear very convincing to people outside the mafia. However, in a very similar trial involving a mafia group from the Camorra of Naples (1982–1983), the legal interactions between the prosecution and the defense revolved around the question of honor, questioning the sexual behavior of the pentito, whose word in the end was not believed (Jacquemet 1996: 217–284).

for having carried them out with his own hand but for having decided on them in the Commission.

Buscetta took the floor:

> In four hundred pages of questioning, I have never touched on the family question of anyone. And the behavior of a man of honor like himself, who talks about my family and personal adventures, is most bizarre. More to the point: the only true thing he has said in the courtroom is that my brother was bound to him by a very deep friendship. But he forgets right now that he sat on the commission that decided the death of my brother and nephew, trampling on him again, even here! He should have avoided speaking about my family.

Transcending the contradiction inherent to a mafia pentito who, if he speaks, loses his honor and discredits his own word, Buscetta showed here that he had passed to the other side, the side of responsibility, a responsibility as penal as it is moral and toward which he pushed his adversary. But the Cosa Nostra members were not charged as individuals. They were charged as members of a "mafia-type association," based on a principle of "collective responsibility" postulating that all the alleged crimes had been perpetrated "within a strategic functional project in the association's global interests" (Chinnici 1992: 53). This premise was, in reality, the outcome of a long investigative process that led the anti-mafia judges to "comprehend the singular criminal episodes in their overall logic and within the dynamics of the crime organization of which they are the expressions" (Chinnici 1992: 98).

This work had been inaugurated by Judge Terranova who, from the mid-1960s, had an inkling of the existence of the criminal coordination group called the Commission.[34] The first Commission—created in 1957 and modeled on the commission established to settle disputes and facilitate relations between American mafia families—was dissolved in 1963 following an exacerbation of conflict that resulted in the First Mafia War, a turf war between mafia families on which the

---

34. The sentences given at the trials against Angelo La Barbera (1964) and Pietro Torretta (1965), which would cost Judge Terranova his life in 1979, are quoted in the *Documentazione allegata alla relazione conclusiva della Commissione parlamentare d'inchiesta sul fenomeno della mafia in Sicilia*, vol. 4 (tome 17: 627, for the "commission").

Corleonese clan had an incendiary effect. At the turn of the 1980s, through his infiltrators, the Corleonese Riina controlled all Palermo families from within. But for this hidden power to come out in the open, he had to become head of the "second Commission," reborn in the mid-1970s. Two men blocked his path who, together with the Corleonese Luciano Leggio, formed part of the triumvirate that headed Cosa Nostra: Gaetano Badalamenti and Stefano Bontade. Both were historical figures from the Sicilian mafia, respected not only by the members of Cosa Nostra but also by the local population and even by politicians who, in turn, found it difficult to interact with the Corleonese "louts," also nicknamed *viddani* (peasants). To deal with his adversaries, Riina launched two operations: one of "treason," which led to Bontade's murder on April 23, 1981; the other of "tragedy," which resulted in Badalamenti's "expulsion." These events are considered as the trigger for the Second Mafia War. In the mid-1980s, a time marked by the mafia's drift into terrorism and a crisis in its internal judicial system (with the Commission having being transformed into a mere instrument of power in the hands of Riina), a number of men of honor on the losing side wished to protect themselves and their family from the indiscriminate violence of the Corleonesi and decided to switch to the side of state justice.

Thanks to the depositions of the justice collaborators, the anti-mafia judges were able to corroborate Terranova's hypothesis and rethink the economy of responsibility of mafia crimes. Nothing was new in the Buscetta theorem; what was new was the condition—the conflict internal to the mafia—under which this description of the mafia emerged and became the foundation for a renewed breakdown of sentences. Two principles were accepted as the basis to prove the responsibility of the Cosa Nostra bosses: 1) no homicide can be perpetrated in a family's territory without go-ahead by its boss; and 2) for larger scale homicides, the consensus of all members of the Commission is necessary.[35] The consequence of these axioms, the foundation of the Buscetta theorem, is the following: "the members of the governing body of Cosa Nostra, the infamous commission, must be called to answer for all these homicides" (U. Santino 1992: 127).

These members were identified as the Corleonesi and their allies, victors of the Second Mafia War, who were thereafter held responsible

---

35. Palermo Court, Investigation Office, *Processo verbale di interrogatorio di T. Buscetta*, 1984, p. 14.

for all subsequent murders: those that they perpetrated within Cosa Nostra to eliminate their enemies, and those that they perpetrated against the numerous agents of the state engaged in the anti-mafia struggle. Yet their "responsibility" was not easy to demonstrate:

> The Court, in its obsessive search for a higher degree of legal certainty of the effective responsibilities of all the accused taken individually, in accordance with the principle of personal responsibility, as stipulated by Article 27, Paragraph 1 of the Constitution, determined that the elements presented were insufficient to close the probative circle, even if it was constituted by a series of sequences valid in themselves, requiring, for the purposes of establishing the responsibility of the defendants taken individually, the subsistence of a material, instrumental or even logical connection, in terms of a causal or co-causal relationship, between the function of the boss and each homicide committed.[36]

As a result, a series of sentences issued at the first stage of the Maxi Trial were revoked on appeal (La Fiura 1992: 190). But on January 30, 1992, the Court of Cassation reconfirmed the original sentences against all members of the Commission, validating the Buscetta theorem. A principle of "collective responsibility"[37] was thereby introduced into the jurisprudence of the mafia trials, which was not only the result of a long and laborious elaboration of doctrine within the legal world but also, as we have observed, the reflection of a concept of crime as a collective act within the mafia universe.

A major advance was achieved at an ontological level: henceforth it was known not only that the mafia *existed* but also how it was governed. Recall the unheard-of sentence opening the Maxi Trial: "This is the case brought against the mafia association Cosa Nostra." Finally the mafia

36. Palermo Court, Assizes Court, *Sentenza contro Abbate Giovanni + 459*, 1987, p. 1462 (quoted in U. Santino 1992: 129).
37. The judges involved in the mafia trials pursued this view of murder as a collective action by exploiting a principle contained in the Italian Penal Code, the theory of the *equivalence of causes* (Article 110), which formalizes the co-responsibility of all those who take part in the same crime by any means, whether moral, executive, or simple collaboration—a principle equally applied to homicide (Article 575). My thanks to the prosecutor of the Antimafia Directorate of the District of Palermo, Gaetano Paci, for clarifying this point.

had been given a *name*; a *body* too, a collective body, one that could be counted by the hundreds of members who sat behind bars in the bunker court room built for the trial. To understand the scope of this event, let us go back a few years, to the end of the 1970s, when the mafia had no legal existence, in order to measure the consequences of this absence or silence of the law on all the statements concerning mafiosi and their (mis)deeds.

CHAPTER 8

The Impastato affair

Mafia: state of violence or state violence?

"Criminal event presumably aimed at provoking a railroad disaster," one learns from the police report (Puglisi and Santino 2005: 21) written, with astonishing efficiency and promptness, after the corpse of a left-wing militant was discovered on May 9, 1978, along the railroad track of the small Sicilian town of Cinisi. Immediately, a rumor began to circulate: "Giuseppe Impastato was killed by the mafia," or, even, "Giuseppe Impastato was killed by mafioso Gaetano Badalamenti." On May 17, 1978, family and friends of Giuseppe "Peppino" Impastato, the activist, asked the public prosecutor's office in Palermo to reopen the file on Impastato's death that the policemen of Cinisi had already closed and sent to the archives. They firmly dismissed the police's suicide finding and argued instead that Impastato had been murdered and that "the mafia" was responsible for it. In the complaint, the family emphasized the anti-mafia campaign that the young politician had led "against the Badalamenti family and against many other alleged mafiosi" (Puglisi and Santino 2005: 40). This is how a detailed investigation into the death of Impastato was opened, one that took twenty-four years to complete, during which his friends and family fought to rehabilitate his memory and him to be officially recognized as a "victim of the mafia."

The Impastato affair, the history of the reversal of charges brought in the murder case of the left-wing activist, is closely tied to the legal and political history of Italy between 1978 and 2002. The murdered activist was against the so-called *compromesso storico* (historic compromise) between the Italian Communist Party and Christian Democracy, initiated by Aldo Moro, president of Christian Democracy in the early 1960s and mid-1970s, and celebrated by certain factions of the Italian left. In 1978, the tensions of the *anni di piombo*—the years of lead that began in the 1960s and were marked by violent left-wing and right-wing terrorist attacks throughout the country—reached their apex when Moro was kidnapped by the Red Brigades, a far left-wing armed guerilla group. May 9, the date on which Impastato's corpse was found in Cinisi, was also the day on which a member of the Red Brigades informed Moro's family by telephone that the body of the kidnapped politician had been left in a car parked in the center of Rome. This national event seemed to corroborate the version of the Cinisi police on Impastato's death: an alleged suicide bomb terrorist attack in Sicily, echoing the Red Brigades's assassination of Moro in Rome.

In the twenty-four years between the beginning and the end of the Impastato affair, a growing number of social actors, be they individuals or committees, clubs, parties, and movements, joined the anti-mafia cause. Certain events of national significance—from Moro's kidnapping and assassination to the Andreotti trial, from *Mani pulite* to the multiple trials that have cast doubt on the Italian ruling class—produced three concurrent effects: a new perception of the mafia phenomenon as a social and public problem (Blumer 2004), whose urgency replaced that of terrorism; an unprecedented attention to anti-mafia commitment as civic and moral action, rather than as a form of subversion; and a redefinition of the state that, by opposing the mafia, acquired a newfound legitimacy and credibility.

In this process, the transformation of the statement "Giuseppe Impastato is a terrorist," as the state police claimed him to have been after his passing, suggesting the death to have been his own mistake and punishment, into the declaration "Giuseppe Impastato is a victim of the mafia" would expose the state's active participation in publicly defaming the young, murdered activist.

The reason why the anti-mafia movement was initially considered subversive becomes clearer if one takes into account the function attributed to the mafia in the shaping of the nation. It is only with the birth of the Italian state in 1861 that the term "mafia" appears in the Italian tongue (Blok 1974: 19). This does not mean that the phenomenon did not *exist* before this date and the speech act of its naming (U. Santino 2000a)—and this is significantly different from witchcraft (Siegel 2006:

218). According to one of the most widely circulated interpretations based on Weberian theory, the mafia has its roots in the incapacity of the new Italian state to guarantee the monopoly of the use of force in regions like Sicily that remained at the margins of the central administration. Faced with pressure from farmers' movements who pushed for the redistribution of land, landowners hired "violent mediators" (Blok 1974: 16), proto-mafia figures who proceeded aggressively against the land-occupiers, the unions organizing them, and the citizens (lawyers, journalists, state agents) who defended the legitimacy of their claims (U. Santino 2000b). If the mafia is a form of violence "organized" by the sociopolitical status quo to protect its own maintenance, the anti-mafia de facto presents itself, from the very beginning, as the more or less radical questioning of this system of power.[1] The anti-mafia fight thus took on, right from the start, a subversive character and thus found itself sanctioned: from the mid-nineteenth to the mid-twentieth centuries, many leaders of the anti-mafia movement were assassinated, and judicial efforts to identify the guilty parties, however focused, systematically resulted in the release of the accused.

Impastato's political activity needs to be seen in this context: it took place in a triangle formed by Partinico, Terrasini, and Cinisi in western Sicily, a region with a strong mafia presence but also one already marked by anti-mafia activism. This was the area where Danilo Dolci, the "Gandhi of Sicily," conducted his non-violent fight against the mafia and the mafiosi. But though the critical objective of this anti-mafia effort was not only the mafia but also the more-or-less stable and formal relations the mafia had forged with the state, its denunciations of these links had remained at the level of a scandal and never grew to have the impact of a political affair that would disrupt the status quo.[2] In the following I discuss the differences in scale, modes of circulation, and social implication between these two forms of indignation: scandal and *affair*.

---

1. On the role of the magistrate and the police in the suppression of farmer revolts and the protection of the interests of landowners and their so-called "mediators," see Di Lello (1994: 55).
2. Cyril Lemieux (2007) studies the conditions that allowed certain rumors to become a scandal. On the scandal as revealing and testing relations of power and norms in a given social space, see Editorial Committee (2005).

From rumor to affair

In the late 1960s, when Impastato began his anti-mafia activity, there were rumors circulating about mafia-related actions taking place around Sicily. Everybody knew the mafiosi and spoke of them in hushed tones, but these were rarely outed publicly. The individuals were also known by the justice system, but this turned a blind eye. As Cyril Lemieux (2007: 390) writes:

> Toleration for transgressions, typical of the gossip-monger, can thus assume a normative character within a group, when it finds itself in a situation of moral schism toward the authorities endowed with punitive powers in its regards (hierarchical superiors, the state, the media, etc.). The respect for this norm, which is translated into a collective, continuous effort to impede the transition to scandal, corresponds to what we usually call—whether we consider the army, the mafia, or professional cycling—the "law of silence" or *omertà*. (Lemieux 2007: 390)

We note, first of all, how authorities and forces of law and order share, at least partly, this social norm with the group that should go punished. This is also shown, with extraordinary visual force and a considerable measure of humor, by one of Zecchin's photographs. The image portrays two policemen standing behind a sign reading "The mafia kills, and so does your silence."[3] This statement still "walks on the legs" of Impastato's comrades (Figure 8). This law of silence or *omertà*, which can be formulated as the social injunction not to see and not to hear, even before the rule not to tell, becomes ever harder to respect when some people set into motion public denunciations whereas "the official version of the facts up to that moment was relegated to the realm of the unofficial" (Boltanski and Claverie 2007: 418).

Impastato and his collaborators took on the responsibility of denouncing mafia figures and activities, through formats ranging from flyers handed out to manifestos pasted on walls, from publishing a clandestine newspaper to creating a new radio station. Until then the people of Cinisi may have chosen not to see and not to hear; but this was not possible anymore once Impastato and his friends called the mafiosi by

---

3. There remains Zecchin's photograph: https://francozecchin.com/continent-sicile/ (Ref. 4362-10).

Figure 8: "The mafia kills, so does your silence – Peppino Impastato's comrades," anti-mafia demonstration (Source: Photo archive Centro Siciliano di Documentazione Giuseppe Impastato).

name in their flyers, documented the damage done by mafia activities through photographs (see chapter 3), and publicly spoke out on Radio Aut about the dysfunctional local administration—thus revealing the intrigues at the heart of the town council of Cinisi, which they nicknamed "Mafiopoli." Even more shocking, these young rebels ridiculed the so-called men of honor, mocked their supposed faith in God, insulted them, and so sullied their most precious form of capital: honor. In this phase, Impastato was in the position of the aggressor, if it is indeed true that "to publicly accuse one or more people is, in any case, to do violence to them, to attack their reputation, the consideration they enjoyed up to that moment or, to put it the old-fashioned way, their 'honor'" (Boltanski and Claverie 2007: 415).

These accusations risked raising the mafia—whose semantic field was widened by the criticism of Impastato and his comrades to include political corruption and environmental degradation—to the level of *scandal*. But, as any accuser who attempted to break the rule of *omertà*, Impastato knew well that "denouncing certain scandals can constitute, to the eyes of the community to which they belong, an even greater fault than that of the scandals themselves"(Lemieux 2007: 390). Badalamenti,

Vito Palazzolo, and the other Cinisi mafiosi had been put to the test of public indignation; but soon the tables were turned against their accusers and these became the "scandal" of their families. Impastato was labelled a "madman,"[4] his comrades, *sfardati* (beggars); and after his death, his friends and relatives who wished to be heard as "witnesses" were dismissed by the police as "accomplices." From the very beginning of their investigation the police discarded the possibility of murder and searched Impastato's house in the hope of finding proof of his supposedly terrorist endeavors. In the 1970s, the accusation of terrorism was often raised immediately to qualify attacks and assassination attempts, only for them later to be revealed as acts carried out by the mafia (Di Lello 1994: 15). When the police found a letter in which the young activist expressed his profound political disappointment and talked about suicidal thoughts, they felt vindicated in their hypothesis and closed the case. Here we witness the repetition of the common customary practice of turning a blind eye to a possible mafia crime. Accepting as normal the collusion between mafia and politics was a constant attitude held by judges and policemen, for whom undertaking investigations against the mafia would have been as unthinkable as it was impossible, given the few legal instruments that were available at the time for such an undertaking. The report released by the commissioner of Cinisi could, thus, have—as for many other mafia cases—marked the end of the investigation.

Yet, parallel to the official investigation, Impastato's comrades began a counter-investigation: they denied the accusation of terrorism that had been raised against their friend and refuted the suicide hypothesis, treating it as an imposture. Soon after the death, they began to use all the means at their disposal to publicly expound their truth. In front of the train tracks at Cinisi station—hastily repaired from the bomb blast that had killed Impastato, with incredible efficacy considering the normal pace of bureaucratic endeavors in Sicily—they hung up a banner reading, in block letters, "GIUSEPPE IMPASTATO ASSASSINATO DALLA MAFIA QUI, 09/05/1978, ORE 01.30" (Giuseppe Impastato killed here by the mafia, May 9, 1978, 1:30 a.m.)"[5] A small distance from the explosion,

---

4. It is noteworthy that in the 1970s any form of denunciation of the mafia was stigmatized as "madness." Let us not forget that in 1974 Leonardo Vitale, the first pentito of the Cosa Nostra, was admitted to a mental health institution after confessing his misdeeds as a mafia member.

5. There remains Zecchin's photograph (https://francozecchin.com/wp-content/uploads/2019/05/3146-10a.jpg).

they found a stone spattered in blood that, upon analysis by a forensic doctor in Palermo, was attested to be compatible with the blood of the victim. They reconstructed the dynamics of Impastato's death as follows: the activist was beaten to death with a rock before he was set down on the tracks with a bomb tied to his chest, in order to simulate a kamikaze terrorist attack. This reconstruction of the deed led to fierce criticism of the police, given that they seemed to have deliberately excluded and covered up any evidence pointing to a murder hypothesis, obscuring traces that could have identified the real killers and thus irremediably compromising the outcome of the investigation.

These people, taking on the role of investigators of the Impastato case, used the evidence they had gathered to claim that the death had been a "murder by mafia" and to call on the court of Palermo to reopen the case. The divergence between these two authorities—the local Cinisi police and the court in Palermo, the Sicilian capital—created a situation that lent itself to the development of an *affair* (Boltanski and Claverie 2007: 420). But what was still missing was a third entity that would launch a counter-denunciation in the name of public opinion—whichever entity that could be (Van Damme 2007: 154).[6]

It was Santino who was to assume this task—legal expert, activist, and scholar of the mafia. For this the social resources, organizational force, and argumentative possibilities of the Sicilian Documentation Center that he had founded in 1977, renamed the Giuseppe Impastato Sicilian Documentation Center after the death of his comrade, played a critical role. A research laboratory, an anti-mafia archive, a cell of political action, and a publishing house at the same time, the center began to publish on the Impastato affair. Over the years and decades, it was this research work that nourished the reading of Impastato's murder as a mafia act, and that made possible the Impastato family's legal effort. Thanks to his legal competence, his rhetorical capacity, and his publicity techniques, Santino assumed the role of denunciator,[7] turning the accusations against those that accused Impastato and taking aim at the collusion between the mafia, the police, and the political authorities of Cinisi. His work began to show that the police authorities had played along with the mafiosi's plans, interpreting the crime scene in exactly

---

6. On the importance of a third figure in the development of an *affair*, see especially Claverie (1998: 185–260) and Boltanski (1990: 255–265).

7. About the role of the denunciator, in the reversal of situations, see Boltanski (1990: 255–366).

the way they had deliberately "devised"—for controlling and pushing police investigations into a particular direction, intimidating witnesses, and contaminating evidence were all well-known mafia tactics (see Di Lello 1994: 137–138). Such non-speech acts, aimed at silencing, belong to the Mafiacraft repertoire of action.

The figure of the activist intellectual was not altogether new on the Sicilian scene. In the 1950s and 1960s, the sociologist and activist Danilo Dolci experimented with different forms of denouncing mafiosi (when identifying them as such had not yet been enabled by the Italian penal code) and their collusion with power: strikes, demonstrations, passive resistance, giving witness in court, etc. But his words had not yet produced an effect at the level of the judiciary, apart from multiple sentences against Dolci himself. This opens the question of what conditions had changed so that, in the Impastato case, a connection between the public space and the judicial arena became possible—a connection typical for an affair.

From vendetta to justice?

For Impastato's friends and relatives to see Palermo's court as a possible avenue of recourse, the latter first had to constitute itself as a legitimate authority, free of compromising association with the mafia, different from how the Cinisi police force appeared. This coincided with important changes that were introduced in the structures, practices, and representations of justice in Italy during the 1970s: the autonomization of the legal authority, separating it from political power; the mutation of the hierarchical equilibrium between civil and criminal law, putting the spotlight on examining magistrates in criminal proceedings; and the admittance of a new generation of legal minds into the ranks of the magistracy, including individuals socialized in the 1968 student uprisings (Vauchez 2004). The nomination of Chinnici as examining magistrate in the mid-1970s and his appointment as head of the Palermo office in 1979 opened up new "possibilities of action"[8] in the city. Suddenly the classification of mafia offences under criminal law became *feasible*: several prosecutors started to think it possible to go after individuals that others before them had refrained from investigating. It is within the Palermo court that, gradually,

---

8. I am borrowing this expression from French political thinker Violaine Roussel (2002: 113) who employs it in an analysis of the dynamics of action that French judges used in the 1990s in investigating political scandals.

an expertise in anti-mafia inquiry emerged. At first, these competencies in the exposure of mafia-related murders were developed by individual magistrates, then they were shared between several, and finally they formed complexes of experiences that became available to all who intended to deal with mafia crime. The indignation at murders of anti-mafia judges inspired young people to take up positions as magistrates, recruits who tended to immediately adhere to the new "model of professional excellence" that was developing in these judicial circles (Vauchez 2004).

Thus, the fact that Impastato's family saw the Court of Palermo as a possible avenue of resource is described in anti-mafia milieus as a historic transition "from vendetta to justice." When Giuseppe Finazzo, one of the men of the Badalamenti clan who had ordered Impastato's murder, was killed on December 12, 1981, the police immediately raided the Impastato family home under the suspicion that the activist's relatives had exacted revenge for his murder. The Giuseppe Impastato Sicilian Documentation Center protested against the police allegation and declared that "the relatives of Peppino gave up the possibility of any form of private revenge, choosing unequivocally the road of justice and anti-mafia commitment (12/20/1981)" (U. Santino 1998: 17–18). In fact, Impastato had himself come from a mafia family. His father, Luigi Impastato (Figure 9), had been condemned to exile for mafia activities during the Fascist period. The family had itself been hit by mafia murders—such as that of his paternal uncle Cesare Manzella, a boss of the mafia family in Cinisi, killed on April 26, 1963, when he was blown to pieces by a car bomb. The family had closely adhered to the law of silence: "If the cops come by, don't talk, don't say anything. *Omertà!*," as Impastato's mother, Felicia Bartolotta Impastato, described what she had been taught (Bartolotta Impastato 1987: 28). Even when Impastato was killed, his relatives advised his brother Giovanni "not to speak" (Bartolotta Impastato 1987: 48). Other neighbors similarly warned his mother that the same fate could happen to her other son, Giovanni, if she talked. She could remember the exact allusion they used: "You have to be careful, because blowing out a candle is nothing for them" (Bartolotta Impastato 1987: 49). One of his father's relatives by marriage, who carried the nickname "Sputafuoco" (Fire-Breathing) in mafia circles, had offered his "help," for purposes of revenge, but Felicia refused. It seems, then, that the Impastato affair occurred at exactly a moment when some Sicilians were prepared to try the legal route.

Indeed, just a few days after Impastato's death, his mother and brother went to Palermo to testify before Judge Domenico Signorino. The

Figure 9: Young Peppino Impastato (front row, third from right) holding the arm of his father (a mafioso), walking alongside one of Baladamenti's brothers. (Source: Family archive Felicia Bortolotta Impastato).

fact that members of a mafiosi family made recourse to the state's justice system could be considered as a historic transgression of the *omertà* code, the central element of its mental and cultural universe. According to folklorist Pitrè ([1889] 1944: 295), *omertà* commands one not to denounce the violence one has suffered to representatives of the law. The fact that members of Impastato's family did so thus can be seen as a sign of change in attitude not only toward the mafia but also toward the state.

In the late 1970s, anti-mafia magistrates such as Falcone began to be known across Sicily. Certain trials ended with sentences against mafiosi, even if "being a mafioso" was not yet recognized as a crime in the Italian penal code. This might then suggest that one might be able to resolve disputes through processes of legal mediation, and that mafia mediation was no longer necessary. However, certain elements from the Impastato case suggest that the move by his relatives cannot necessarily be read as a sign for a "modernized" form of social relations. Both the words spoken by Impastato's mother and the reaction of the magistrate who gathered her testimony—himself a Sicilian—recall the "traditional" conception of justice. Felicia called Judge Chinnici (Judge Signorino's successor) a "gentleman," a term that, in Sicilian, designates a man who is "honest, generous, and ready to fight in order to defend honor," and is used precisely to describe "men of honor." In Sciascia's book *Il giorno della civetta* (Sciascia [1961] 1990), a paradigmatic example of a Sicilian novel, it is mafia boss Don Mariano Arena who is called a "gentleman." The application of the word to anti-mafia magistrates thus seems to impose on them the idealized image of a mafia avenger. Anti-mafia judges unwittingly participated in this process of translation. Here is a rendition by Impastato's mother of a dialogue between her and the judge:

> Twice I spoke with Chinnici and he has acted like a gentleman. He says: "Don't worry. In Cinisi, those mafiosi reduced your son to pieces."

> I said to him: "My son wasn't made to pieces, he didn't tolerate injustice against the innocent."

> "We're here to carry out justice, to help the people." (Bartolotta Impastato 1987: 55)

The terms used in this interaction suggest that we are not witnessing a crisis of "archaic" justice but a critical moment in which the mediators have changed. For some Sicilians, the "men of peace" (a term which Impastato's mother applied to her mafioso relative, Cesare Manzella) are no longer the mafiosi but, rather, the anti-mafia judges.

When Impastato's mother spoke to representatives of the state, she explained her appeal to them by saying that she could not stand the idea that the memory of her son be sullied by the ignominy of the terrorist act of which he had been accused,[9] an appeal that the Giuseppe Impastato Sicilian Documentation Center described as animated by the will to "save the memory of Peppino." But is not defending his memory also a way of reestablishing his honor? The mother's appeal to Judge Chinnici gave the latter a power that had formerly been granted only to mafiosi: the power to wash infamy away, to renew the honorability of a dishonored family from calumny (an accusation that in mafia parlance goes by the name of *tragedia*).

This assimilation of anti-mafia magistrates such as Chinnici, as "men of peace," or "men of honor," a pattern we saw above in relation

9. "Neither terrorist nor suicide. My son was murdered!" Interview of Felicia Bartolotta by Mario Francese, *Il Giornale di Sicilia*, May 18, 1978. Mario Francese was murdered in his turn by the mafia on January 26, 1979.

to Falcone, is better explained if we consider it within an economy of forms: just like the state, the mafia—at least in the form it assumed in Sicily through the association known as Cosa Nostra—makes use of a tribunal, of iron-clad rules likened to laws, and of a complex system of sanctions to apply to transgressors. There is thus a structural equivalence between the internal functioning of the Sicilian mafia and that of a legal institution.[10] This *isomorphism*—to take up the concept defined by Paul DiMaggio and Walter Powell (1983)—is in fact recognized by both parties. Chinnici postulated the existence of a "mafia tribunal" (Zingales 2006: 59). Falcone considered it an instance of regulation internal to the organization (Falcone 1994: 37). These mechanisms led to the instituting, toward the late 1970s, of a commission that Judge Scarpinato defined as "a system of composition of conflicts through organs of internal jurisdiction" (Scarpinato 1998: 84). Livio Pepino, another Italian magistrate committed in the anti-mafia struggle, admitted that mafia justice is

> a parallel justice founded on different values but, in its way, efficient and punctual....In this way, the mafia subtracts from the state the powers and prerogatives over which it [the state] should enjoy a monopoly, according to the contemporary conception of political organization, and thus becomes an institution that is, in some sense, homologous to it. (Nebiolo and Pepino 2006: 9)

But even if we recognize certain characteristics of traditional justice within anti-mafia justice, the latter is nonetheless grounded in a new legal model.

Impastato: From "terrorist" to "mafia victim"

Hearkening back to the state of urgency that brought legal minds to the frontlines of the fight against terrorism during the Years of Lead, certain Italian magistrates raised in the anti-mafia struggle found a new terrain on which to come to the defense of democracy. New investigative strategies (such as working in teams or pools), new conceptual

---

10. This was already noticed by jurists such as Giovanni Fiandaca (1995: 21–28), who takes up an essay published in 1917 by Sicilian jurist Santi Romano. For a broader discussion on the mafia as a "legal system," see Puccio-Den (2015: 36–39).

schemes (such as that of the "organization"), new juridical figures (such as the pentito, the repentant mafioso), initially created to confront terrorism, were now applied to the mafia. Taking up Vauchez's analysis once more, we can speak of a "transfer of skills," instruments, juridical categories, and conceptual schemes from the anti-terrorism to the anti-mafia sphere. But this time the critique of the state was amplified, and the anti-mafia movement attracted the support of social groups that, up to then, had not felt addressed (such as students, teachers, businessmen, or priests) because they had considered these conflicts as simply ones between rival groups. The mafia losing its consensus by using terrorist methods, the popularity of certain anti-mafia magistrates grew even more. It remains to be understood what conditions allowed for the institutionalization, if not the sacralization, of what, at first, was a subversive movement.

The anti-mafia movement that spread during the 1980s could be defined as a "common domain of specialization" (Roussel 2002: 157) in which magistrates, police, politicians, intellectuals, and journalists acted synergistically. Denouncing the mafia and its relationship with politics no longer belonged to the register of action of "madmen" or "beggars," of marginal groups seen with suspicion.

Impastato's murder inscribed itself into the historical plot of a country in which the mafia and power were tied together. But for protests against this to have an effect in the legal sphere, it was first necessary to alter the Italian penal system. In fact, to say that Impastato was "killed by the mafia" did not make any penal sense in 1978. No juridical definition of the mafia in its criminal form was available then; the murders committed by mafiosi were thus judged to be a matter of common law criminality. The legal efforts of jurists and magistrates constantly ran up against the difficulty of establishing evidence due to the particular modalities of mafia-related criminal action. Chinnici described this in 1983 during a meeting of the National Association of Italian Magistrates in the following way:

> It is certain that, concerning mafia murders, it is often hard to establish a direct relation between who commissions the murder and who actually carries it out; just as one can never verify—because it is almost insubstantial—the relationship between the executor of a crime and the victim. (Zingales 2006: 60–61)

Only in the wake of the assassination of General Dalla Chiesa on September 3, 1982, did the Italian parliament approve the law that had been proposed by the regional secretary of the Italian Communist Party, La Torre (himself assassinated a few months earlier, on April 30). The promulgation of the Rognoni–La Torre law created a juridical framework within which mafia murders would be punished "as such," given that belonging to a mafia-like criminal association had become a crime. From this moment on, the assertion "Giuseppe Impastato was assassinated by the mafia" could lead to a trial for "participating in a mafia association." This involved a certain way of describing the links between the executors and the instigators of a crime. Judge Chinnici was one of the first to describe these connections. While the unitary nature of the mafia organization was still posed in terms of conjecture, Chinnici had intuited the ties between the murders of La Torre and Dalla Chiesa.[11] This intuition was a threat for the men of honor, because it threatened to bring to light the connections that united those who ordered mafia assassinations and those who carried them out. Magistrates who dared to follow this path, which led to a much clearer definition of the responsibilities of the individual mafiosi, were systematically assassinated. Chinnici himself became a mafia victim on July 29, 1983.

After Chinnici's assassination, the Impastato trial was taken on by Caponnetto, the new head of the Palermo investigative office, now constituted by a group of magistrates specializing in trials against mafia associates, the anti-mafia pool. The sharing of information within this office allowed for the growth of a shared perspective on the mafia phenomenon, and the development of a new epistemological model that identified the Sicilian mafia as a single organization with a hierarchical structure, thus breaking away from the former view of it as formed by small groups that lacked connections between them. The principle of co-responsibility between executors and instigators of a murder already existed in Article 110 of the Italian penal code: "When more people participate in the same crime, each of them will receive the sentence established for that crime," which is applicable even in the case of murder (art. 572) by virtue of the juridical theory of the "equivalence of conditions." Nonetheless, the way murders were commissioned and carried out in Cosa Nostra made it extremely difficult to establish a causal chain for homicidal acts. In the Impastato trial, as in other trials against mafiosi, the pentiti testimonies were crucial in that they offered missing pieces

---

11. This is what emerges from the sentence handed down in the trial of the mafiosi accused of massacring Judge Chinnici Court of Assizes of the Court of Appeal of Caltanissetta, June 26, 2002, n14).

that allowed for the reconstruction not only of the scene of the murder but also of what Scarpinato called its "*ob-scene*" side, the behind-the-scene, where the planning of the murder had taken place.

Before the decisive intervention of a pentito, Caponnetto had to recognize his own impotence: during sentencing in the Impastato trial, in May 1984, he admitted finding himself before the juridical impossibility of identifying those responsible for the murder. Even though the Rognoni–La Torre law had allowed for the indiction of members of a mafia association, responsibility in the penal code was strictly defined in terms of the individual perpetrator. Even if there was not enough evidence to permit the attribution of the crime to a specific mafioso but it was clear that the Badalamenti clan was involved in the act, there was no way it could be allocated to the whole group. Thus, though it was known that Impastato was killed by the mafia, it was still not possible to demonstrate which specific mafiosi were criminally liable for the murder (U. Santino 1998: 76). Without specific knowledge of the inner functioning of the mafia organization and the decision-making structure of murderous acts perpetrated in Sicily, Article 416 *bis* of the penal code was an empty tool, a legislative device without any agency or efficacy.

Even if the Impastato trial had allowed for the rehabilitation of the memory of a left wing activist, in that he was no longer considered a terrorist, the impunity of the assassins left the Giuseppe Impastato Sicilian Documentation Center and the Impastato family dissatisfied, which is why they once again asked the Palermo court not to close the case. Among those who signed a petition promoted by the center were numerous anti-mafia groups that had formed throughout the country during the course of the trial (U. Santino 1998: 86–87), proving that this had drawn the attention, interest, and concern of ever vaster sectors of the Italian society. This extension of contestation during the 1980s had the effect of "desingularizing the victim" (Boltanski 1990), typical of an *affair*.

A new phase of the Impastato trial opened at the Palermo office in the late 1980s. A file collated by the Giuseppe Impastato Sicilian Documentation Center, and entitled *Notissimi ignoti* (the very known unknowns)[12]—which sarcastically played with the fact that those who remained unknown to justice were notoriously mafiosi and assassins—named Badalamenti and Palazzolo as having ordered the killing and

---

12. The title was borrowed from an Italian film made in 1959 by Mario Monicelli, *I soliti ignoti*.

listed concrete evidence for this (drawing on Santino's training as a jurist). It was Falcone who took on the case, at the same time as the "exterminations" committed by the Corleonesi in the Second Mafia War led the losing families to seek protection from the state and to collaborate. Falcone began to draft a legal framework for the phenomenon of "repentance," defining the conditions for when testimonies of collaborators can be used as legal evidence (Falcone 1994: 33–65). The Impastato trial thus formed the basis for the testing of new judiciary categories, like the charge of "association with the mafia," the deployment of new investigative tools in fighting the mafia, like the anti-mafia pools and the use of pentiti, and the confirmation of a new model of thinking of the mafia as a unitary, hierarchical, and centralized organization.

We know that by virtue of the second postulate of the Buscetta theorem—according to which the Sicilian mafia has a pyramid structure and includes a commission, the Cupola, a decision-making body—the heads of the organization could be considered responsible for all mafia crimes. This theorem had universal application and could be applied even to minor trials, such as that of Impastato. In the early 1970s, Badalamenti belonged to the triumvirate at the top of the commission, together with Stefano Bontade and Luciano Leggio. His responsibility for the Impastato murder could easily have been demonstrated if he had still belonged to it in 1978. But Buscetta declared that in that period Badalamenti was no longer a member of the triumvirate, because he had been put aside (*posato*) by the Corleonesi as punishment for a misdemeanor. As a result of Buscetta's testimony at the Impastato trial, the hypothesis that Badalamenti had been the one to order Impastato's murder was disproven and the investigation came to a dead end. And once more, the Palermo court decided to close the case.

The incapacity of the justice system to identify the guilty parties in the murder of Impastato had repercussions for his relatives who had been claiming for a long time the status of "victims of the mafia." Backed by the Giuseppe Impastato Sicilian Documentation Center, Impastato's mother had tried to claim damages from the state. But Minister of the Interior Antonio Gava responded in 1990 that because the responsibility of the mafia in the murder of her son had never been proven, she could not claim the title of "victim of the mafia." Yet, the political situation of the early 1990s was considerably different from that in the late 1970s. In 1992 the *Mani Pulite* inquiry was put in place to investigate the corruption of the Italian political class. Launched by the prosecutor's office in Milan, the case was progressively extended to other Italian

cities, exposing a whole network of businessmen who had illicitly funded political parties in exchange for "favors." In 1993, Gava was himself
charged with collusion with a mafia organization. The Cusani trial of
1994, setting out from this investigation and screened on national television, completed the process of "degradation" of governmental elites
(Giglioli, Cavicchioli, and Fele 1997). The Milan magistrate, supported
by the media and backed by public opinion, declared the behavior of the
political class illegitimate, anti-democratic, and unethical. Italy had progressed far from the period when magistrates would look the other way
and "turn a blind eye" to this type of behavior. Christian Democracy were
severely weakened by this scandal and the Italian Socialist Party was so
decimated as to nearly vanish from the political scene. In this context,
the anti-mafia struggle became an integral part of the delegitimization
of the system of power that had governed Italy since the Second World
War, a system in which the mafia, with its widespread capacity for controlling votes, had been a crucial factor.

It is in these circumstances that Andreotti, one of the most eminent
members of the Italian Parliament, was accused in 1993, by the Palermo
prosecution, of participation with the mafia association Cosa Nostra. The
collusions of part of the ruling class with the mafia had been denounced
more than once, but up to that point the political elite had not been affected by legal action. But when the mafia violence reached its apex in
1992, with the murders of Falcone and Borsellino and their entourages,
the anti-mafia section of the Palermo court was able to attempt what
would have been unthinkable just a year earlier: laying a charge against
politicians for collaborating with the mafia (Briquet 2007: 81–82, 117).
Public indignation at the mafia's attempt to intimate Italians by taking
an increasingly confrontational approach and intensifying its "strategy of
tension"[13] led to tighter protection measures of state representatives. This,
in turn, led to an increasingly spectacular demonstration of destruction
by the mafiosi who from this moment began to be regarded as terrorists.

Where public criticism of the mafia and corruption was not tolerated
in the 1970s—when Impastato and his comrades were relegated to the
realm of psychological deviance and social marginality—by the 1990s it

---

13. This expression is found in texts produced by anti-mafia magistrates on
    the basis of testimonies provided by pentiti of the Corleonese clan. For a
    rereading of this period and its political backdrop, see the debate following
    the trial on the so-called "Trattativa" (state-mafia bargaining) (Fiandaca
    and Lupo 2014).

had acquired a new legitimacy. Bringing mafiosi and corrupt politicians to justice became imaginable, available for mobilization not only by investigating magistrates but also by common citizens, often grouped together in anti-mafia associations as corporate entrepreneurs, consumers, or witnesses. Leaders of opposition parties, journalists, and intellectuals knew they could count on a public ready to "open their eyes" to political scandals. Unlike twenty years earlier, it was no longer an intolerable affront to call Cinisi "Mafiopoli," especially not once the term *Tangentopoli* (city of bribes), to designate the generalized system of corruption reigning over Italian cities, had become widely used. To be accused of complicity with the mafia no longer remained a rumor: such an accusation had excellent possibilities of developing into a real scandal that, if taken on by the justice system, could lead to sentences for the accused.

But the path of the Impastato affair intersected not only with criticism of Italy's political system but also with criticism of the "terrorist" methods within Cosa Nostra itself. Growing dissent within the Sicilian mafia augmented the number of those willing to collaborate with the law. Among these was Salvatore Palazzolo, a man of honor from Cinisi, whose confessions were to provide essential evidence for solving the Impastato case. In 1994, the Giuseppe Impastato Sicilian Documentation Center, supported by a myriad of anti-mafia groups, again urged the court to reopen the case. New evidence was provided by Salvatore Palazzolo who declared that even if it was true that Badalamenti had been squeezed out of the Cupola at the time of Impastato's murder, he still had enough local clout in Cinisi town to organize the elimination of this young activist. Indeed, in 1996 Salvatore Palazzolo formally identified Badalamenti as the one who had ordered Impastato's murder.

This was not why the Impastato family received damages. The document given by the government in answer to the request for compensation explained that the technique of reparation existed solely for "victims of terrorism" or of "subversion of the democratic order." Felicia Bartolotta Impastato then appealed to the president of the Republic of Italy with the aim of demonstrating that her son's murder was nothing other than yet another episode of "mafia terrorism." The text of the appeal—signed by her but drafted by Santino—argued that the state had wrongly interpreted the 302/90 law on which it based its refusal of the application:

> In particular cases, the criminal organization named Cosa Nostra pursued its ends using the strategy of terror....Every murder committed by the criminal organization named Cosa Nostra, be it toward

men of the state who do their job or simple citizens who, for the very fact of exercising the fundamental rights sanctioned by the Constitution, represent a danger for the criminal organization, with the end of intimidating the state and society and to affirm the force of the organization itself, every such murder cannot but have a subversive-terroristic nature in itself.

"Given this," the jurist proceeds,

...with the present appeal we ask for the cancellation of the decision given that, tracing an exclusively bureaucratic and unrealistic line of demarcation between terroristic murder acts and mafia-related murder acts, denied the special donation specified by the law 302/90 to Ms. Bartolotta, mother of Giuseppe Impastato. (U. Santino 1998: 196–203)

On March 13, 1998, twenty years after his murder, the Palermo prefecture declared him an "innocent victim of the mafia" and granted his family reparations corresponding to this status. Five years later, in 2002, Badalamenti was formally identified as instigator of the murder (Figure 10).

Figure 10: Peppino Impastato's mother flanked by Felicetta, her daughter-in-law, and Anna Puglisi. (Source: Photograph by Pino Manzella.)

Testing the state

Through the Impastato affair, we have seen how, in a span of twenty years, the mafia ended up being identified with terrorism, not ideologically but at least in the form of extreme violence against the state. To describe this transformation as caused by a preceding change of values would be to fall prey to a "retrospective illusion" (Roussel 2002: 283, 292). In the same way that Violaine Roussel interpreted the political scandals rocking France in the same years, I have here preferred to concentrate on the series of small changes or "shifts" produced in the course of the clashes, to explain what, at different levels of analysis, shaped the Impastato affair.

To choose this case study as a privileged position from which to view this shift means to recognize the role of this *political form* (Boltanski and Claverie 2007) as agent of transformation of the juridical, political, and social order, and to recognize in it a testing of the state (Linhardt 2012). If it is true that this is "the moment destined to qualify and requalify the entities tied to a relevant question" (Dodier 2003: 31), the Impastato affair contributed to the conversion of the mafia issue into a national debate and transformed a localized event into a state *affair*, putting into question, right during the crisis of the First Republic, the entire political class.

The pragmatic perspective adopted here does not consider collectives (the mafia, the state, the victims) as fixed, already constituted social entities but rather describes the processes that shape them over time (Boltanski 1990: 23). The diffusion of the mafia phenomenon, often compared to the contagion of the plague in the nosographical model disseminated at all levels of society (see chapter 2), imposed on Italians the feeling of being progressively concerned by it. On the one hand, public position-taking for the anti-mafia cause produced a common front. On the other hand, the normative processes that led to the promulgation of the Rognoni–La Torre law, confirmed by the mafia trials which put into test its definitions, conferred ontological stability to the mafia. But the mafia and the anti-mafia movement are not the only two entities transformed in the course of this affair, almost as though they had swapped their roles with respect to the constitutive order: the one, previously claimed as an element of the state order (Di Lello 1994), now delegitimized as terrorist; the other, previously denounced as terrorist and ostracized for its critical views, now legalized and recognized as a legitimate form of political and moral struggle. Hearkening back to the notion of *épreuve d'État*, as defined in French pragmatic sociology, we can consider mafia violence as a "testing of the state." Falcone (1994: 115) wrote:

> It is not yet understood that in the fight against the mafia it is, no doubt, essential to remove the social and economic causes, but that it is no less important to reestablish the authority of the state, in all its articulations, in entire regions in which, up to now, it has not made its presence felt.

Undoubtedly, the anti-mafia justice project has contributed to the existence of the state in Sicily. From the earliest investigations, Falcone (1994: 137) endeavored to spread, in his professional milieu, "that collective awareness of the gravity of the mafia phenomenon which is indispensable for it to not be related to a merely local matter." Through his anti-mafia investigation method Falcone intended to show "that these problems do not belong to this or that office, to this or that police force, but are problems that belong to the State, and that we are all at the service of a single State." This same principle brought him to announce the creation of new investigative tools and devices when he was nominated to the position of Director of Criminal Affairs at the Ministry of Justice in 1991: the Direzioni Distrettuali Antimafia and the Direzione Nazionale Antimafia (Falcone 1994: 124–125).[14] The hoped-for "constitution of nuclei of judiciary police, highly specialized, centralized, and structured, capable of intervening in every part of the national territory in strict collaboration with local police and jurisdiction" (Falcone 1994: 317) would not only have ensured a shared vision of the mafia but would also, and especially, have made visible the unitary character of the Italian state. In a country in which unification was slow, late, and has remained somewhat incomplete, the fight against the mafia inspired a revalorization of the idea of homeland, one that had been discredited by the tragic experience of nationalism during the Fascist period.

In 1978, only a few hundred Sicilians escorted Impastato's coffin as it was driven through Cinisi, past closed doors and windows (Figure 11).

---

14. The anti-mafia divisions (Direzioni Distrettuali Antimafia) exist in all Italian cities in which there is a court of appeal. The Direzione Nazionale Antimafia, with its headquarters in Rome, is in charge of coordinating all anti-mafia inquiries in Italy in order to build a data bank on the mafia phenomenon.

Figure 11: Peppino Impastato's funeral procession: "Driven by Peppino's ideas and bravery, we will carry on." (Source: Photograph by Paolo Chirco.)

In 1992, fifty thousand people from all over Italy participated in the state funeral of Falcone, Morvillo, and three of their bodyguards. The following year more than one hundred thousand publicly commemorated the Capaci massacre. During the quarter century between the murder of Impastato and his recognition as a victim of the mafioso Badalamenti, mafia violence and the repressive response by the state opened questions on the limits of legitimate force in a democracy (Sciascia 2002), just as the Italian state was acquiring new legitimacy. It should not be assumed that there is linearity across the process of naming and judging the mafia, and reasserting the state monopoly of legitimate violence. The current absence of spectacularly violent Cosa Nostra attacks should not be read as a victory of the state or the law, or as a reaffirmation of the legitimate monopoly by the state of physical force, but as a return to the regime of invisible violence. Falcone (1994: 123) had indeed warned: "Contrary to common thinking, in fact, mafia power is the highest precisely where its external manifestation is at a minimum, that is, where life seems to pass in total tranquility." After his death in May 1992, the arrest of Riina in

January 1993, and his substitution in the mafia by his right-hand man Provenzano, Italy thus found itself in a new mutation that reconfigured not only the relation between state and mafia but also the power relations within Cosa Nostra (see chapter 10). Once the violence inside the Cosa Nostra and in the whole country had subsided, the most urgent issue for magistrates was no longer that of punishing the perpetrators or the instigators of mafia murders but rather of sanctioning the forms of complicity that the mafia could find beyond the criminal world. The locus of the investigation moves from the "obscene" to the inner self, the scene of the awareness, of the unconscious, and of the intentionality of crime.

CHAPTER 9

The Aiello trial

On intentionality in mafia crimes

What constitutes evidence and proof in mafia crimes? And what part does intentionality have in such criminal acts? To answer these questions, I draw on material from legal and judicial sources on Cosa Nostra. This Sicilian mafia has served as the reference point for Italian jurists trying to understand mafia-type organizations and characterize their activities as criminal offences. Besides being crucial to defining the "crime of participation in a mafia-type organization" (*associazione di tipo mafioso*), introduced by the Rognoni–La Torre law to the Italian Penal Code in 1982, the concept of intentionality lies at the center of the judicial categories—in particular, *concorso esterno* (external complicity)—that were then worked out to sanction actions that aided and abetted the mafia without the person doing them being a member of the mafia.

The question of intentionality is central to discussions about how to legally characterize a "mafia crime." Investigators, magistrates, and lawmakers were faced with crimes for which the motives were obscure, not only because these motives were hidden under the law of silence (*omertà*) but also because these crimes were organized so as to clearly separate the principal, who gives the order, from the agent, who executes it. To be effective, the campaign against the mafia could not just sanction criminal offenses as such; it had to trace criminal actions back to the murderous intent and reconstitute the material and logical relations between principal and agent.

The distinction between principal and agent is not simply a precaution, to make the killer's motives inscrutable during investigations. Cosa Nostra requires of whoever wants to join that they obey orders by carrying out actions with neither intent nor reason. Before formal initiation, the qualities that turn the postulant into a man of honor are tested through crimes and offences he is required to commit without hesitation and, above all, without asking questions. As he silently learns crime, the postulant is trained to experience his membership in the mafia as subjugation for which he has to sacrifice his own discernment. The pentito Salvatore Cucuzza,[1] for example, recalled having committed his first murder well before his official admission into Cosa Nostra: he shot a street vendor in cold blood, without even a vague inkling why someone selling fruit and vegetables had to be killed by the mafia. This is what Cucuzza calls "killing someone without the intention of killing him."

Initiation, as the pentito Francesco Paolo Anzelmo[2] pointed out, was also the occasion when the postulant "opened his eyes," as he might be let in on what happened behind the scene in various affairs, including murder. However, nothing would be disclosed to him about the crimes he had been asked to perpetrate. Prison, too, is a place where information is passed between veterans and new recruits or even between men of honor of the same rank but from different families. Mafiosi have to respect the law of silence toward outsiders but are obliged to tell the truth to each other—an ideal in contradiction with the concealment practices that the Corleonesi adopted as part of their strategy, in particular during the Second Mafia War in the early 1980s. In the mafia world, the rules about what to say and what to keep for oneself are very complicated: the reputation of a man of honor, as well as his survival, depends on him knowing when to hold his tongue. Not asking anyone about the reason for a murder nor using other avenues to find out, such is the very essence of membership in Cosa Nostra: unconditional and silent commitment to the organization.

The initiatory ceremony already described (see chapter 7), where the novice has to shoot an image of Christ to become a *fratuzzo* (brother), clearly illustrates the parallel drawn between murder and initiation. This

---

1. Salvatore Cucuzza, interview with author, Servizio centrale di protezione dei testimoni e collaboratori di giustizia, Rome, November 2009. He died in 2014.
2. Francesco Paolo Anzelmo, interview with author, Servizio centrale di protezione dei testimoni e collaboratori di giustizia, Rome, December 2010.

means that "as he had shot the Lord, so he would have no trouble killing his brother or father, if the society wanted him to" (Gambetta 1993: 263). In fact, when the organization sentences someone to death, it prefers giving the execution order to a member of the victim's biological family. What makes this practice possible—abolishing as it does any feeling of humanity in the murderer—is that men of honor perceive, or at least describe the act of killing as *unintentional* or unwitting. They thus dissociate themselves from their actions, justifying their acts by claiming that they did not commit them in their own interest but for the sake of the organization.

This stance does not, of course, hold up in the courtroom where the accused are held responsible for their actions as individuals. As Donald Davidson (2008: 106) has explained, a person is capable of doing something "intentionally" without ever having chosen, decided, or having had the intention of doing so. When a mafioso must, before a judge, account for the actions that he committed "without any intent," one possibility is to abjure his "belief," like the aforementioned pentiti,[3] and thus come to doubt the ideology underlying his actions. However, the falseness of a belief or the illusory nature of a value or desire do not prevent this belief, value, or desire being considered as reason for an action (Davidson 2008: 120) and thus serving as grounds for attributing the action to the person who did it. A mafioso, whether or not he has turned informant, and whether or not he had the intent (a reason concerning him and belonging to him) to kill someone, is—once he has killed someone intentionally (by consciously pursuing plans to perpetrate the murder)—to be recognized as guilty. He has to serve a sentence. The lack of a plausible motive by the agent who executes the crime leads magistrates, then, to look elsewhere for the primary motive.

Decision-making in Cosa Nostra

In Cosa Nostra, the initiative for committing a crime always comes from higher up. We already know that, at the top of this hierarchical system of domination, was the Commission that made decisions about operations to be undertaken. This body, which assembled the bosses of the various districts (*capimandamento*) of Palermo, rendered verdicts to

---

3. On repentance by mafiosi as a form of religious conversion, see Puccio-Den (2014).

punish violations of Cosa Nostra rules. Although membership of the Commission or the way it worked changed over time, Cosa Nostra has always had a hierarchical decision-making structure. During the bloody 1980s and until the early 1990s, the carrying out of punishments was assigned to "soldiers" or placed in the charge of a "fire group" belonging to Cosa Nostra's elite. According to the Cosa Nostra ideology, the people killed are not personal enemies but individuals harmful to the organization, because they violated its rules or threatened its prestige, resources, or power.

This opens the question of how prosecutors can trace a crime perpetrated by the mafia to its instigators when faced with low-ranking mafiosi who knew nothing about the circumstances of their own acts or with a group charged indistinctly with a series of murders. Article 41 of the Italian Penal Code considers the intent to kill and the actual act of killing as equivalent under condition that the intent is formulated as an actual order. This principle fits with the mafia's own internal conception of its crimes: relative indifference about the actual role played in a murder (gunman, lookout, driver of the escape vehicle, thief of the vehicle, etc.), interchangeability of these roles (the person giving the order might become the actual killer), and dilution of responsibility within a "fire group" or even the whole organization. The association's very name, Cosa Nostra, connotes a blurring of identities and intents, even for the purpose of murder.

From an anthropological point of view, as formulated by Perig Pitrou, prescription is the "first action performed in an itinerary"; and therefore, the order to kill, the impetus of an action, can be seen as the first act leading up to murder. In this "delegation of agency" (Pitrou 2012: 97–98), the actual perpetrator is the instigator since the agent is only obeying this higher authority. Prosecutors, therefore, had the task not just of following the traces from the spilled blood and the words backwards, so as to reconstruct the events that led up to the murder, but also of producing the material and verbal evidence that constitutes proof. It is no easy task to return to the initial act of speech when investigating a world reigned by the law of silence.

Proof of a mafia crime

How, therefore, can one establish proof in a mafia-related crime? Article 416 *bis*, introduced into the Italian Penal Code in 1982 to define "participation in a mafia-type organization" (*associazione di tipo mafioso*), provides for a prison sentence of three to six years for members of such an organization. What is sanctioned is membership, since it implies the intent to harm society, even if such a malicious intent has not (yet) been realized through any malevolent act. The postulate is that partners in crime are punished not for their material involvement in a specific criminal act but due to the shared purpose of committing such crimes, as implied by their membership of the organization. This postulate hardly differs from the type of commitment made by neophytes when, during initiation, they declare their readiness to work for Cosa Nostra (and, if need be, carry out criminal actions) and accept that their bond of subjugation and obedience to the mafia should override any other allegiance.

Passed in 1982, the Rognoni–La Torre law was not informed by an insider's understanding of this world of crime—such knowledge would be acquired only later, thanks to the pentiti. The law was based, rather, on types of behavior that were identified by the Sicilian politician and jurist La Torre as being mafia-like—even though at the time the existence of Cosa Nostra as an organization in its own right was still a matter of conjecture. These forms of behavior are of interest to us because they bring the relationship between intent and act into play.

Three specific forms of behavior were posited as typical of a mafia organization in contrast with those of ordinary crime: intimidation, subjugation, and *omertà*. Article 416 *bis* considers as a mafioso any person who uses or "intends to use" intimidation, without necessarily committing an actual act of violence, simply for drawing profit from the organization's capacity for frightening, a capacity with roots in the "public's memory" of its malicious acts (Turone 2008: 115–118). This comportment might be manifested as a mere attitude: "Even in the absence of words or gestures that are unambiguously intimidatory." Threats might be expressed latently through "advice from a friend, a silent presence, simple warnings" (Turone 2008: 20–21). This capacity for intimidation is part of the organization's "joint legacy," from which every one of its members profits (Turone 2008: 120). The two other forms of behavior, or methods, stem from the first: systematic intimidation creates the condition for subjugation and *omertà*, which obstruct the individual's engagement with public authorities. Lawmakers did not draw a profile of mafiosi as violent but rather as persons who silently, latently, insidiously menace society with potential violence, without it necessarily becoming actual. Obviously, this aura of intimidation has to be verifiable; proof of the mere intent to intimidate does not suffice (Turone 2008: 118).

Assuming that an agent is a reflexive subject who belongs to a community of such subjects (or "interpreters"), detecting intentionality is a hermeneutic, interactive operation of attributing meaning (Davidson 2001). This places us in the realm of the explanations and rationalizations advanced by such a subject wishing to justify what they have done. These explanations imply a set of beliefs, desires, moral conceptions, social conventions, and cultural values that enable people to define an intentional act as an action accomplished "for a given reason." This reason leads to redescribing the action and its meaning. The assumption here is that what people say about their acts necessarily corresponds to what they believe about them. Otherwise we are dealing not with a disclosure of explanations or reasons but with an imposture, a lie for dissimulating the link between action and intention so as to shift focus toward other motives, which are easier to mention because they are less likely to be severely punished. The question of dissimulating one's real intentions, not new in the philosophy of action (Davidson 2008), has also appeared in the legal practices of the institutions that judge violent crimes (Komter 1998). It becomes even more incisive for persons who, like the justice collaborators, are summoned to reconstruct events that might reach back several dozens of years (before they turned state witness) and to explain their intentions—intentions not at all explicit at the time of the events reported on, when the man of honor lived under a different code (that of *omertà*) and a different condition (that of subjugation to Cosa Nostra).

For all these reasons, the difficulty of establishing proof through testimony at the trials against mafiosi led to the adoption of probative strategies and investigatory techniques that took advantage of the technological advances of the late twentieth century: wire-tapping and hidden microphones for eavesdropping. Thanks to the evidence thus collected, magistrates were able to reconstruct mafia-related social interactions with the help of network analysis.[4] Investigators were thus able to verify what they had suspected for a long time, namely that members of the mafia maintained relations with persons who, though not formally affiliated with the organization, contributed in various ways to its prosperity—what was legally possible to qualify as "external complicity." This sparked controversy among state prosecutors who were investigating mafia crimes and raised the question of how to bring findings of this

---

4. A very good example of this in the social sciences is given in Paolo Campana's (2011) study of a Camorra network in Aberdeen.

sort into the judicial realm to make it possible to charge prominent professionals and politicians for aiding a mafia-related criminal conspiracy.

The Cuffaro controversy

The Aiello trial (2005–2008) presents us with the arraignment of nineteen persons on charges ranging from participation in a mafia-type organization to external complicity (*concorso esterno*) to simple or aggravated *favoreggiamento* (helping someone evade police investigations). The debate in legal circles about what charges to press against one of the major defendants—Salvatore Cuffaro, politician and at the time president of Sicily—provides us with insight into the legal categories invoked. As the trial proceeded, the arguments presented as proof shed light on all facets of the notion of intentionality in mafia crimes. The differing social classes of the accused was evidence of the entanglement of legality and illegality in politics, business, finance, and the public administration. It raises the question as to what extent these men were aware that their behavior was aiding and abetting a criminal organization.

The Aiello trial came out of an investigation launched in 1999 by Paci, prosecutor in the Anti-mafia Directorate of the District of Palermo.[5] Microphones hidden in the living room of Guttadauro, a doctor and mafia boss (who had previously been convicted of participation in a mafia-type organization), exposed a series of extortions, homicides, and acts of malfeasance linking the mafia to business and politics. However, the investigation, which ran under the name Ice Operation, came to a premature halt when Cuffaro alerted Guttadauro to the wiretap and the latter stopped using his living room for mafia-related business.

In a parallel investigation that started in 2002, disclosures by pentito Giuffré led to identifying Aiello, a doctor who owned several clinics but also a businessman in the construction industry, as being close to Cosa Nostra head Provenzano. A piece of paper (*pizzino*) found in Riina's pockets when he was arrested in January 1993 had brought up the name of Aiello. The pentito Brusca had recounted during a hearing that, in the late 1980s, he also had received a *pizzino* (small letter) from Provenzano (see chapter 10) in which the then fugitive leader told him to treat Aiello "as if he were his own person," a euphemism used to indicate that the doctor was to be considered as "Cosa Nostra." Informed by

5. Gaetano Paci, interviews with author, Palermo, August 2006.

Cuffaro of the investigation into his activities, Aiello managed to avoid the police wiretapping by drawing in two technicians, Giuseppe Ciuro and Giorgio Riolo, who were working for the Anti-mafia Division of Investigation.

On November 5, 2003, Aiello, Ciuro, and Riolo were arrested. Aiello was charged with "participation in a mafia-type organization"; the other two were indicted on "external complicity." Cuffaro was not yet called in for questioning because the prosecutors in Palermo could not agree on the indictment. Michele Prestipino and Maurizio De Lucia were advocating a charge of *favoreggiamento aggravato*: helping someone elude police investigations, in line with Article 378 of the Penal Code, with the aggravating circumstance that this help went to a mafia organization (Article 416 *bis*). Prosecutor De Lucia[6] explained the pertinence of this charge as well as the risks involved with a charge of external complicity. The latter would, according to him, result in a fiasco (as in the Andreotti trial), with high costs for both the justice system, the public image of the judiciary, and, ultimately, the anti-mafia campaign. Prosecutor Paci in contrast, was arguing that a charge of external complicity would be more relevant and effective. First of all, it would not require proof for the willingness to help Cosa Nostra as such, but proof for the consciousness of occasionally or intermittently helping the organization would suffice. The charge of *favoreggiamento aggravato*, in his estimation, would however require the demonstration that this help had been given with the clear intent of helping the mafia. Moreover, the offense of *favoreggiamento aggravato* did not take into account the full scope of the acts committed and of their grave effects. The fact that a politician serving as president of Sicily had helped notorious men of honor elude police investigation reinforced and legitimated the criminal organization. Furthermore, it blocked police wiretaps and judicial inquiries, which could have led to the arrest of several accomplices of Cosa Nostra, including its boss, Provenzano. For these reasons, Paci argued in favor of the charge of external complicity. In the end, those who supported the latter charge were, like Paci, ousted from the investigation and trial, or withdrew from the case, like prosecutor Antonino Di Matteo who brought another legal action against the accused, the second trial against Cuffaro, named the *Cuffaro bis*, which ultimately ended in a dismissal of proceedings.

The Aiello trial ended in January 2008 with Cuffaro's conviction for *favoreggiamento semplice*: Sicily's president was sentenced to five years

---

6. Maurizio De Lucia, interviews with author, Palermo, October 2005.

imprisonment. The court reduced the charge from *aggrovato* to simple *favoreggiamento*, without the aggravating circumstance of mafia, because it deemed that Cuffaro had helped "some mafiosi" elude police investigations without wanting to aid the mafia as such. In January 2010, however, the court of appeal recognized aggravating circumstances and increased the sentence to eight years. In January 2011, in turn, the Court of Cassation upheld this conviction, confirming that Cuffaro had been found guilty of *favoreggiamento aggravato* for consciously favoring Cosa Nostra.

Consciousness of the crime

The judgment from the Aiello trial, all 1,623 pages of it, presents the arguments used for the convictions. Drawing from this source,[7] I discuss in this and the next section several points that shed a legal and jurisprudential light on the question of intentionality in mafia crimes.

The Aiello court emphasized that the crime of participation in a mafia-type organization has two aspects: an objective one, implying that the individual is part of the criminal organization (because, for example, he has been formally initiated), and a subjective one, implying *affectio societatis scelerum*, namely the "individual's consciousness…of being part of a criminal organization and of placing his own conduct in the organizational and operational context of this very organization."[8] The court reserved the possibility of attributing this crime to individuals for whom no proof had been made of formal affiliation with Cosa Nostra, on the basis that these persons had showed a "conduct that constitutes an objectively functional contribution or help for the conservation and reinforcement of the organization's structure."[9] Reaching beyond the criterion of membership and the intention to be part of the mafia, the judges shifted the focus onto acts of behavior.

The trial repeatedly reaffirmed the ontological grounding of the Rognoni–La Torre law: members of Cosa Nostra were "conscious of being durably associated with the implementation of a criminal project independently of, and beyond, the fact of actually perpetrating crimes

---

7. *Aiello + 14* ruling by Judge Vittorio Alcamo, January 18, 2008 (hereafter referred to as the "Alcamo ruling").

8. Alcamo ruling, p. 44.

9. Alcamo ruling, p. 43.

planned by the organization."[10] This consciousness entailed the "willing-ness to participate in, and contribute actively to,…the activities of an or-ganization in which the contribution of each partner is part of the whole, of the realization of a common program that thus becomes a common cause."[11] The defense's arguments—that the accused actually took part in a mafia-type organization but without their knowledge, "without hav-ing consciousness" of it being a criminal organization—were rejected outright since "no one nowadays can seriously maintain that they do not know about the mafia's existence, operational modalities and unlawful goals." For this reason, "adhering, in whatever way, to this organization, by making a considerable, significant contribution, represents a conscious form of accepting Cosa Nostra's rules and sharing its purposes."[12] Once postulated, this axiom placed on magistrates the task of "clearly defining what corresponds to subordination, toleration, conscious acceptance, or else membership in relation to Cosa Nostra's existence and actions."[13] The judges' job was to strike the right balance in evaluating this range of moral attitudes.

Let us now examine the charge of external complicity and the diver-sity of roles by which individuals either "participated" in a mafia-related organization or "contributed" to its prosperity from the outside. "Par-ticipants" would be individuals who are members of the mafia, whereas "contributors" would aid the organization, perhaps temporarily or irreg-ularly, or for a single action. This contribution becomes an offence since it sustains and reinforces a criminal organization. Nonetheless, some ju-rists pointed out the contradiction of how a behavior that is temporary can contribute to a crime that is permanent (Grosso 1994).[14]

Despite the difference in "psychological attitude" between a willing-ness to contribute occasionally to the goals of a criminal society or persis-tently, consciousness and intentionality are much the same in both cases. For persons who contribute to the mafia from the outside, however, this intentionality or willingness is "depleted even as it is realized."[15] Intent and act, we might say, necessarily coincide in the case of contributors,

---

10. Alcamo ruling, p. 44.

11. Alcamo ruling, p. 45.

12. Alcamo ruling, p. 54.

13. Alcamo ruling, p. 79.

14. See Grosso (1994) for a discussion of the differences between the categories of mafia crimes.

15. Alcamo ruling, p. 64.

whereas the two are separable in the case of actual members. Recall that members of the mafia fall under the sanction of the law even though their intentions are not necessarily realized through criminal actions. They have a "typical" behavior ontologically characterizing them as mafiosi whereas contributors have an "atypical" behavior characterizing a single action in their lives.[16] What is missing in the latter case is the *affectio societatis*, the "willingness to be part of the organization"[17]—not the awareness of the organization's methods and goals. After all, contributors might help and support the criminal organization just as effectively as participating members. In fact, they "know and want that their contribution is for the purpose of realizing, even partially, the group's criminal plans."[18] We can imagine the difficulty magistrates had of proving what an individual "knows" and "wants."

The *favoreggiatore* of the mafia interferes in the proper course of justice so as to "favor" mafiosi by helping them elude investigations. As is known, "Cosa Nostra's power has grown over time thanks to its capacity to infiltrate the state and appropriating confidential information through the disloyalty of state representatives."[19] It is, therefore, quite difficult to establish the difference between the simple abetting of crime (*favoreggiamento semplice*) and aggravated abetting of crime (*favoreggiamento aggravato*) when help is provided to a member of a tightly knit, unitary organization where a single act might have repercussions on the whole. Magistrates should, therefore, be able to develop an overarching vision of the mafia that links the particular to the general—in comparison with the fragmentary picture emerging from former anti-mafia investigations. Furthermore, they should have the moral qualities for evaluating, case by case, whether a suspect was aware of the more far-reaching effects of his single acts. This entails a conception of human beings as subjects fully endowed with a sense of criticism. But does this conception hold for the men produced by the mafia?

It is language that modifies the ontology of action, hence the implicit force of *knowing how to keep silent*, this skill specific to certain contexts of political violence and domination, acquired by controlling the tools of language and by imposing silence (or, in a visual register, by *invisibilization*). Here Mafiacraft is the inverse of witchcraft, since it reveals how

16. Alcamo ruling, pp. 65–66.
17. Alcamo ruling, p. 84.
18. Alcamo ruling, p. 114.
19. Alcamo ruling, p. 125–126.

power—in those places where it does not construct legal and cognitive frameworks to criminalize certain behaviors and certain social or ethnic categories (Fassin 2017)—deconstructs, disconnects, and obscures large swathes of its own criminal action. *Keeping silent* is also a powerful way to *make someone do something*, since as long as it is covered by silence, and thus disconnected from the subject's will, the action does not fully belong to the actor, who does not consider himself to be the author in a full sense. *Knowing how to keep silent* and knowing how to *make someone do something* thus appear as two techniques of power centered on the possibility of *disconnecting* the subject from his own language,[20] a way of *subjugating* or de-subjectifying him. Anthropologists have developed theories of ritual action—also characterized by a discrepancy between the act and the language used to describe it, a condition that entails a loss of meaning of the performed action (Humphrey and Laidlaw 1994)—that can be extremely useful in analyzing mafia crime as a modality of action.

Criminal action as a form of social action

In her study of the dilemmas faced by Dutch magistrates who had to evaluate the degree of responsibility of individuals for extremely violent crimes—based on a year of observation in courtrooms in Amsterdam, Utrecht, and Haarlem—Martha Komter (1998) uses ethnomethodological methods and linguistic analysis to study the interactions between the various parties to the cases. Pointing to the problems of dealing with defendants who denied the acts of which they were accused (Komter 1998: 22), she underscores defendants' moral ambivalence, a mixture of admission of guilt and denial. Some of them recalled being in a semi-conscious state during the crime and described how at a certain moment they turned from agents into spectators of their murderous acts (Komter 1998: 48). Others, under questioning, stated that they realized the atrocity of their deeds only after the fact (Komter 1998: 53). This raises a critical question: might what was interpreted in the judicial context as a strategy of defense—defendants being reticent about telling the whole truth, their difficulty in describing precisely what they had done and assigning it a meaning (Komter 1998: 49)—rather stem from the particular nature of the criminal act? This would imply that criminals adopt

---

20. Another example of this organized disconnection is torture (Perret 2013).

a position toward their criminal acts, cognitive resources, and language competence that differs fundamentally from that held in everyday life.

The magistrates who wrote the ruling in the Aiello trial did not conceal their discomfort with their assignment to "trace with certainty the bounds between: the condition of pure subordination; the sharing, partially and temporarily, in the goals; and the willing and conscious adherence to the rules established by the Cosa Nostra."[21] This task is all the harder because the sparing use of language by men of honor gives rise to shared forms of denial. Men of honor do not have to provide justifications for their actions, nor search for them in their conscience. A trial raises the curtain on the crime's *ob-scene*, and the murderous intent comes into the spotlight—sometimes as revelation even to the defendants as they reconstruct events a posteriori. That is the time when murderers—at least those who do not remain confined to silence—give a meaning to actions they had undertaken in what we might call an automated state of mind.

Judges investigating mafia crimes are in the same predicament as anthropologists studying rites: both inquire into acts that might be performed mechanically, without the persons involved knowing their precise meaning. When questioned by Caroline Humphrey and James Laidlaw, participants in the *puja* ceremony (widely observed in Jainism) replied, "the *puja* is meaningless." This reply served as the starting point for a long study of rites as a form of action that "severs the link, present in everyday activity, between the 'intentional meaning' of the agent and the identity of the act which he or she performs" (Humphrey and Laidlaw 1994: 2).

Maurice Bloch (2004) examined a category of acts (including rites) that are not rooted in the intentionality of those who perform them. When, for example at the request of anthropologists eagerly looking for interpretations, informants try to explain ritual performances, they refer to earlier scenes or events as the grounds of their acts, or else are satisfied with quoting sources of authority in justification. This "quoting" underlies "deference," the fundamental mechanism of ritual acts. In the endless regress of the quest for meaning, the agent is in a position of nonreflexivity, "so that his intentionality, and thus his understanding, disappear or become irrelevant to the text" (Bloch 2004: 130). Their action is fully absorbed in self-effacement. Such an agent becomes "transparent," performing gestures of which they do not grasp the meaning (even though

---

21. Alcamo ruling, p. 127.

they are sure it exists). They become the recipient of interpretations previously made by others. For this reason, interpreters—whether judges or anthropologists—are caught in a continuous spiral of searching for an ever elusive meaning.

"Ritual commitment" resembles involvement in the mafia: "it results from a positive act of acquiescence in a socially stipulated order" (Humphrey and Laidlaw 1994: 5), with the implication of suspending one's own critical capacity in recognition of a higher authority: "a kind of abandonment of the examination of the truth of the quoted statement," where "one can assume that what has been said is true without making the effort of understanding" (Bloch 2004: 126). The essence of a rite (and of a mafia-related act) depends precisely on this relationship of subordination, we may say subjugation (*assoggettamento*): "the degree of ritualization of action corresponds to the degree to which actions are felt to be stipulated in advance and thereby separated from people's intentions in acting" (Humphrey and Laidlaw 1994: 12). According to these two anthropologists, this approach is not restricted to ritual, since the "quality of ritual action" inheres in other types of action, such as theatrical performances, games, customs, conventional patterns of behavior, or actions conducted under order: "Here, as in few other human activities, the actors both *are*, and *are not*, the authors of their acts" (Humphrey and Laidlaw 1994: 5, emphasis added).

This helps us better understand the feelings of perplexity of the antimafia magistrates who, when interrogating mafiosi about their murderous acts, obtained responses similar to those received by anthropologists questioning those who perform ritual acts: "We do this because we have been ordered to act in this way" (Bloch 2004: 125). We understand the frustration felt by the judges who were trying to identify the mastermind behind mafia-related crimes but stumbled upon a black box. As Bloch (2004: 131) has explained: "These apparently frustrating answers combine explicitness concerning deference and awareness of imprecision about who exactly is the originating mind behind the practice." In explanations of ritual action, the indeterminacy of the original intention is structural: "It is not possible to identify clearly an original intentional being" since those who perform rites are "deferring to invisible and indeterminable others" (Bloch 2004: 128). What about defendants who identify as source of their action an entity as abstract and impersonal as Cosa Nostra? Prosecutors had the titanic labor of reconstructing the motives for crimes. Again, Bloch's (2004: 131) comment is insightful:

"Scrutiny of the source of authority inevitably leads the inquirer into an endless regress."

How then can the guilt of individuals be established who have cleared themselves of any responsibility for their acts by pushing intentionality onto a higher entity (higher in rank and in willpower) to the point of naming God as the ultimate source of inspiration—as did mafia boss Provenzano, famous for garnishing his written instructions with quotations from the Bible? This raises again the question of belief, as we shall see in the next and last chapter. According to philosopher Hilary Putman (quoted in Bloch 2004: 135):

> people are almost conscious of the fact that they are constantly relying on the understanding of others and that they normally act in terms of beliefs they do not fully understand, but which they hold valid because of their trust in the understanding of others.

The magistrates who judge mafia crimes have to examine behaviors lodged in the coils and folds of defendants' minds, between consciousness and unconsciousness, sincerity and dishonesty, belief and deceit. Since men of honor justify their acts by invoking a set of values and ideals in which they "believe," it opens the question of how to, legally and morally, evaluate malicious actions that are motivated by "good intentions." Pierre Smith (quoted by Humphrey and Laidlaw 1994: 9) wrote that women and children summoned to undergo rites of initiation "believe, or are supposed to believe, or at least are supposed to act as if they believed." The task of anthropologists is to explore this "as if" in ritual, criminal, and other types of action. Ontological changes—from things being as if they were true to things having the consistency of truth—are hanging by a wording, pronounced, denied, or affirmed. This will become apparent in next chapter, which analyzes the justifications of criminal acts provided by non-repentant mafiosi.

CHAPTER IO

The Provenzano code

On initiation, again

While anthropologists and sociologists neglected the initiation rituals of the men of honor, considering them as superstitious practices, Judge Falcone saw them as significant:

> One can smile about it, as with an archaic ceremony, or consider it a joke. But it has to do instead with an extremely serious matter, which engages the individual for the rest of his life. To come to belong to the mafia means to become a convert to a religion. One never stops being a priest. Or a Mafioso. (Falcone and Padovani 1997: 97)

To take the mafiosi seriously, and to take seriously what they themselves take seriously: this was the lesson of the judge who, in order to fight the mafia phenomenon but also due to authentic intellectual curiosity and sincere human interest, sought to penetrate the mental and cultural universe of Cosa Nostra. The descriptions of the rites of initiation, as revealed by several pentiti, allow us to determine the sacral nature of the relationship linking the men of honor.

The following scene took place in Catania in 1963, as told by pentito Antonino Calderone to sociologist Pino Arlacchi in the early 1990s. In the scene we find a number of candidates who wished to join the mafia, each one accompanied by his *padrino* (godfather) who leads the initiation of his ward and carries out the requisite gestures.[1] Among them was Calderone with his godfather, Uncle Peppino.[2] Calderone takes up the story:

> At this point Uncle Peppino took a needle and asked, "What hand do you shoot with?"
> "With this one," I answered.

> So he pricked my finger, making it bleed and letting some of the blood fall over a small sacred image. I looked at it. It was Our Lady of the Annunciation, the patron saint of Cosa Nostra, whose day was March 25th.

> Uncle Peppino lit a match and brought its flame to a corner of the image, asking me to take it into my hand and to hold it until it was completely burned. I closed my hands in a seashell shape—I was full of emotion and sweating at this point—and I saw the image turn into ash. Meanwhile, Uncle Peppino asked me to repeat the oath after him. According to this formula, if an affiliate should ever betray the commandments of Cosa Nostra, he should be made to burn like the sacred image. (Arlacchi 1992: 59)

Despite certain adaptations, to which we will return later, this ritual has remained intact from the early nineteenth century onwards.[3] With its similarities to a baptism because of the presence of a godfather and his initiatory role into a new community, the mafia initiation creates a spiritual kind of relationship[4] that is irreversible and overtakes all other types of relationships. "You cannot leave or betray Cosa Nostra, because it is beyond everything. It comes before your father and your mother, your wife and your children," explained Calderone (Arlacchi 1992: 58).

---

1. *Parrinu*, the Sicilian term for *padrino*, also means "priest."
2. Certain functions that are elsewhere carried out by the paternal uncle are in Sicily carried out by the godfather (see D'Onofrio 2004: 57). It is noteworthy that these roles often coincide in Cosa Nostra.
3. At the end of his book *The Sicilian Mafia* (2003), Diego Gambetta provides a series of descriptions of the rite of initiation, the oldest of which dates back to 1884. All other variants cited in this chapter are taken from his book.
4. Spiritual parenthood inscribes the bond of friendship into a sacred horizon, thus removing it from the vagaries of profane time and making it irreversible (D'Onofrio 2004: 87).

And it is by mirroring Christian characters and rites (the godfather, the Madonna) that the "mafia family" affirms its superiority over the so-called carnal family, according to the model of the Sacred Family: like Jesus, the mafia "son" is reborn under the sign of the Sacred Virgin and the godfather (the child's "social" father, as Joseph was for Christ) and under these saintly auspices, he is required—and ready—to renounce his biological family.

One such radical interpretation of the evangelical precept to "abandon one's own being and abandon one's family" was that of St. Francis of Assisi, whose Rule affirms: "If someone comes to me and does not hate his father and mother, his wife and children, his brothers and sisters, and even life itself, he cannot be my disciple" (Reg. 21 I). But it is precisely the literal relation to the Scriptures that distinguishes fundamentalism as a closed system, in which language has a merely prescriptive value, from religion understood as an open system, which leaves space for symbolic, metaphorical, exemplary, and illustrative uses of language (Kaufmann 2013). More than once, the "made man," thus the man made by the mafia, will be asked to kill one of his relatives or made to fall into a trap, in order to test his complete devotion to Cosa Nostra and to destroy any residual sentiment he might still hold toward his family. The initiation serves as a language of legitimation, an abstract cultural frame through which to inscribe concrete actions that would otherwise be difficult to justify.

If this model of affiliation to a new social and spiritual family is, in and of itself, quite exhaustive, particularly in Sicily, by which relationships between godparents and godchildren are held to be "nobler" than biological ones (D'Onofrio 2014: 62),[5] another type of family relationship also overlaps with it, that of the brotherhood.[6] In fact, as two pentiti explained,[7] the principal bond instituted by the rite of initiation is not the (vertical) one between father and son but rather the (horizontal) one between those who were initiated or "combined" (*cumminati*) on the same day. Thanks to the mediation of the Madonna, the common mother whose ashes are mixed with their blood, the novitiates

---

5. Strangely, Sicilian anthropologist D'Onofrio makes no mention of the mafia's use of the relationship between godparent and godchild.

6. In its sociological aspects, this model was studied by L. Paoli (2000).

7. Salvatore Cucuzza and Francesco Paolo Anzelmo, interviews with author, Servizio centrale di protezione dei testimoni e collaboratori di giustizia, Rome, 2009 and 2010.

become "brothers." The words of pentito Leonardo Messina's godfather expressed this clearly: "He also reminded me that, from that moment on, my brothers would be components of Cosa Nostra and the interests of Cosa Nostra were superior even to my own interests and to those of my carnal family" (cited by A. Dino 2008: 62). The act that metonymically designates initiation, the "puncture" (*punciuta*), embodies its very meaning: everything resides in this "combination," the mystical union of life and death, blood and ash; an almost chemical procedure through which the candidate is assimilated to and by the mafia to the point of total identification, which is reflected in certain formulas of presentation used in front of third parties: "This man and I are the same thing," or "He is cosa nostra" (literally, our thing).

This new brotherhood, one of sharing the same substance, could explain the absolute ban for a "combined man" to have sexual relations with the woman of another "combined man" (one of the Cosa Nostra's principal "commandments"). Following the redefinition of the social and familial relations brought on by the initiation, such a relationship would be equivalent to "incest of the second type," consisting in "two same-sex blood relatives sharing the same sexual partner" (Héritier 1979: 219). This relationship, explains French anthropologist Françoise Héritier, drawing on the theory of humors, is sanctioned by law in Western societies because it produces not the union of contraries, as in "normal" sexual relations, but rather joins secretions from individuals who are of the same nature (brothers, sisters) through the shared partner. One can well wonder whether it is not this principle because of which the Cosa Nostra sanctions this type of adultery within the "Mafia Brotherhoods" (Paoli 2000)—and only this—with death. A vast literature tells of the divine sanctions incestuous lovers run up against. And we will see later on how mafiosi "believe" themselves to be interpreting God's will when they commit (such a) murder.

The ritual constitution of a community of brothers also evokes another Catholic rite, that of communion. In this sense, the bloody image of Our Lady is also an annunciational figure for the sacrifice of Christ, a sacrifice that the novitiate relives in his own flesh:

> As this saint is burned and in these few drops of my blood, I shall pour out all my blood for this *Brotherhood*; and just as these ashes cannot return to their original state and this blood in its proper state, I, too, cannot renounce the *Brotherhood*. (cited by Paoli 2000: 82, emphasis in original)

Theological models intersect with literary models, which also allow for the emergence of the significance of the brotherly bond and the irrevocable nature of the pact. One of these is the initiation scene as told by Natoli in *I Beati Paoli*. Well-known by mafiosi at the time of publication in the early twentieth century thanks to its serialization in the *Giornale di Sicilia*,[8] a daily newspaper, this story of a mythical sect from the early eighteenth century,[9] which had as its mission the defense of the weak, the punishment of injustice, and the protection of victims, is still told to Cosa Nostra candidates during the rite of initiation, as a reassuring, idealizing frame of commitment that they underwrite with criminal association. In Natoli's novel, the neophyte is accompanied into an underground cavern beneath the city of Palermo and adorned like a sanctuary:

The chief asked: "Your name is Andrea Lo Bianco?"

"Yes, most illustrious one."

"Here there are no illustrious ones, there are only brothers," the officiant answers.

Then, he cuts a cross into the initiate's arm, dips a feather into it and hands it to him, asking him to affix a cross on the New Testament and to swear:

"That your body and your soul belong now and forever to this venerable society of the Beati Paoli, in service of justice, in defense of the weak, against any violence and power of government, of sirs, of priests." (Natoli 1971: 122–123)

Beyond myth, members of the Calabrian *'ndrine*, or 'Ndrangheta groups called *Vangelisti* (evangelicals), are marked by a cross-shaped incision on their shoulders (Dino 2008: 55). It is also true that the practice of marking a vote or a profession of faith in one's own blood is known in Christianity (Albert 1997: 387–388). But when blood is used by the

---

8. Luigi Natoli—under the pseudonym William Galt—wrote *I Beati Paoli* especially for the *Giornale di Sicilia*, publishing it in 239 episodes from May 6, 1909 to January 2, 1910.

9. The events narrated in the novel take place during the period 1698—1719.

signatory as ink with which to seal a contract with a transcendent power, what comes to mind more directly are pacts with the devil.

"Every piece of paper is good. You will sign with a small drop of blood," Mephistopheles says to Faust, in Goethe's work. This indifference to what paper is used to make the contract is reflected in one of the swearing-in formulas of the mafia rite of initiation: "Like paper I burn you, as saint I adore you…" (Dino 2008: 52). But despite this premise, burning a sacred image is nonetheless an iconoclastic act. This blasphemous dimension is clearly acted out in the initiation ceremony of the *Fratuzzi* di Bagheria that we already met in chapter 7:

> The neophyte was led to a large room where a figure of Christ was hung. He was given a pistol and, without trembling, had to shoot him with a bullet to show that, just as he had shot the Lord, so he would have no trouble killing his brother or father, if the society wanted him to. After that the candidate became a *fratuzzo* [small brother]. (Gambetta 1993: 263).

Transposing, in palimpsestic manner, different versions—ancient and present, real and literary—of the mafia's rite of initiation, we see an equivalence between two acts: signing with one's own blood and shooting and spilling another's blood. Thus we are in a position to observe a detail of the initiation to which no commentator has given much importance, despite the fact that we are dealing with a criminal group: the fact that the finger that is pricked is the one that pulls the trigger. Through the initiate's first homicide, which can be decided on during the course of the ceremony or can even precede it,[10] the "made man" ratifies his contract with Cosa Nostra and gives proof of his worthiness. But if writing one's signature with blood and killing represent two gestures that come to be ratified symbolically in the rite of initiation, what happens when we move from the metaphorical use of writing to real writing as part of the criminal practices of the mafia?

---

10. The possibility that the first homicide might precede the initiation was indicated in various life stories, such as that of Leonardo Vitale, Cosa Nostra's first pentito, and that of collaborator Salvatore Cucuzza as he told me personally.

Writing, killing, commanding

The paradox of mafia power is that, to be efficient, it has to show the public that it exists while, to avoid state repression, it has to hide its existence. The use of the language of symbols responds to these two requirements: things speak on their own and allow anyone who wants to send a message to remain in the shadows. The symbolic use of objects or the objectified bodies of animals to create intimidating scenes is well-known: an ex-voto in the shape of a heart perforated by a gun, an empty tomb, a dead bird, a horse's head, left on the path of a person meant to be threatened—all these can constitute an initial warning. If this person "does not wish to understand," then it will be on his corpse on which the next message will be left, this time as warning to others who also might not want to listen. The killer leaves his mark on the victim's body, first riddling it with bullets, then subjecting it to a treatment that establishes a metaphorical relationship between the punished transgression and the punishment, according to the codified repertoire that was introduced in chapter 7, such as money stuffed in the mouth to indicate the greed of the victim, a stone in the mouth to indicate the disregard of *omertà*, or castration for the adulterer of a mafia wife. The murder transforms the body of the victim into an object to be read, deciphered, and interpreted.

This representation exists in the Christian tradition too, where martyred, stigmatized bodies are a "page written by Christ" (Charuty 2008: 34). In the criminal universe, this system of signs gives us an entrance to different hermeneutic operations: within Cosa Nostra, the deciphered symbols warn potential transgressors of mafia norms of the punishment they might encounter; on the outside, the clues put on victims' corpses bring policemen, prosecutors, experts, and forensic doctors to formulate hypotheses about the perpetrators of the murder. In the same way in which professionals analyze the trace left by the assassin like a signature that can lead them to his identity, so, too, mafiosi move in a web of signs that, if manipulated well, allow them to claim responsibility for a murder, in order to gain prestige, or hide responsibility by placing fake evidence that will implicate someone else. If, on the one hand, the pen of the magistrate is a weapon,[11] men of honor, on the other, use their weapons to "sign" their murders: individually, to ratify the pact with Cosa Nostra

---

11. Various songs and popular Sicilian ballads figure the pen as the lethal weapon wielded by the magistrate against the people. Magistrates like Cesare

and, collectively, to transform the "few drops" of blood spilled during initiation into a homicidal communion. Through every new bloodletting, the sacrifice of Christ is renewed, and the mafia community is revived.

To be efficacious, the symbols have to be recognized. The mafia murder has to speak for itself. Clues left at the scene of a crime ought to be interpreted according to Cosa Nostra's internal norms so as to remove them from the specter of arbitrary violence. Yet, the mechanism by which Cosa Nostra constructed a collective "sense" of its crimes was disrupted under Riina's leadership. His progressive seizure of power over the course of the 1980s coincided with two significant changes in the mafia's regime of communication: first, the increased use of gossip and "tragedy"—the discreditation of an individual, by circulating false rumors about him—as privileged modalities for the diffusion of information; and, second, the dramatic increase of the practice of *lupara bianca*—the complete disappearance of a person by killing and dissolution in acid. The "white shotgun" made invisible the message deposited on the corpse, making its reading and interpreting impossible. These two practices formed a double strategy of power, with the aim of disseminating confusion and discord among mafia families, a tactic to divide and conquer. Deprived of internal procedures of control, understanding, and the regulation of violence, Cosa Nostra was in a state of chaos when Provenzano, the Corleonese boss who took power after Riina's arrest on January 15, 1993, began to use writing as a new means of internal communication.

Riina's methods were considered as too brutal even by standards internal to Cosa Nostra. Under Provenzano, they were substituted by new instruments of power, *pizzini* (small letters) that were praised for their discretion and efficiency, particularly after the spectacular and useless massacres of 1992 and 1993 (to which, it should be said, Provenzano, comrade-in-arms to Riina during the campaign of terror launched by the Corleonesi, had also greatly contributed). Provenzano's slow, patient weaving of a web of mafia correspondents did contain the risk of implosion. Yet after a long career as bloody and brutal killer, the new boss had the intuition that it was time to close rank and pull in the men of honor who had felt lost in the constantly shifting chessboard of mafia alliances, untrusting and unhappy with the long period of dangerous internecine struggles. This is precisely what the other bosses

---

Terranova had been shot for being the (sole) signatories of rulings involving members of the Cosa Nostra.

asked of him: "Many lies are in our way, not to mention tragedies… .I hope that these things can be resolved between us so as to bring some tranquility to our province after the hurricane that has hit us recently" (Palazzolo and Prestipino 2007: 199), wrote the Caltanissetta vice-representative; Alessio (alias Matteo Messina Denaro)[12] stated: "I wish to tell you that I am for dialogue and pacification as you asked me and I respect your will, for how it has always been" (Palazzolo and Prestipino 2007: 186).

Historian Jean Hébrard (1991: 197) affirms the positive impact that writing can have in regulating violence: "correspondence allows for the avoidance of direct confrontation, to sweeten relations of dependence, to introduce forms of rudimentary civility in potential conflicts, and perhaps also to put law on one's side." It seems then that the appropriation of writing by a group that, up to that point, had banned it is a sign that presages a "civilizing process" (Elias 2000). The use of the letter as instrument to neutralize conflict—to affix a doxa, to avoid the uncontrolled proliferation of rumor, to dissolve inner controversies before they degenerate—avoids the recourse to murder that, after the bloody 1980s, was now again reserved for correcting the irreparable. Writing appears at the height of violence, in a process that finds a corollary in the Catholic world, when exercises written by mystical saints came to substitute bloody penitentiary practices (Albert 1997: 399–400). A new principle of action, a new rule is affirmed at the heart of Cosa Nostra: before one spills blood, it is better first to let rivers of ink flow. In this move the relationship of equivalence between rite of initiation and criminal practice seems to have been reversed.

According to legal sources and corroborated by the declarations of several pentiti, 1993 was marked not only by an inversion in the use of violence but also by a drastic reduction in the traditional rites of initiation. This internal transformation of Cosa Nostra, which seems to have modified both the modalities of admission and the boundary of the organization, led anti-mafia magistrates to re-define the criteria by which they characterized the mafia universe, and thus to recognize all of Provenzano's correspondents as "organic" elements of the association. For the magistracy, the mafia was thus no longer defined as "the organization of all those who have sworn their allegiance" (Arlacchi 1992: 26) to it but the clandestine web constituted by the circulation of *pizzini*.

12. Matteo Messina Denaro is considered as the new head of Cosa Nostra, after Provenzano's arrest in April 2006.

This raises an important question: have these writings perhaps replaced the blood pact sealed with the Madonna[13] and become the "shared substance" that allows members of Cosa Nostra to think of themselves and constitute themselves as brothers?[14]

There are many episodes in Cosa Nostra's history that confirm the force of its previous prohibition on writing. To cite just two: the man of honor Michele Cavataio was killed in the Viale Lazio massacre in 1969 for having in his possession an organizational chart of the Palermo mafia families; and in 1970 a coup attempt by Prince Valerio Borghese in collaboration with mafioso Luciano Liggio failed when mafiosi refused to provide them with a list of all affiliated members (Arlacchi 1992: 75, 98). Indeed, the passage from interdiction to promotion of writing produces a reconfiguration of existing power relations.[15] From a homicidal communion to a communion of writers, the founding contract of a fraternity of equals (at least formally) is transformed into a paternalistic system in which the hierarchy of men of honor is defined according to their nearness or distance, in epistolary terms, from the supreme leader. The Provenzano Code,[16] as was well understood by the magistrates who found and deciphered the boss's letters, is first and foremost a social code.

The silent action of *pizzini*

Inside an extensively underlined and annotated Bible, which the police found in a small hut in which Provenzano lived, was the following *pizzino*:

---

13. See Albert-Llorca (1993: 199) on written communication with Catholic divinities as "contract." It is worth noting that in Sicily *pizzini* are also written messages sent to saints to ask for intercession.
14. Herrou (2008: 43) suggests that the diffusion of religious texts in communities of Taoist monks could play a similar role in creating a brotherhood. I used the expression "consanguinity of texts" in relation to an Aragonese community torn apart by memories of the conflict of the Spanish Civil War where scripts of a religious drama were circulated and established blood relations (Puccio-Den 2009: 48–52).
15. See Goody (1977) on hierarchical reorganizations prompted by the introduction of writing in societies with oral traditions.
16. I here refer to the title of Palazzolo and Prestipino's book, *Il codice Provenzano* (2007).

In any place, or part of the world, in which I find myself, in any hour
I might have to communicate with Y....Be they words, opinion, facts,
writing. To ask God his suggestion, guidance, assistance; that His will
be done. Order may arrive to be executed for the Common Good.
(Palazzolo and Prestipino 2007: 266)

It was this *pizzino* that gave rise to the hypothesis that Cosa Nostra was strategically using the Scriptures for its communications. Read
from an anthropologist's point of view, this fragment of "correspondence
with the Heavens" returns us to the question of the relationship between
mafia and religion: How should we understand professions of faith and
acts of devotion made by mafiosi? What role should we assign to the cult
objects and the holy books with which they surround themselves, and
which follow them into the intimacy of their hideouts? By considering
them as external signs of a "superficial religiosity,"[17] we would fall prey
to a moral prejudice, ignoring the possibility of a deeper dimension of
at least some of these devotional manifestations. Given the case that
interests us here, if we cannot penetrate the inner motivation of someone like Provenzano—just as it is difficult to look inside the inner self
of any other human being—then we at least need to understand which
connections can be established between practices of writing that put religion into play and other aspects of the life of the Cosa Nostra boss: the
administration of a vast web of affairs, the management of crime, the
necessity of justifying it—even to himself—and the self-legitimation of
the mafia enterprise.

The incipit of Provenzano's letters is always the same: "Dearest, with
the wish that this will find you in Excellent Health, as I can tell you of
myself," and the same goes for the closing: "May the Lord Bless you
and protect you."[18] It is this fixed character that ensures the "sacrality
of the statements of power" in the kind of language that characterizes
totalitarian regimes (Fabre 1997: 39). We might say that these fixed formulas constitute the "ceremonial conditions of performativity" (Charuty
2008: 34) of the *pizzini*: through them, these bits of paper, typed on an

---

17. Alessandra Dino (2008: 67), an important point of reference for studies of
the relationship between mafia and religion, defines the religiosity of the
mafiosi in terms of "morality of exteriority."

18. Apart from the *pizzini* published in Palazzolo and Prestipino (2007), I have
been able to consult a collection of around three hundred *pizzini* collected
as part of the prosecution of Provenzano by prosecutor De Lucia.

Olivetti typewriter as mere, humble administrative dispatches, assume a liturgical solemnity. Hybridizing sacrality and familiarity, these missives recall the founding model of an epistolary genre in the Catholic world: St. Paul's epistles. One finds the same rhetorical artifice to establish communication on an otherwise asymmetric plane, the same "formulas of institutional humility" to compensate for such asymmetry, the same jurisprudential role assigned to letters (Boureau 1991: 131–137). And it is entirely possible that these parallels were not lost on the Cosa Nostra boss, who was an assiduous, almost compulsive, reader of the Bible.

The *pizzini* became legal documents and served as arguments from authority in reunions that the highest levels of mafiosi held in absence of their "boss of bosses,"[19] read aloud and subjected to a form of collective exegesis that made the proceedings recall the Apostles commenting on the word of Christ. It is worth noting that part of the unease we feel in reading Provenzano's letters derives from the fact that they were meant to be read aloud, as discursive means whose operativity was tied to the social and performative context for which they were produced. Circumscribed by religious formulas, these humble scraps let slip references to legal language, another model of authentification and legitimation for the Cosa Nostra boss: "Seek the truth before speaking, and remember that it is never enough to have a single form of proof to reason with; to be certain in one's reasoning, one needs three forms of proof, in addition to correctness and coherence"; or, "We have to be patient, wait to hear the other bell, after which we see what needs to be done" (Palazzolo and Prestipino 2007: 203, 209). Prosecutor Prestipino commented: "Power is exercised in the contradiction of parts."

This aloof position allowed Provenzano to impose his will by obscuring his power. He managed to occupy such power mobilizing one of the most powerful argumentative levers of epistolary writing (Boureau 1991: 147), distance and the presumption of objectivity, so much so that the letters seemed to intervene in answer to external demands: "I, with the will of God, want to be a servant; command me, and if possible, with calm and reservation, we can see how to proceed"; or, "If he knows that you are the holder, why do you go through me? I am not interested that things go through me. If they need to, or wish to go through me, like you, I am born to serve" (Palazzolo and Prestipino 2007: 203, 230). In truth,

---

19. I have been able to read transcriptions of some of these reunions in the legal files related to Operation Gotha during which several of Cosa Nostra bosses were arrested on June 20, 2006.

Provenzano presented (imposed) himself as the indispensable mediator through which to resolve all the problems that coursed through the association, even (and especially) the most banal ones, because that is how power insinuates itself:[20]

> They sought me because a hammer of ours was stolen, along with two welders, which I ask you to find out about, and communicate with me, not directly to them…tell me so I might communicate it to those who recommended them. (Palazzolo and Prestipino 2007: 175)

Since the origin of the mafia phenomenon (Blok 1974), mediation has been a principal function of the Cosa Nostra. Indeed, the latter was the only association to have institutionalized, in different forms but systematically and with continuity, an entity—the Commission—that was in charge of solving conflicts between its different families. This function was at least partially performed by Provenzano's correspondence. But this boss of Cosa Nostra had a very particular style: "I hope with the will of God to fix a bit everything I can do for you, for everyone;" "we have to limit ourselves and to accommodate Divine Providence by the means that it allows us;" "but we pray to our good God, that He may guide us to do Good works. For everyone" (Palazzolo and Prestipino 2007: 141–142, 139). As far as we can see, the mediation proposed by Provenzano was not violent, but insidiously sweet, like the presence in Sicilian society of Cosa Nostra during the period when Provenzano, under the nickname *Zio Binnu* (Uncle Bernardo), was directing it (1993–2006). Or maybe sweetness was only the mask of the violence that threatens to explode in certain rare missives: "In hoping that I have been as clear as possible, I conclude my letter, and with the will of God, that this may reach you because it is a bomb" (Palazzolo and Prestipino 2007: 188) Also, Provenzano's rhetoric always called into account other "contacts" (in mafia parlance) higher than him: "My adored Lord Jesus Christ, teach us how to understand and speak as the spirit of God and the spirit of Christ do. I pray that you show me spiritual things" (Palazzolo and Prestipino 2007: 266).

This aspect of absolving oneself from any responsibility, or of transferring responsibility to other beings, real or transcendent, may well have its roots in Catholicism:

---

20. See Foucault (1995) on the "infinitely small" of political power.

Because—as Judge Scarpinato explains—in Catholic religion the relationship with God is managed by a "cultural mediator," a priest,
and every social segment expresses from within a "cultural mediator"
that consents to an unproblematic rapport with God. (Scarpinato
and Mongovero 2012: 159–181)

Nino Fasullo, priest and member of the Congregation of the Most
Holy Redeemer who has for years engaged the question of the attitude
of the Catholic church toward the mafia, goes further and locates the
foundation of mafiosi religion in "a theology founded on the assumption
of the point of view of God." The result of this doctrine, he states, "is not
so much to lower God to the level of the mafioso, but to heighten the
mafioso to the plane of God" (Fasullo 1996: 43). In so doing, the mafioso
becomes a divinity on earth who enjoys excellent relations with God and
is an incontestable interpreter and scrupulous executor of the divine will.
Forms of veneration have been noticed even for other Cosa Nostra bosses,
such as Messina Denaro, nicknamed *lu Siccu* in Sicilian (*il secco* or "the thin
one") who was invoked as a saint: *a lu Siccu lo dobbiamo adorare* (we have
to adore *lu Siccu*); *lu beni veni di lu Siccu* (all good comes from lu Siccu),
or *lu vulissi viriri almeno un momento* (I would like to see him for a single
moment) (Dino 2008: 73). The nicknames attributed to mafia bosses—for
example, *il papa* (the Pope) for Michele Greco, *U Signuri* (the Lord) for
Antonino Mangano, and *Madre Nature* (Mother Nature) for Giuseppe
Graviano—suggest a popular will to recognize in them superior beings.
But what made Provenzano set up a hierarchically organized web of small
and large mediators or "messengers," all under his direct command, was
the systematization of what Bloch (2004: 128–137) calls "deference," a
principle of delegation of authority. This linguistic expedient, employed in
ritual action, in which actors are used to motivate their actions by reference to abstract entities like "our ancestors" or "traditions," is a powerful
mechanism of de-responsibilization. Silent instruments of surreptitious
mafia action, the *pizzini* are a spiritual exercise of detachment from the
act performed.

For Provenzano, the *pizzini* inserted themselves into a process of as-
cension, one that was not only political but also metaphysical. First of all
this was because the scribe enjoyed a panoptic perspective, seeing that he
painstakingly archived not only all letters he received but also copies of all
those he had sent: like God, he was omnipotent because he was omnisci-
ent. Like the divine eye, he saw all but remained invisible. The humble
writing activity inscribed itself, then, in a much wider spiritual project,

following a Christian tradition in which writing and atonement went hand in hand,[21] mimicked by the withdrawal of the boss, living off bitter herbs, dressing poorly, and finding solace in shepherds' huts. Finally, the paper trail was a guarantee of the "rightness" of calculations (Gardey 2008: 224–227), an accounting of human and divine justice. Through it, Provenzano could identify himself with the God of the reparation theology who rigorously allocates punishment in proportion to sin, "keeps count, weighs, calculates." As Fasullo (1996: 44) explains: "The mafia right to kill is an integral part of a geometric culture of order, of debt and duty, of precision and punishment, of payment and of balance." It is probably for this daily act that the "boss of all bosses" was nicknamed *u ragiunieri* (the accountant) and previously, when still working alongside the "beast" Riina, *u tratturi* (the tractor). It is a conversion of power from an exercise of brute violence, mechanically quashing everything in its path, into an authority that imposes itself mutedly, through small acts of writing, accounting, and measurement, that the *pizzini* seem to have miraculously and magisterially accomplished.

Provenzano did not use the strength of writing in the manner of the anti-mafia movement or the anti-mafia judges, namely to order or clarify the meaning of things. Rather, he perverted the power of writing to hide the real power behind his religious formula and kind advice. Writing was a means of silencing other men of honor, to impose his personal decisions *as if* they came from somewhere or someone else: Providence, Bible, God. Provenzano preferred to write than to speak because he could leave much more unspoken in letters than in speech. The men of honor, as well as the magistrates and experts who deciphered them, became exegetes of what was implied in these small pieces of paper, thereby soundlessly crafting and solidifying relationships of power between themselves and their boss.

Mafiacraft proposes an anthropological paradigm for thinking about the mafia, as well as other phenomena linked to power and its relation to language and silence. Intimidation, *omertà,* and subjugation, the three forms of behavior that jurist La Torre identified to define the mafia—in its essence, we could say—are spread across many other non-Italian and non-criminal contexts. Mafiacraft is thus a study of the *form of silence,* and its substance. We have explored the latter through various social, legal, and cognitive tools developed to combat the mafia in Italy since the 1970s, when to pronounce, write, or photograph the word "mafia"

---

21. See Albert (1997, chap. 9) on the case of mystical saints.

was a revolutionary act, literally something *unheard*, an aggression and transgression of a taboo, comparable to removing the mask of a masked individual during carnival (Puccio 2002). Mafiacraft ends with a writing act accomplished by a man of honor, showing the path traveled and the reversal achieved: weakened by public protests and state repression, the Cosa Nostra is now summoned to provide for itself evidence of its existence.

I set out from the ethnographic observation of different contexts and milieus (activist, associative, legal, judicial, civic) in which there lurked behind the question "What is the mafia?" another question: how to construct the *know-how* and *know-how-to-say* relevant to and effective for breaking the silence. This led me to see what this silence is *made* of, how it is maintained, and what, in turn, it allows to be maintained. At this juncture, it seems possible to conclude that silence enables the maintenance of a state of *semantic uncertainty*, which also has a very high degree of performativity because it allows everything to be done, and someone to do it, without anyone being responsible for it, thus facilitating all kinds of violence. There is a subtle difference between whether it is done *without being known* or *without being made known*, one that is linked to "good faith" or "bad faith" and to the belief and power systems associated with it (Ogilvie 2006). The latter are also based on speech and non-speech acts or speech "acts of silence" (Basso 1970) that anthropologists can describe and analyze. This, at least, is the challenge that Mafiacraft, an ethnography of deadly silence, has set itself.

Forms of extreme violence can creep in and nestle within this uncertain space between speech and silence, but also creative ways of being in the world, as I have shown in other works on art (Delle Notti and Puccio-Den 2016), on the night (Puccio-Den 2016), and on dance (Puccio-Den 2017b). Mafiacraft is thus one stage of a larger, multidimensional project that aims not only to deal with phenomena that evade qualification (and thus scientific description) but also to invent innovative and creative methodological tools to empower ethnographers dealing with "invisible things" (Puccio-Den forthcoming).

Invisible things

> Of all the changes of language a traveler in distant lands must face,
> none equals that which waits him in the City of Hypatia, because the change regards not words, but things.
> —Italo Calvino, *Invisible Cities*

In Italo Calvino's novel *Invisible Cities*, Marco Polo tells Kublai Khan that a traveler should not be concerned with finding correspondences between words and things when coming across novel places but rather consider that one word may address two different things. Likewise, when the anthropologist faces questions such as "Am I closer to a jaguar than to another man?" or "May we share some qualities with mountains or forests?" (cf. Descola 2013), he or she is probing systems of categorization of the real and the unreal, challenging the boundaries between visible and invisible things. Embarking on a similar ontological and epistemological revisitation of the umbrella term "mafia" was the actual challenge of the Mafiacraft project.

Take the following example. A judge asks the defendant Mini at the 1883 Amoroso trial, "Weren't you part of the mafia?" and the defendant replies, "I don't know what that means." One could be tempted to gloss the response as a lie. This excerpt from a historical trial, the epigraph to Henner Hess's (1998) book about the mafia, was never subject to a proper scrutiny to understand what Mini's dismissal of signification entailed. Neither have any anthropologists who followed Hess tackled this task. One could then begin by associating the function of the signifier "mafia" with the reflections on mana terms by Lévi-Strauss (1987: 62–63) who notes how some systems of signification are sustained by semantic vacuums, allegedly empty signifiers, or notions capable of incorporating all kinds of meanings and laying the groundwork for the invisible substance of power. Geschiere (2010: 234) has a similar concern when he approaches such a fleeting subject as witchcraft: "a panacea concept of considerable power, because of its kaleidoscopic character; and anthropological writings seem to reinforce this tendency rather than to defuse it." The words "mafia" and "witchcraft" share the same semantic ambiguity: this is where lies their performative power of terrifying by threatening social, political, or religious life with unpredictable harm. But we must be careful not to confuse the analysis with the dispositions of the topic.

In order to clarify what we, social scientists, mean when we refer to witchcraft, let us return to the concept's origins. When explaining the genesis of witchcraft as a term which, "used loosely in Tudor and Stewart England,…applied to virtually every kind of magical activity or ritual operation that worked by occult methods," Keith Thomas (1970: 48–49) pointed out that, at a certain moment in history, the "bewildering variety of semantic usage" of the term was subsumed by a religious category with legal consequences, the "heretical belief—Devil Worship." In 1982, the Rognoni–La Torre law—a watershed moment for Mafiacraft—introduced the "mafia" into the penal code, completing the work of endless interpretation of this word, which served the mafia's own cunning purposes. Witchcraft can, however, be approached as a discursive formation, to scrutinize how the deployment of the term has had political effects. This was the approach followed by Ginzburg (2002) when casting light on phenomena such as "witch trials," comparing the repression of terrorism to a "witch hunt." The same was true for the fight against the mafia (Sciascia 2002). At this level, witchcraft acts as a historical metaparadigm illustrating how social facts founded on mere conjectures have been stabilized by the use of legal categories and repressive measures—as was the case for popular practices associated with witchcraft and witches, before being criminalized by the Inquisition (Ginzburg 1980, 1983). In a similar fashion, Mafiacraft aims to become an anthropological metaparadigm describing how a range of real and widespread illegal practices (thus, aggression, extortion, smuggling, money laundering, fraud, murder), concealed by government complicity, have been tolerated or considered as more or less nonexistent by certain groups, and have been publicly "grouped" or "counted-as-one" by others, to borrow Alain Badiou's (2005: 4) famous concept. This social "counting-as-one" has given full consistency to a new signifier where the mafia is a special kind of criminal association and a mafioso is a member of a mafia-type association.

By translating mafia into another term such as criminal organization, we would incur the same problem affecting early anthropologists who attempted to translate mana into energy, merely replacing a floating signifier (Lévi-Strauss 1987: 63) with an equally mysterious thing: Our Thing, Cosa Nostra. After Geschiere (1998: 1253) criticized witchcraft as a reductive term for a set of African notions that could be better represented by more neutral concepts such as "occult force" or "special energy," he came to recognize that the widespread use of this wording by Africans makes it impossible to avoid it in anthropological analyses. Let us recall also that Ludwig Wittgenstein (2009: 270) questions another floating signifier, imagination: "One ought to ask," he writes, "not what images are or what goes on when one imagines something, but how the word 'imagination' is used." As invisible wrongdoing, witchcraft and mafia occupy the same ontological space of those things whose very existence is put into doubt, sources of misunderstandings between outsiders and insiders who "may have other things on their minds" (Geschiere 2010: 235) when referring to these words. That is why the first step of Mafiacraft was an extensive ethnographic survey on the multifarious ways in which the word "mafia" was translated, interpreted, and used in different contexts. Being more interested in this process of translation than in the "real" meaning of the word, I deferred the issue of what the mafia *is* to obtain a better understanding of how the word *works* (mafia-craft). This was the first task of Mafiacraft as an alternative methodology for investigating the mafia phenomenon.

Maybe a better understanding of the mafia phenomenon could be obtained by an acknowledgment that some topics—such as witchcraft or mafia—require one to adopt a position of "epistemological pluralism" (Geschiere 2001: 645) which recognizes for some things the (magical) faculty of being and not being at the same time (Jewsiewicki 2001: 626). Maybe if social scientists are finally unable to find a proper answer to the question "Does the mafia exist?" it is because they are taking a "*regard scholastique*" (Geschiere 2010: 249), trying to objectify social facts that, like witchcraft or mafia, draw their strength from the ambiguity of their ontology. And maybe, to clarify the ontological issue at stake regarding the mafia, we have to analyze questions that arise when we tackle other invisible things. When I studied the Virgin Mary (Puccio-Den 2009: 183-230), it was not in order to decide whether the Virgin Mary exists or not. It was rather to interrogate how social actors make the Virgin Mary exist: by which devices, acts, gestures, things, and words. It was rather to understand in which ontology, or in which regime of reality or truth, the Virgin Mary does exist. As stated by Herzfeld (2005, 47), "inasmuch as facts are constructions of realities, they have the same ontological status as other perceived realities." Designed as a material history of moral ideas, Mafiacraft describes ethnographically how the anti-mafia, as a movement claiming the existence of the mafia, was a Copernican knowledge revolution made of concrete actions, operating procedures, tangible objects, legal devices, and work practices to make the mafia exist. Mafiacraft focuses on the ontological consequences of these activities, whether grassroots or institutional, not to decide on the existence or nonexistence of the mafia but in order to describe the ontologies in the minds of the social and political actors involved. In the next step, Mafiacraft is a program for ethnographically capturing the silence by focusing on the mechanisms used to deny reality based on the hypothesis that the work or labor of silence—to adopt the helpful term suggested by Marco Santoro (2019)—defines the terms in which the mafia *exists*.

Another qualification is in order regarding the complex relationship between talk and silence. I have previously underlined some epistemological similarities between witchcraft and Mafiacraft; nonetheless these ethnographic devices deal with two different levels of reality and thus require two specific methods. "Witchcraft" may be employed as an analytical concept, a paradigm shaped by ethnographic theory to scrutinize discourses (Favret-Saada 1980) or speech acts such as rumors (Bonhomme 2016) aimed to generate performative malicious effects. "To talk, in witchcraft, is never to inform," writes Favret-Saada (1980: 9–10):

> informing an ethnographer, that is, someone who claims to have no intention of using the information, but naïvely wants to know for the sake of knowing, is literally unthinkable....Similarly, it is unthinkable that people can talk for the sake of talking.

Favret-Saada goes on to argue that what Malinowski called "phatic communication"—allegedly purposeless speech acts and polite small talk—does not exist in the Bocage, the French countryside where she did her fieldwork. Rather, she argues, "when interlocutors for whom witchcraft is involved talk about nothing (that is about anything except what really matters) it is to emphasize the violence of what is not being talked about" (Favret-Saada 1980: 10). Deadly words thus contain the seed of a theory of performativity of deadly silences or, one could rather argue, a reflection on the violence of non-definitional speech acts. Mafiacraft aims to explore ethnographically how such speech "acts of silence" (Basso 1970) and circumlocution (which Mini's answer to the judge epitomizes) have constituted the mafia reality and mode of existence.

Mafiacraft follows the footsteps of the research perspectives opened by Basso (1970: 226) by describing and analyzing specific acts of silence in such situations where "the status of the focal participant is marked by ambiguity." But it underlines the political implications of this ambiguity. This is where it feeds into a political anthropology of silence, by aiming to inquire how non-definitional states constructed by a pragmatic use of silence create, manipulate, or reinforce dissymmetry. This construct, "craft," or labor, is precisely the work of the mafia: Mafiacraft. Here two levels of reality have to be distinguished: while the social representation of the mafia is shaped by words and images, mafia as such is shaped by silence. Thus, anti-mafia wording processes make the mafia exist, para-doxically, at the same time as they dissolve the mafia's power to exist through silence—through silent acts (*omertà*), silent threats (intimida-tions), and silent obedience (subjugation) that substantiate its existence.

Earlier scholars, such as Di Bella (2008), have acknowledged the work of silence as a type of speech act in Sicily. However, Di Bella's work lo-cates silence's matrix in Sicilian "popular culture" or folklore. In my work, I refuse to categorize silence as a sort of "folk act" but illustrate how it has become a modality of political action. Drawing on Mitchell's (2006) seminal article, Mafiacraft is an anthropological survey that examines the political process through which the powerful distinction between the state and the mafia has been produced, taking seriously the elusiveness of the boundary between these two entities, and analyzing their co-con-struction. Mafiacraft considers the efforts to demarcate this boundary as a "technique" of the modern state, alerting us to the role played by social scientists in reinforcing this distinction. The state's contribution to this "craft work" calls for a refined model of the state's action. If witchcraft could be deployed by different state powers as a coercive apparatus to invent innocent victims and occult practices, and qualify them as witches and witchcraft, in our Mafiacraft the state is constantly subject to an ideological splitting: some institutional representatives have decided to conceal a cluster of criminal activities through silence, while others have worked to expose these wrongdoings and build conceptual categories, concrete devices, and legal tools able to grasp the mafiosi and bring them to justice. Mafiacraft illustrates this dual-track process: what mafia does with silence is inferred by what anti-mafia undoes with words. Speech acts and writing events pave the way to confronting the power of silence that could be studied through the entire spectrum of its figures: the unsaid, the tacit, the implicit, the denied.

Much work has been done by historians, sociologists, and anthropologists that provides insights into the "historical and political conditions" (Schneider 2019: 625) of the emergence, and current vitality, of the mafia: my critical stance by no means aims to diminish their substantial contributions to the debate. I am rather concerned with the epistemological implications of certain ex-post descriptions of mafia events perceived as stemming from precise historical, social, and economic situations, which could provide a biased view of the inferential chain. In other words—drawing on Roussel's analysis of the transformation of the practices of magistrates with the increase of political-financial scandals in France from the 1990s onward—we should not succumb to the "retrospective illusion" (Roussel 2002: 283) of social and political conditions that could be themselves conditioned by other factors. Mafiacraft points out the radical transformation of categories of knowledge entailed by the advent of a new generation of lawyers, magistrates, and investigators. As in Giovanni Levi's (1988) book *Inheriting Power: The Story of an Exorcist*, Mafiacraft is a new narrative where the focus is shifted to the agency and the creativity of some social actors (Geschiere 1998: 1271), like Judge Falcone whose description of the mafia phenomenon modified once and for all its ontological status (no one in Italy nowadays is allowed to posit that the mafia does not exist). Mafiacraft is not a criticism but a reconsideration of current approaches to the mafia phenomenon that aspires to become an alternative project. As an anthropological program of research, it seizes the opportunity to take a different perspective on the mafia, one which does not view it solely as a phenomenon linked to a specific historical and political context.

The real and urgent problem about the mafia was how to address it from a legal point of view; which implied the question of how to cope with the "semiotic force of specific acts of silence" (Herzfeld 2019: 620) like intimidations or implicit instigations to kill. This was the work of "responsibilization" (Walker 2019: 638), a term grounded in a wide range of legal and moral processes (Lacey 2016) that challenge our neoliberal models of description of the self. It is striking that direct interventions by some African states, notably Cameroon, in witchcraft affairs (Geschiere 1998) are coeval with the emergence of mafia trials in Italy. Similarly to witchcraft, the mafia is possibly one of the "ways in which people try to cope with the baffling modern changes" (Geschiere 2010: 247) produced by the birth of centralized nations. Similarly to witchcraft in African countries, the use of the term "mafia" was disqualified for "primitivizing" (Geschiere 2010: 235) Sicily, a region at the periphery of Italy's modernization. The global dimension of the mafia phenomenon is well known (Armao 2000; U. Santino 2007), but there have been few attempts in anthropology at examining the specific linkages between mafia and globalization (Campana 2011; Varese 2012), as does Geschiere (2010: 246) when interpreting witchcraft as a device for articulating the local and the global scale, the periphery and the center, traditions and the market. Such innovative frameworks for interpreting the mafia phenomenon were firstly elaborated by judges such as Falcone than by anthropologists. Mafiacraft is grounded in this effort to withdraw the mafia from its archaizing and "local" settings, showing how pervasively silence acts in the political strategies of modern states.

Witchcraft is in the realm of religion what the mafia is in the realm of politics: a discursive reality (but not only) that emerged concurrently to the metanarrative called "modernity" for supporting modern forms of power through the efficacy of the secret (Geschiere 2010: 251). Mafiacraft has the ambition of opening the debate about the mafia to these issues of moral and political anthropology. Now it is time to show how the mafia topic should renew such themes as responsibility (Puccio-Den 2017a). In regard to the difference between witchcraft and Mafiacraft, I already noted that both concepts are employed to address what Douglas (1980: 49–73) called "systems of accountability." In a collection entitled *Competing Responsibilities: The Ethics and Politics of Contemporary Life*, Susanna Trnka and Catherine Trundle (2017) have underlined how neoliberal rhetoric reifies the "responsible subject," thus minimizing the myriad forms of individual and collective responsibility with which people may engage in their everyday lives. Questioning responsibility thus opens up new avenues that lay the groundwork for future work about the clash of normative systems in a neoliberal state. This could stimulate a reflexive critique on the global scale about how compulsory worldwide norms clash with local conceptions and practices of accountability, inserting the mafia, and *omertà*, within a wider debate on legal pluralism.

Omertà is an ideological device defining the very borders of humanity. For the people affected by the (non-)speech act of *omertà*, mafia's strategic use of silence upsets the very idea of humanity and human rights, the bases of democracy and of the rule of law. The issue at stake regarding "responsibilization" is: How does a democratic state, with a judiciary inspired by the liberal principle of strictly personal liability, deal with the problems linked to the judgment of a collective entity, the mafia? Responsibility could be interpreted as a speech regime at the opposite end of the spectrum of silence. The former supposes a speech act whereby the "I" is the privileged point of view of the agent on his or her actions. Thus, let us assume that silence does not allow this kind of speech act, leaving the action in a state of indeterminacy about its author. That is crucial with regard to the collective entity or form of criminal action that is of interest to us. Responsibility—as a new quality of action that the Italian state demanded from the mafiosi when they were held accountable for their criminal acts—put into question honor as a collective good and shared substance ("Our Thing"). What is at stake with "responsibilization" is a profound alteration of the ontology of the action when the mafiosi were forced to respond individually for acts they had committed collectively within the social, moral, and cognitive framework of Cosa Nostra. Studying ontological changes in a specific context is thus a way of considering ontologies as not fixed once and for all. It is a method of introducing temporalities in structures.

The mafia challenges the categories of knowledge shaped by the state. Many magistrates, politicians, lawyers, activists, and ordinary citizens have paid an actual and high price for changing perceptions of and mindsets regarding the mafia. Debates on this issue, when genuine, are always highly controversial. So was Mafiacraft (Ferme 2019). Hopefully the strength of anthropology as a mode of critical thinking will live up to this challenge.

References

Abate, Ida. 1997. *Il piccolo Giudice: Profilo di Rosario Livatino*. Messina: Armando Siciliano.

Accati, Luisa. 1998. *Il mostro e la bella: Padre e madre nell'educazione cattolica dei sentimenti*. Milan: Raffaello Cortina.

Agamben, Giorgio. 2000. *Le temps qui reste*. Paris: Rivages.

———. 2002. *L'aperto: L'uomo e l'animale*. Turin: Bollati Boringhieri.

Albera, Dionigi, Anton Blok, and Christian Bromberger. 2001. *L'anthropologie de la Méditerranée: Anthropology of the Mediterranean*. Cahors: Maisonneuve et Larose, Maison Méditerranéenne des Sciences de l'Homme.

Albert, Jean Pierre. 1997. *Le sang et le ciel: Les saintes mystiques dans le monde chrétien*. Paris: Aubier.

Albert-Llorca, Marlène. 1993. "Le courriel du ciel." In *Écritures ordinaires*, edited by Daniel Fabre, 183–221. Paris: POL, Centre Georges Pompidou.

Alongi, Giuseppe. (1886) 1977. *La Maffia nei suoi fattori e nelle sue manifestazioni: Studio sulle classi pericolose della Sicilia*. Palermo: Sellerio.

Amurri, Sandra, ed. 1992. *L'Albero Falcone*. Palermo: Fondazione Giovanni e Francesca Falcone.

Andreotti, Giulio. 1995. *Cosa loro: Mai visti da vicino*. Milan: Rizzoli.

Anscombe, Elisabeth. 1958. *Intention*. Oxford: Blackwell.

Antolisei, Francesco. 1966. *Manuale di diritto penale*. Milan: Giuffré.

Ardener, Edwin. 1975a. "Belief and the problem of women." In *Perceiving women*, edited by Shirley Ardener, 1–17. London: Malaby Press.

———. 1975b. "The problem revisited." In *Perceiving women*, edited by Shirley Ardener, 19–27. London: Malaby Press.

Ardener, Shirley, ed. 1975. *Perceiving women*. London: Malaby Press.

Arlacchi, Pino. 1992. *Gli uomini del disonore: La mafia Siciliana nella vita del grande pentito Antonino Calderone*. Milan: Arnoldo Mondadori Editore.

———. 1994. *Addio Cosa Nostra: I segreti della mafia nella confessione di Tommaso Buscetta*. Milan: Biblioteca Universale Rizzoli.

———. 1995. *Il processo: Giulio Andreotti sotto accusa a Palermo*. Milan: Rizzoli.

———. 2007. *La mafia imprenditrice: Dalla Calabria al centro dell'inferno*. New ed. Milan: Il Saggiatore. First published as *La mafia imprenditrice: L'etica mafiosa e lo spirito del capitalismo* (Bologna: Il Mulino, 1983).

Armao, Fabio. 2000. *Il sistema mafia: Dall'economia del mondo al dominio locale*. Turin: Bollati Boringhieri.

Atkins, Chloë G. K., Keith Brownell, Jude Kornelsen, Robert Woollard, and Andrea Whiteley. 2013. "Silos of silence, stress, and suffering: Patient and physician experiences of MUPS and diagnostic uncertainty." *AJOB Neuroscience* 4 (3): 3–8. doi: 10.1080/21507740.2013.796324

Austin, John Langshaw. 1970. *Quand dire, c'est faire*. Paris: Gallimard. First published as *How to do things with words* (Oxford: Clarendon, 1962).

Badiou, Alain. 2005. *Being and event*. Translated by Oliver Feltham. London: Continuum. First published as *L'Être et l'événement* (Paris: Seuil, 1988).

Banfield, Edward C. 1958. *The moral basis of a backward society*. Glencoe: Free Press.

Barthes, Roland. 1980. *La chambre claire: Note sur la photographie*. Paris: Gallimard.

———. 2005. *Leçon: Leçon inaugurale de la chaire de sémiologie littéraire au Collège de France prononcée le 7 janvier 1977*. Paris: Seuil.

Bartolotta Impastato, Felicia. 1987. *La mafia in casa mia*. Palermo: La Luna.

Basso, Keith. 1970. "'To give up on words': Silence in western Apache culture." *Southwestern Journal of Anthropology* 26 (3): 213–230. doi: 10.1086/soutjanth.26.3.3629378

Battaglia, Letizia. 1999. *Passion, justice et liberté: Photographies de Sicile*. Arles: Actes Sud.

————, and Franco Zecchin. 1989. *Chroniques siciliennes*. Paris: Centre National de la Photographie.

————. 2006. *Dovere di cronaca/The duty to report*. Rome: Peliti associate.

Becker, Howard S. 1981. *Exploring society photographically*. Evanston: Mary and Leigh Block Gallery.

Bensa, Alban, and Eric Fassin. 2002. "Les sciences sociales face à l'événement." *Terrain: Anthropologie et sciences humaines*, no. 38: 5–20. doi: 10.4000/terrain.1888

Bernand, Carmen, and Serge Gruzinski. 1988. *De l'idolâtrie: Une archéologie des sciences religieuses*. Paris: Seuil.

Bloch, Maurice. 2004. "Ritual and deference." In *Rituals and memory: Toward a comparative anthropology of religion*, edited by Harvey Whitehouse and James Laidlaw, 128–137. Lanham: AltaMira Press.

Blok, Anton. 1974. *The mafia of a Sicilian village, 1860–1960: A study of violent peasant entrepreneurs*. New York: Harper and Row.

————. 2001a. "La mafia d'un village sicilien." *Ethnologie Française* 31 (1): 61–67. doi: 10.3917/ethn.011.0061

————. 2001b. *Honour and violence*. Cambridge: Polity.

Blumer, Hebert. 2004. "Les problèmes sociaux comme comportements collectifs." *Politix*, no. 67: 185–199. doi: 10.3406/polix.2004.1630

Boltanski, Luc. 1990. *L'amour et la justice comme competences: Trois essais de sociologie de l'action*. Paris: Métailié. Translated by Catherine Porter as *Love and justice as competences: Three essays on the sociology of action* (Cambridge: Polity Press, 2012).

————. 1993. *La souffrance à distance: Morale humanitaire, medias et politique*. Paris: Métailié.

————. 2009. *De la critique: Précis de sociologie de l'émancipation*. Paris: Gallimard.

————, and Elisabeth Claverie. 2007. "Du monde social en tant que scène d'un procès." In *Affaires, scandales et grandes causes: De Socrate à Pinochet*, edited by Luc Boltanski, Elisabeth Claverie, Nicolas Offenstadt, and Stephane van Damme, 395–452. Paris: Stock.

————, and Laurent Thévenot. 1991. *De la justification: Les économies de la grandeur*. Paris: Gallimard.

Bonhomme, Julien. 2016. *The sex thieves: Anthropology of a rumor*. Translated by Dominic Horsfall. Chicago: Hau Books. First published as *Les voleurs de sexe: anthropologie d'une rumeur africaine* (Paris: Seuil, 2009).

Bonnain, Rolande, and Fanch'Elegoët. 1978. "Les archives orales: pour quoi faire? Les archives orales. Définition." *Ethnologie Française* 8 (4): 348–355.

Bourdieu, Pierre. 1965. "The sentiment of honor in Kabyle society." In *Honor and shame: The values of Mediterranean society*, edited by John G. Peristiany, 193–241. London: Weidenfeld and Nicholson.

———. 2012. *Sur l'État: Cours au Collège de France 1989–1992*. Paris: Seuil.

Boureau, Alain. 1991. "La norme épistolaire, une invention médiévale." In *La correspondance: Les usages de la lettre au XIXème siècle*, edited by Roger Chartier, 127–157. Paris: Fayard.

Briquet, Jean-Louis. 2007. *Mafia, justice et politique en Italie: L'affaire Andreotti dans la crise de la République, 1992–2004*. Paris: Karthala.

Buscetta, Tommaso. 1999. *La mafia ha vinto*. Milan: Arnoldo Mondadori Editore.

Caisson, Max. 1995. "L'Indien, le détective et l'ethnologue." *Terrain: Anthropologie et sciences humaines*, no. 25: 113–124. doi: 10.4000/terrain.2856

Calvino, Italo. 1997. *Invisible cities*. Translated by William Weaver. London: Vintage. First published as *Le città invisibili* (Turin: Einaudi, 1972).

Campana, Paolo. 2011. "Eavesdropping on the mob: The functional diversification of mafia activities across territories." *European Journal of Criminology* 8 (3): 213–228. doi: 10.1177/1477370811403442

Campana, Paolo. 2013. "Understanding then responding to Italian organized crime operations across territories." *Policing: A Journal of Policy and Practice* 7 (3): 316–325. doi: 10.1093/police/pat012

Catanzaro, Raimondo. 1992. *Men of respect: A social history of the Sicilian mafia*. New York: Free Press.

Catino, Maurizio. 2019. *Mafia organizations: The visible hand of criminal enterprise*. Cambridge: Cambridge University Press.

Champeyrache, Clotilde. 2007. *Les sociétés du crime: Un tour du monde des mafias*. Paris: CNRS Éditions.

Charuty, Giordana. 2008. "Les scènes du texte." In *Du corps au texte: Approches comparatives*, edited by Brigitte Baptandier and Giordana Charuty. Nanterre: Société d'Ethnologie.

Chinnici, Giorgio. 1992. "Processi per omicidio a Palermo." In *Gabbie vuote: Processi per omicidio a Palermo dal 1983 al maxiprocesso*, edited by Giorgio Chinnici, Umberto Santino, Giovanni La Fiura, and Ugo Adragna, 202–224. Milan: Franco Angeli.

————, Umberto Santino, Giovanni La Fiura, and Ugo Adragna. 1992. *Gabbie vuote: Processi per omicidio a Palermo dal 1983 al maxiprocesso*. Milan: Franco Angeli.

Chinnici, Rocco. 2006a. "Mafia: Aspetti e problemi giuridici e giudiziari." In *Rocco Chinnici: L'inventore del "pool" antimafia*, edited by Leone Zingales, 21–39. Arezzo: Limina.

————. 2006b. "L'acquisizione della prova nei processi di mafia." In *Rocco Chinnici: L'inventore del "pool" antimafia*, edited by Leone Zingales, 57–69. Arezzo: Limina.

Claverie, Élisabeth. 1992. "Sainte indignation contre indignation éclairée: L'affaire du Chevalier de La Barre." *Ethnologie française* 22 (3): 271–290.

————. 1994. "Procès, Affaire, Cause: Voltaire et l'indignation critique." *Politix* 26: 76–85.

————. 1998. "La naissance d'une forme politique: L'affaire du Chevalier de la Barre." In *Critique et affaires de blasphème à l'époque des Lumières*, edited by Jacques Cheyronnaud and Philippe Roussin, 185–260. Paris: Honoré Champion.

Clifford, James. 1996. *Malaise dans la culture: L'ethnographie, la littérature et l'art au XXe siècle*. Paris: École nationale supérieure des Beaux-Arts.

————, and George Marcus, eds. 1986. *Writing culture: The poetics and politics of ethnography*. Berkeley: University of California Press.

Cohen, Yves. 1997. "Des lettres comme action: Staline au début des années 1930 vu depuis le fonds Kaganovic." *Cahiers du Monde Russe* 38 (3): 307–345.

Conord, Sylvaine. 2007. "Usages et fonctions de la photographie." *Ethnologie Française* 37 (1): 11–22. doi: 10.3917/ethn.071.0011

Corbier, Mireille. 2006. *Donner à voir, donner à lire: Mémoire et communication dans la Rome ancienne*. Paris: CNRS.

Crotty, Michael. 1996. *Phenomenology and nursing research*. Sydney: Churchill Livingstone.

D'Agati, Mauro. 2010. *Napule shot*. Göttingen: Steidl Books.

D'Ambrosio, Loris. 2002. *Testimoni e collaboratori di giustizia*. Padua: CEDAM.

Davidson, Donald. 2001. *Inquiries into truth and interpretation*. Oxford: Oxford University Press.

———. 2008. *Actions et événements*. Translated by Pascal Engel. Paris: Presses Universitaires de France. First published as *Essays on actions and events* (Oxford: Clarendon, 1980).

De Certeau, Michel. 1982. "Corps mysticus ou le corps manquant." In *La fable mystique*, Vol. 1. Paris: Gallimard.

Delle Notti, Gherardo, and Deborah Puccio-Den. 2016. "Topografía de la noche: La nocturnidad de un magistrado antimafia." In *Las cosas de la noche: Una mirada diferente*, edited by Aurore Monod-Becquelin and Jacques Galinier, 67–75. Mexico: Centro de Estudios Mexicanos y Mesoamericanos.

Descola, Philippe. 2013. *Beyond nature and culture*. Translated by Janet Lloyd. Chicago: University of Chicago Press. First published as *Par-delà nature et culture* (Paris: Gallimard, 2005).

De Sutter, Laurent. 2016. *Théorie du kamikaze*. Paris: PUF.

Di Bella, Maria Pia. 2008. *Dire ou taire en Sicile*. Paris: Éditions du Félin.

Dickie, John. 2006. *Cosa Nostra*. Bari: Editori Laterza.

Didi-Huberman, Georges. 2009. *Quand les images prennent position*. Paris: Les Éditions de Minuit.

Di Lello, Giuseppe. 1994. *Giudici*. Palermo: Sellerio.

Di Lorenzo, Maria. 2000. *Rosario Livatino: Martire della giustizia*. Rome: Paoline.

DiMaggio, Paul J., and Walter W. Powell. 1983. "The iron cage revisited: Institutional isomorphism and collective rationality in organizational fields." *American Sociological Review* 48 (2): 147–160. doi: 10.2307/2095101

Dino, Alessandra. 2002. *Mutazioni: Etnografia del mondo di Cosa Nostra*. Palermo: La Zisa.

———. 2006 "'Ai pentiti non credo…': La percezione sociale dei collaboratori di giustizia in Sicilia." In *Pentiti: I collaboratori di giustizia, le istituzioni, l'opinione pubblica*, edited by Alessandra Dino, 209–256. Rome: Donzelli Editore.

———. 2008. *La mafia devota: Chiesa, religione, Cosa Nostra*. Bari: Editori Laterza.

———, ed. 2009. *Criminalità dei potenti e metodo mafioso*. Milano: Mimesis Edizioni.

———. 2013. "Au royaume des discours incomplets: Ambiguïté et malentendu dans la conversation entre mafieux." *Revue des Sciences Sociales*, 50: 52–59.

Dodier, Nicolas. 2003. *Leçons politiques de l'épidémie de sida.* Paris: Éditions de l'École des Hautes Études en Sciences Sociales.

Donadieu-Rigaut, Dominique. 2005. *Penser en images les ordres religieux (XIIe–XVe siècles).* Paris: Éditions Arguments.

D'Onofrio, Salvatore. 2004. *L'esprit de la parenté: Europe et horizon chrétien.* Paris: Éditions de la Maison des Sciences de l'Homme.

———. 2014. *Les fluides d'Aristote: Lait, sang et sperme dans l'Italie du sud.* Paris: Les Belles Lettres.

Douglas, Mary. 1980. *Edward Evans-Pritchard.* Glasgow: Fontana.

Dubois, Philippe. 1990. *L'acte photographique.* Paris: Nathan.

Dulong, Renaud. 1998. *Le témoin oculaire: Les conditions sociales de l'attestation personnelle.* Paris: Éditions de l'École des Hautes Études en Sciences Sociales.

Ebano, Gabriella. 2005. *Felicia e le sue sorelle: Dal secondo dopoguerra alle stragi del '92–'93: Venti storie di donne contro la mafia.* Rome: Ediesse.

Editorial Committee, eds. 2005. "À l'épreuve du scandale." Special issue, *Politix*, no. 71.

Ehrenberg, Alain. 1991. *Le culte de la performance.* Paris: Calmann-Lévy.

Elias, Norbert. 2000. *The civilizing process: Sociogenetic and psychogenetic investigations.* Rev. ed. Translated by E. Jephcott. Malden: Blackwell. First published as *Über den Prozeß der Zivilisation* (Basel: Haus zum Falken, 1939).

Fabre, Daniel. 1997. "Seize terrains d'écriture." In *Par écrit: Ethnologie des écritures quotidiennes,* edited by Daniel Fabre, 1–56. Paris: Éditions de la Maison des Sciences de l'Homme.

Fabre, Thierry, and Deborah Puccio, eds. 2002. "Retrouver Palerme." Special issue, *La pensée de midi,* no. 8.

Faeta, Francesco. 1993. "La mort en images." *Terrain: Anthropologie et sciences humaines,* no. 20: 69–81. doi: 10.4000/terrain.3059

Falcone, Giovanni. 1994. *Interventi e proposte (1982–1992).* Milan: Sansoni.

———, and Marcelle Padovani. 1997. *Cose di Cosa Nostra.* Milan: Biblioteca universale Rizzoli. First published in 1991.

Fassin, Didier. 2009. "Les économies morales revisitées." *Annales* 6 (64): 1237–1266.

———. 2017. *Punir: Une passion contemporaine.* Paris: Seuil.

Fasullo, Nino. 1996. "Una religione mafiosa." *Segno* 179: 39–46.

Favret-Saada, Jeanne. 1980. *Deadly words: Witchcraft in the Bocage.* Translated by Catherine Cullen. Cambridge: Cambridge University Press. First published as *Les Mots, la mort, les sorts* (Paris: Gallimard, 1977).

Ferme, Mariane. 2019. "Crafting mafia: Performative and material practices." *HAU Journal of Ethnographic Theory* 9 (3): 596–598.

Ferrando, Stefania, Deborah Puccio-Den, and Alessia Smaniotto, eds. 2018. *Sociologia dell'indignazione: Genesi e trasformazione di una "forma politica."* Turin: Rosenberg and Sellier.

Fiandaca, Giovanni. 1995. "La mafia come ordinamento giuridico: Utilità e limiti di un paradigma." *Il Foro Italiano* 118 (2): 21/22–27/28.

———, and Salvatore Lupo. 2014. *La mafia non ha vinto: Il labirinto della trattativa.* Bari: Editori Laterza.

Foucault, Michel. 1978. *An introduction.* Vol. I of *The history of sexuality.* Translated by Robert Hurley. New York: Pantheon Books.

Foucault, Michel, 1995. *Discipline and punish: The birth of the prison.* 2nd ed. Translated by Alan Sheridan. New York: Vintage.

Fraenkel, Béatrice, 1992. *La signature: Genèse d'un signe.* Paris: Gallimard.

———. 2002. *Les écrits de septembre: New York 2001.* Paris: Textuel.

———. 2007. "Actes d'écriture: Quand écrire c'est faire." *Langage et société* 121–122 (3–4): 101–112. doi: 10.3917/ls.121.0101

Franchetti, Leopoldo. 1993. *Condizioni politiche e amministrative della Sicilia.* Rome: Donzelli. First published in 1877.

Gambetta, Diego. 1993. *The Sicilian mafia: The business of private protection.* Cambridge, MA: Harvard University Press.

Garapon, Antoine. 2010 *Bien juger: Essai sur le rituel judiciaire.* Paris: Odile Jacob.

Gardey, Delphine. 2008. *Écrire, calculer, classer: Comment une révolution de papier a transformé les sociétés contemporaines.* Paris: La Découverte.

Garfinkel, Harold. 1967. *Studies on ethnomethodology.* Englewood Cliffs: Prentice-Hall.

Gensburger, Sarah and Marie-Claire Lavabre. 2005. "Entre 'devoir de mémoire' et 'abus de mémoire': La sociologie de la mémoire comme tierce position." In *L'histoire entre mémoire et épistémologie: Autour de Paul Ricœur,* edited by Bertrand Müller, 76–95. Lausanne: Payot.

Gerbino, Aldo, ed. 1991. *La rosa dell'ercta, 1196–1991: Rosalia Sinibaldi: Sacralità, linguaggi e rappresentazione.* Palermo: Edizioni Dorica.

Geschiere, Peter. 1998. "Sorcellerie et modernité: Les enjeux des nouveaux procès de sorcellerie au Cameroun. Approches anthropologiques et historiques." *Annales: Histoire, Sciences Sociales* 53 (6): 1251–1279.

———. 2000. "Sorcellerie et modernité: retour sur une étrange complicité." *Politique africaine* 79 (3): 17–32.

———. 2001. "Regard académique, sorcellerie et schizophrénie (commentaire)." *Annales* 56 (3): 643–649.

———. 2005. *Sorcellerie et politique en Afrique.* Paris: Éditions Karthala.

———. 2010. "Witchcraft and modernity: Perspectives from Africa and beyond." In *Sorcery in the Black Atlantic*, edited by Luis Nicolau Parés and Roger Sansi, 233–258. Chicago: University of Chicago Press.

———. 2013. *Witchcraft, intimacy and trust: Africa in comparison.* Chicago: University of Chicago Press.

Giglioli, Pier Paolo, Sandra Cavicchioli, and Giolo Fele. 1997. *Rituali di degradazione: Anatomia del processo Cusani.* Bologna: Il Mulino.

Gilmore, David D., ed. 1987. *Honor and shame and the unity of the Mediterranean.* Washington: American Ethnological Association.

Ginzburg, Carlo. 1980. *The cheese and the worms: The cosmos of a sixteenth-century miller.* Translated by John Tedeschi and Anne C. Tedeschi. Baltimore: Johns Hopkins University Press. First published as *Il formaggio e i vermi: Il cosmo di un mugnaio del '500* (Turin: Einaudi, 1976).

———. 1983. *The night battles: Witchcraft and agrarian cults in the sixteenth and seventeenth centuries.* Translated by John Tedeschi and Anne C. Tedeschi. Harmondsworth: Penguin. First published as *I benandanti: Stregonerie e culti agrari tra cinquecento e seicento* (Turin: Einaudi, 1966).

———. 1986. "Spie: Radici di un paradigma indiziario." In *Miti, emblemi, spie: Morfologia e storia*, 158–93. Turin: Einaudi.

———. 1989a. "Witchcraft and popular piety: Note on a Modenese trial of 1959." In *Clues, myths and the historical method*, 1–15. Baltimore: Johns Hopkins University Press.

———. 1989b. "Clues: Roots of an evidential paradigm, " In *Clues, myths and the historical method*, 87–113. Baltimore: Johns Hopkins University Press.

———. 2002. *The judge and the historian: Marginal notes on a late-twentieth-century miscarriage of justice.* Translated by Antony Shugaar. London: Verso. First published as *Il giudice e lo storico: Considerazioni in margine al processo Sofri* (Turin: Einaudi, 1991).

Giunta, Francesco. 1991. "Santità ed eremitismo nella Sicilia normanna." In *La rosa dell'ercta, 1196–1991: Rosalia Sinibaldi: Sacralità, linguaggi e rap-prentazione*, edited by Aldo Gerbino, 21–27. Palermo: Dorica.

Goffman, Erving. 1974. *Les rites d'interaction*. Translated by Alain Kihm. Paris: Les Éditions de Minuit.

Goody, Jack. 1977. *The domestication of the savage mind*. Cambridge: Cambridge University Press.

Griaule, Marcel. 1952. "L'enquête orale en ethnologie." *Revue Philosophique de la France et de l'Étranger*, no. 142: 537–553.

———. 1957. *Méthode de l'ethnographie*. Paris: PUF.

———. 1966. *Dieu d'eau: Entretiens avec Ogotemmêli*. Paris: Fayard.

Grosso, Carlo Federico. 1994. "La contiguità alla mafia tra partecipazione, concorso in associazione e irrilevanza penale." In *La mafia, le mafie: Tra vecchi e nuovi paradigmi*, edited by Fiandaca Giovanni and Constantino Salvatore, 192–216. Bari: Editori Laterza.

Hale, Charles. 2001. "What is activist research?" *Items and Issues* 2 (1–2): 13–15.

Haney, C. Allen, Christina Leimer, and Juliann Lowery. 1997. "Spontaneous memorialization: Violent death and emerging mourning ritual." *Omega* 35 (2): 159–171. doi: 10.2190/7U8W-540L-QWX9-1VL6

Hébrard, Jean. 1991. "La lettre représentée: Les pratiques épistolaires popu-laires dans les récits de vie ouvriers et paysans." In *La Correspondance: Les usages de la lettre au XIXᵉ siècle*, edited by Roger Chartier, 279–365. Paris: Fayard.

Héritier, Françoise. 1979. "Symbolique de l'inceste et de sa prohibition." In *La fonction symbolique: Essais d'anthropologie*, edited by Michel Izard and Pierre Smith, 209–243. Paris: Gallimard.

———. 1984. "Le sang du guerrier et le sang des femmes." *Les Cahiers du GRIF*, no. 29: 7–21.

———, and Margarita Xanthakou, eds. 2004. *Corps et affects*. Paris: Odile Jacob.

Herrou, Adeline. 2008. "Quand les moines Taoïstes se mettent en texte." In *Du corps au texte: Approches comparatives*, edited by Brigitte Baptandier and Giordana Charuty, 43–74. Nanterre: Société d'ethnologie.

Herzfeld, Michael. 1980. "Honour and shame: Problems in the comparative analysis of moral systems." *Man* 15 (2): 339–351. doi: 10.2307/2801675

———. 1997. *Cultural intimacy: Social poetics in the nation-state*. New York: Routledge.

———. 2005. "Practical Mediterraneanism: Excuses for everything, from epistemology to eating." In *Rethinking the Mediterranean*, edited by William V. Harris, 45–63. Oxford: Oxford University Press.

———. 2019. "The reality of inchoateness." *HAU Journal* 9 (3): 619–624. doi: 10.1086/706544

Hess, Henner. 1998. *Mafia and mafiosi: Origin, power and myth*. New York: New York University Press. First published as *Mafia: Zentrale Herrschaft und lokale Gegenmacht* (Tübingen: Mohr, 1970).

Hirschauer, Stefan. 2006. "Puttings things into words: Ethnographic description and the silence of the social." *Human Studies* 29 (4): 413–441.

Humphrey, Caroline and James Laidlaw. 1994. *The archetypal actions of ritual: A theory of ritual illustrated by the Jain rite of worship*. Oxford: Clarendon Press.

Jacquemet, Marc. 1996. *Credibility in court: Communicative practices in the Camorra trials*. Cambridge: Cambridge University Press.

Jameson, Fredric. 1990. "Cognitive Mapping." In *Marxism and the interpretation of culture*, edited by Cary Nelson and Lawrence Grossberg, 347–360. University of Illinois Press.

———. 1991. *Postmodernism: Or, the cultural logic of late capitalism*. Durham: Duke University Press.

Jamin, Jean. 1977. *Les lois du silence: Essai sur la fonction sociale du secret*. Paris: François Maspero.

Jamous, Raymond. 1981. *Honneur et baraka: Les structures sociales traditionnelles dans le Rif*. Cambridge: Cambridge University Press.

Jewsiewicki, Bogumil. 2001. "Pour un pluralisme épistémologique en sciences sociales." *Annales: Histoire, Sciences Sociales* 56 (3): 625–641.

Karsenti, Bruno. 2012. *Moïse et l'idée de people: La vérité historique selon Freud*. Paris: Le Cerf.

Kaufmann, Laurence. 2013. "Le silence des agneaux: L'hospitalité libérale à l'épreuve du fondamentalisme." *SociologieS*, no. 11: 1–10.

Kidron, Carol A. 2009. "Toward an ethnography of silence: The lived presence of the past in the everyday life of holocaust trauma survivors and their descendants in Israel." *Current Anthropology* 50 (1): 5–27. doi: 10.1086/595623

Komter, Martha.1998. *Dilemmas in the courtroom: A study of trials of violent crime in the Netherlands.* Mahvah: Lawrence Erlbaum.

Lacey, Nicola. 2016. *In search of criminal responsibility: Ideas, interests and institutions.* Oxford: Oxford University Press.

La Fiura, Giovanni. 1992. "'Imputati dichiaranti' nelle motivazioni della sentenza di primo grado del processo di Palermo." In *Gabbie vuote: Processi per omicidio a Palermo dal 1983 al maxiprocesso*, edited by Giorgio Chinnici, Umberto Santino, Giovanni La Fiura, and Ugo Adragna, 170–201. Milan: Franco Angeli.

Laidlaw, James. 2014. *The subject of virtue: An anthropology of ethics and freedom.* Cambridge: Cambridge University Press.

La Licata, Francesco. 2002. *Storia di Giovanni Falcone.* Milan: Feltrinelli.

Lemieux, Cyril. 2007. "L'accusation tolérante: Remarques sur les rapports entre commérage, scandale et affaire." In *Affaires, scandales et grandes causes: De Socrate à Pinochet*, edited by Luc Boltanski, Élisabeth Claverie, Nicolas Offenstadt, and Stephane van Damme, 367–394. Paris: Stock.

Le Roy Ladurie, Emmanuel. 1975. *Montaillou, village Occitan.* Paris. Gallimard.

Levi, Giovanni. 1988. *Inheriting power: The story of an exorcist.* Translated by Lydia G. Cochrane. Chicago: University of Chicago Press.

Lévi-Strauss, Claude. 1962. *The savage mind.* Chicago: University of Chicago Press. First published as *Le pensée sauvage* (Paris: Plon, 1962).

———. 1987. *Introduction to the work of Marcel Mauss.* Translated by Felicity Baker. New York: Routledge and Kegan Paul. First published as *Introduction à l'oeuvre de Marcel Mauss* (Paris: Presses Universitaire de France, 1950).

Linhardt, Dominique. 2012. "Avant-propos: Épreuves d'État." *Quaderni*, no. 78: 5–22.

Lodato, Saverio. 1994. *Diciotto anni di mafia: Una guerra che non sarà infinita.* Milan: Biblioteca Universale Rizzoli.

———. 1996. *Diciotto anni di mafia.* Milan: Biblioteca Universale Rizzoli.

———, and Roberto Scarpinato. 2008. *Il ritorno del principe.* Milan: Chiarelettere.

———, and Marco Travaglio. 2005. *Intoccabili: Perché la mafia è al potere. Dai processi Andreotti, dell'Utri e C. alla normalizzazione. Le verità occultate sui complici di Cosa Nostra nella politica e nello Stato.* Milan: Rizzoli.

Loraux, Nicole. 1997. *La cité divisée: L'oubli dans la mémoire d'Athènes*. Paris: Payot.

———. 2010. "Blessures de virilité." *Revue française de psychosomatique* 38 (2): 157–174.

Lucentini, Umberto. 2003. *Paolo Borsellino*. Milan: Edizioni San Paolo.

Lupo, Salvatore. 1988. "'Il tenebroso sodalizio': Un rapporto sulla mafia palermitana di fine Ottocento." *Studi Storici* 29 (2): 463–489.

———. 1999. *Histoire de la mafia des origines à nos jours*. Paris: Flammarion.

———. 2007. *Che cos'è la mafia? Sciascia e Andreotti, l'antimafia e la politica*. Rome: Donzelli.

Macaluso, Ennio. 1995. *Giulio Andreotti tra Stato e mafia*. Soveria Mannelli: Rubbettino.

Manzini, Vincenzo. (1908–1919) 1983. *Trattato di diritto penale.* Turin: Utet.

Margry, Peter Jan, ed. 2008. *Shrines and pilgrimage in the modern world: New itineraries into the sacred*. Amsterdam: Amsterdam University Press.

———, and Cristina Sánchez-Carretero. 2007. "Memorializing traumatic death." *Anthropology Today* 23 (3): 1–2. doi: 10.1111/j.1467-8322.2007.00508.x

Marino, Gian Carlo. 1964. *L'opposizione mafiosa (1870–1882): Baroni e mafia contro lo Stato liberale*. Palermo: Flaccovio.

Masson, Michel. 1999. *Matériaux pour l'étude des parallélismes sémantiques*. Paris: Presses de la Sorbonne Nouvelle.

Mead, Margaret, and Gregory Bateson. 1942. *Balinese character, a photographic analysis*. New York: Academy of Sciences of New York.

Mitchell, Timothy. 2006. "Society, economy, and the state effect." In *The anthropology of the state: A reader*, edited by Aradhana Sharma and Akhil Gupta, 169–186. Malden: Blackwell.

Montanaro, Silvestro, and Sandro Ruotolo. 1995. *La vera storia d'Italia: Interrogatori, testimonianze, riscontri, analisi. Gianfranco Caselli e i suoi sostituti ricostruiscono gli ultimi vent'anni di storia italiana*. Naples: Pironti.

Mosca, Gaetano. (1949) 2002. *Che Cosa è la mafia*. Bari: Editori Laterza.

Mubi Brighenti, Andrea. 2008. *Tra onore e dignità: Per una sociologia del rispetto*. Trento: Università degli Studi di Trento.

Natoli, Luigi, 1971. *I Beati Paoli*. Palermo: Flaccovio.

Nebiolo, Marco, and Livio Pepino, eds. 2006. *Mafia e potere*. Turin: EGA Editore.

Neppi Modona, Guido. 1994. "Il difficile confine tra responsabilità politica individuale e responsabilità penale." In *La mafia, le mafie: Tra vecchi e nuovi paradigmi*, edited by Giovanni Fiandaca and Salvatore Constantino, 177–191. Bari: Editori Laterza.

Nicaso, Antonio. 2010. *La mafia spiegata ai ragazzi.* Milan: Mondadori.

Nisticò, Vittorio. 2001. *Accadeva in Sicilia: Gli anni ruggenti dell'Ora di Palermo.* Palermo: Sellerio.

———, 2004. *L'ora dei ricordi.* Palermo: Sellerio.

Nora, Pierre, ed. 1984–1992. *Les lieux de mémoire.* Paris: Gallimard.

Ogilvie, Bertrand. 2006. "La mort en face." *Incidence* 2: 9–21.

Padovani, Marcelle. 1987. *Les dernières années de la mafia.* Paris: Gallimard.

Palazzolo, Salvo, and Michele Prestipino. 2007. *Il codice Provenzano.* Bari: Editori Laterza.

Pantaleone, Michele. 1970. *Il sasso in bocca: Mafia e Cosa Nostra.* Bologna: Cappelli Editore.

Paoli, Letizia. 2000. *Fratelli di mafia: Cosa Nostra e 'Ndrangheta.* Bologna: Il Mulino. English language edition: *Mafia Brotherhoods: Organized Crime, Italian Style* (New York: Oxford University Press, 2003).

Pastoureau, Michel. 1993. "Introduction à la symbolique médiévale du bois." In *L'arbre: Histoire naturelle et symbolique de l'arbre, du bois et du fruit au Moyen Âge*, edited by Michel Pastoureau, Gaston Duchet-Suchaux, Christiane Klapisch-Zuber, and Danièle Alexandre-Bidon, 25–40. Paris: Cahiers du Léopard d'Or.

Pepino, Livio. 2005. *Andreotti, la mafia, i processi: Analisi e materiali giudiziari.* Turin: Ega Editore.

Peristiany, John G. 1965. "Honour and shame in Cypriot highland village." In *Honour and shame: The values of Mediterranean society*, edited by John G. Peristiany, 171–190. London: Weidenfeld and Nicholson.

Perret, Catherine. 2013. *L'enseignement de la torture.* Paris: Seuil.

Petrucci, Armando. 1980. *La scrittura: Ideologia e rappresentazione.* Turin: Einaudi.

———. 1995. *Le scritture ultime: Ideologia della morte e strategie dello scrivere nella tradizione occidentale.* Turin: Einaudi.

Pierce, Charles Sanders. 1978. *Écrits sur le signe.* Paris: Le Seuil. First published in 1931.

Piette, Albert. 1992. *Le mode mineur de la réalité: Paradoxes et photographies en anthropologie.* Louvain-la-Neuve: Peeters.

Pitrè, Giuseppe. (1889) 1944. *Usi e costumi, credenze e pregiudizi del popolo siciliano*. Vol II. Firenze: G. Barbera.

Pitrou, Perig. 2012. "La divination dans la Sierra Mixe (Mexique) comme forme d'action sur le monde." In *Deviner pour agir: Regards comparatifs sur des pratiques divinatoires anciennes et contemporaines*, edited by Jean-Luc Lambert and Olivier Guilhem, 87–109. Paris: Éditions de l'École pratique des hautes études.

Pitt-Rivers, Julian. 1965. "Honor and social status." In *Honor and shame: The values of Mediterranean society*, edited by John G. Peristiany, 21–71. London: Weidenfeld and Nicholson.

———. 1991. "La maladie de l'honneur." In *L'honneur: Image de soi ou don de soi, un idéal équivoque*, edited by Marie Gautheron, 20–36. Paris: Autrement.

———. 2001. "The moral sanctions of the Pueblo: Niknames and vitos." In *L'anthropologie de la Méditerranée: Anthropology of the Mediterranean*, edited by Dionigi Albera, Anton Blok, and Christian Bromberger, 149–156. Cahors: Maisonneuve et Larose, Maison Méditerranéenne des Sciences de l'Homme.

Principato, Teresa, and Alessandra Dino. 1997. *Mafia donna: Le vestali del sacro e dell'onore*. Palermo: Flaccovio.

Prost, Antoine. 1984. "Le monument aux morts." In *Les lieux de mémoire*. Vol. 1 of *La république*, edited by Pierre Nora, 195–255. Paris: Gallimard.

Puccio, Deborah. 2001. "L'ethnologue et le juge: L'enquête de Giovanni Falcone sur la mafia en Sicile." *Ethnologie française* 31 (1): 15–27. doi: 10.3917/ethn.011.0015

———. 2002. *Masques et dévoilements: Jeux du féminin dans les rituels carnavalesques et nuptiaux*. Paris: CNRS Éditions.

———. 2007. "De la sainte pèlerine au juge saint: les parcours de l'Antimafia en Sicile." *Politix* 19 (77): 107–130.

Puccio-Den, Deborah. 2009. *Les théâtres de "Maures et Chrétiens": Conflits politiques et dispositifs de reconciliation (Espagne, Sicile, XVIIe–XXIe siècle)*. Turnhout: Éditions Brepols.

———. 2014. "Être un 'repenti' de la mafia, entre droit et religion (Italie, 1973–2013)." In *Justice, religion, reconciliation*, edited by Yazid Ben Hounet, Sandrine Lefranc, and Deborah Puccio-Den, 95–108. Paris: L'Harmattan.

———. 2015. "Tribunaux criminels et fictions de justice: La 'commission' de la mafia sicilienne." *Droit et société*, 89 (1): 35–53.

———. 2016. "Introducción: 'Nocturnidades'." In *Las cosas de la noche: Una mirada diferente*, edited by Aurore Monod Becquelin and Jacques Galinier, 18–29. Mexico: Centro de Estudios Mexicanos y Centroamericanos.

———. 2017a. "Introduction: La responsabilité," *L'Homme* 223–224 (3–4): 5–32. Translated by Cadenza Academic Translations as "On responsibility." https://www.cairn-int.info/article-E_LHOM_223_0005--on-responsibility.htm#

———. 2017b. "Faire danser." *Psychanalyse* 38 (1): 73–89.

———. 2019a. "The social life of what? Some comments on Theodoros Rakopoulos's article 'The social life of mafia confession: Between talk and silence in Sicily'." *Current Anthropology* 60 (1): 138–139. doi: 10.1086/701596

———. 2019b. "Mafiacraft: How to do things with silence." *HAU Journal* 9 (3): 599–618. doi: 10.1086/706546

———. 2019c. "Invisible things." *HAU Journal* 9 (3): 642–649. doi: 10.1086/706547

———. Forthcoming. *Ethnographier le silence, ethnographier la nuit.* Nanterre: Société d'ethnologie.

Puglisi, Anna. 2005. *Donne, mafia e antimafia.* Trapani: DG Editore.

———, and Umberto Santino. 2005. *Cara felicia: A Felicia Bartolotta Impastato.* Palermo: Centro Siciliano di Documentazione Giuseppe Impastato.

Quine, Willard van Orman. 1960. *Word and object.* Cambridge, MA: MIT Press.

Rakopoulos, Theodoros. 2018. "The social life of mafia confession: Between talk and silence in Sicily." *Current Anthropology* 59 (2): 167–191. doi: 10.1086/697237

Renda, Francesco. 1997. *Storia della Mafia.* Palermo: Sigma Edizioni.

Ricœur, Paul. 1995. "Le concept de responsabilité: Essai d'analyse sémantique." In *Le juste*, 41–70. Paris. Éditions Esprit.

———. 2000. *La mémoire, l'histoire, l'oubli.* Paris: Éditions du Seuil.

Rodeghiero, Lucia. 1998. "L'antropologo e la sua ombra: Il ruolo dell'informatore nella costruzione della rappresentazione etnografica." In *Etnografia e culture: Antropologi, informatori e politiche dell'identità*, edited by Ugo Fabietti, 19–37. Rome: Carocci.

Roussel Violaine. 2002. *Affaires de juges: Les magistrats dans les scandales politiques en France.* Paris: La Découverte.

Ruta, Carlo, ed. 2014. *Pio La Torre legislatore contro la Mafia: Interventi e discorsi parlamentari.* Rome: Edizioni di Storia e Studi Sociali.

Salvio, Paula. 2012. "'Eccentric subjects': Female martyrs and the antimafia public imaginary." *Italian Studies* 67 (3): 397–410.

———. 2014. "Reconstructing memory through the archives: Public pedagogy, citizenship and Letizia Battaglia's photographic record of mafia violence." *Pedagogy, Culture and Society* 22 (1): 97–116. doi: 10.1080/14681366.2013.877620

Sánchez-Carretero, Cristina. 2006. "Trains of workers, trains of death: Some reflections after the March 11th attacks in Madrid." In *Spontaneous shrines and the public memorialization of death*, edited by Jack Santino, 333–347. New York: Palgrave Macmillan.

Santino, Jack. 2004. "Performative commemoratives, the personal, and the public: Spontaneous shrines, emergent ritual, and the field of folklore (AFS Presidential Plenary Address, 2003)." *Journal of American Folklore* 117 (466): 363–372.

———. 2006. *Spontaneous shrines and the public memorialization of death.* New York: Palgrave Macmillan.

Santino, Umberto. 1992. "Mafia e maxiprocesso: Dalla 'supplenza' alla 'crisi della giustizia'." In *Gabbie vuote: Processi per omicidio a Palermo dal 1983 al maxiprocesso*, edited by Giorgio Chinnici, Umberto Santino, Giovanni La Fiura, and Ugo Adragna, 97–178. Milan: Franco Angeli.

———. 1994. *La borghesia mafiosa.* Palermo: Centro Siciliano di Documentazione Giuseppe Impastato.

———. 1995. *La mafia interpretata: Dilemmi, stereotipi, paradigmi.* Soveria Mannelli: Rubbettino.

———. 1998. *L'assassinio e il depistaggio: Atti relativi all'omicidio di Giuseppe Impastato.* Palermo: Centro Siciliano di Documentazione Giuseppe Impastato.

———. 2000a. *La cosa e il nome: Materiali per lo studio dei fenomeni premafiosi.* Soveria Mannelli: Rubbettino.

———. 2000b. *Storia del movimento antimafia: Dalla lotta di classe all'impegno civile.* Rome: Editori Riuniti.

———. 2007. *Mafia e globalizzazione.* Trapani: DG Editore.

Santoro, Marco. 2007. *La voce del padrino: Mafia, cultura, politica.* Verona: Ombre Corte.

———. 2015, *Riconoscere le mafie: Cosa sono, come funzionano, come si muovono.* Bologna: Il Mulino.

————. 2019. "Mafiacraft, witchcraft, statecraft, or the politics of mafia knowledge and the knowledge of mafia politics." *Hau Journal* 9 (3): 631–637. doi: 10.1086/707726

Scarpinato, Roberto. 1996. Caratteristiche e dinamiche degli omicidi ordinati e eseguiti da Cosa Nostra. *Segno* 22 (176): 75–94.

————. 1998. "Cosa Nostra e il male oscuro della dispersione del Sé." In *La mafia dentro: Psicologia e psicopatologia di un fondamentalismo*, edited by Girolamo Lo Versi, 78–92. Milan: Franco Angeli.

————, and Domenico Mongovero. 2012. "Dio, Mafia e potere: Dialogo tra Roberto Scarpinato e mons. Domenico Mogavero." In "La Chiesa gerarchica e la Chiesa di Dio," special issue, *Micromega* 7: 159–181.

Schneider, Jane. 1971. "Of vigilance on virgins: Honor, shame and access to resources in Mediterranean societies." *Ethnology* 10 (1): 1–24. doi: 10.2307/3772796

————. 2019. "Mafiacraft" and mafia activity: A dynamic and changing interaction." *Hau Journal* 9 (3): 625–630. doi: 10.1086/706545

————, and Peter Schneider. 1976. *Culture and political economy in western Sicily*. New York: Academic Press.

————. 2003. *Reversible destiny: Mafia, antimafia and the struggle for Palermo*. Berkeley: University of California Press.

Schneider, Peter. 1969. "Honor and conflict in a Sicilian town." *Anthropological Quarterly* 42 (3): 130–154. doi: 10.2307/3317036

Sciascia, Leonardo. 1990. *Il giorno della civetta*. Turin: Einaudi. First published in 1961.

————. 1993. *Dalle parti degli Infedeli*. Milan: Adelphi. First published in 1979.

————. 2002. *A futura memoria (se la memoria ha un futuro)*. Milan: Bompiani. First published in 1989.

————. 2013. *Storia della Mafia*. Barion: Palermo.

Sgroi, Salvatore Claudio. 2014. "Le traduzioni del *Giorno della Civetta* di Leonardo Sciascia nelle lingue indoeuropee (romanze e germaniche) e non (ungherese, finnico e cinese) e la resa dei dialettalismi: Un caso paradigmatico (*Quaquaraqua*)." *Ricognizioni, Rivista di lingue, letterature e culture moderne* 2 (1): 187–224. doi: 10.13135/2384-8987/783

Shuqair, Noura. 2019. "The aesthetic of cognitive mapping: An approach to arts-based research and critical artmaking." *Synnyt/Origins*, no. 2: 360–380.

Siebert, Renata. 1994. *Le donne, la Mafia*. Milan: Il Saggiatore.

Siegel, James. 2006. *Naming the witch*. Stanford: Stanford University Press.

Simmel, Georg. 1906. "The sociology of secrecy and of secret societies." *American Journal of Sociology* 11 (4): 441–498.

Smith, Dennis. 2006. *Globalization: The hidden agenda*. Cambridge: Polity Press.

Spera, Enzo. 1977. "Ex voto fotografici e oggettuali." In *Puglia ex voto*, edited by Emanuela Angiuli. Bari: Biblioteca provinciale De Gemmis, pp. 233-247.

Stajano, Corrado, ed. 2010. *Mafia: L'atto d'accusa dei giudici di Palermo*. Rome: Editori Riuniti.

Stille, Alexander. 1995. *Nella terra degli infedeli: Mafia e politica nella Prima Repubblica*. Translated by Paolo Mazzarelli. Milan: Arnoldo Mondadori. First published as *Excellent cadavers: The mafia and the death of the first Italian republic* (New York: Pantheon, 1995).

Taylor, Charles. 1989. *Sources of the self: The making of modern identity*. Cambridge: Harvard University Press.

Tedlock, Dennis, and Bruce Mannheim, eds. 1995. *The dialogic emergence of culture*. Urbana: University of Illinois Press.

Thomas, Keith. 1970. "The relevance of social anthropology to the historical study of English witchcraft." In *Witchcraft: Confessions and accusations*, edited by Mary Douglas, 47–80. New York: Routledge.

Thompson, Edward Palmer. 1991. "The moral economy reviewed." In *Customs in common: Studies in traditional popular culture*, 259–351. London: Merlin Press.

Traïni, Christophe. 2008. "Émotions, paradoxes pragmatiques et valeurs sociales: Les ressorts de l'engagement." Habilation treatise, Université Paris I–Panthéon Sorbonne.

Trnka, Susanna, and Catherine Trundle, eds. 2017. *Competing responsibilities: The politics and ethics of contemporary life*. Durham: Duke University Press.

Turone, Giuliano. 2008. *Il delitto di associazione mafiosa*. Milan: Giuffré Editore.

Van Damme, Stéphane. 2007. "Grandeur, affaire et épreuve libertine au XIIe siècle: le cas de Théofile de Viau." In *Affaires, scandales et grandes causes: De Socrate à Pinochet*, edited by Luc Boltanski, Élisabeth Claverie, Nicolas Offenstadt, and Stephane van Damme, 151–176. Paris: Stock.

Varese, Federico. 2012. "How mafias take advantage of globalization: The Russian mafia in Italy." *British Journal of Criminology* 52 (2): 235–253. doi: 10.1093/bjc/azr077

Vauchez, Antoine. 2004. *L'institution judiciaire remotivée: Le processus d'institutionnalisation de la "nouvelle justice" en Italie (1960–2000).* Paris: LGDJ.

Virmani, Arundhati, ed. 2016. *Political aesthetics: Culture, critique and the everyday.* New York: Routledge.

Vivilaki, Victoria, and Martin Johnson. 2008. "Research philosophy and Socrates: Rediscovering the birth of phenomenology." *Nurse Researcher* 16 (1): 84–92. doi: 10.7748/nr2008.10.16.1.84.c6755

Walker, Harry. 2019. "Dislocating responsibility." *HAU Journal* 9 (3): 638–641. doi: 10.1086/706763

Wittgenstein, Ludwig. 2009. *Philosophical investigations.* Translated by G. E. M. Anscombe. Malden: Basil Blackwell. First published in 1953.

Zecchin, Franco. 1993. *La conta.* Palermo: Edizioni della Battaglia.

———. 2016. "Aesthetics as critique: A photographic inquiry into the mafia." In *Political aesthetics: Culture, critique and the everyday,* edited by Arundhati Virmani, 87–105. New York: Routledge.

Zeitlin, Steve. 2006. "Oh did you see the ashes come thickly falling down? Poems posted in the wake of September 11." In *Spontaneous shrines and the public memorialization of death,* edited by Jack Santino, 99–117. New York: Palgrave Macmillan.

Zempleni, András. 1996. "Savoir taire: Du secret et de l'intrusion ethnologique dans la vie des autres." *Gradhiva,* no. 20: 23–41.

Zingales, Leone. 2006. *Rocco Chinnici, l'inventore del "pool" antimafia.* Arezzo: Limina.

Index

A

Abate, Ida, 100

actions: collective, 32, 91, 176; concrete, 221, 238; harmful, 14; indirect, 14; judicial, 24; legal, 147, 169, 195, 210; malicious, 217; moral, 180; penal, 58; political, 6, 29, 66, 107, 185, 239; ritual, 20, 214, 216, 232

activists, 4–5, 25, 29, 60, 65, 71, 83, 91, 179, 185–86, 234; young, 117, 184, 196

administration: central, 181; dysfunctional local, 182; public, 209

adultery, 161–62, 222

Africa, 16, 125, 237, 240, 241

Alberti, Gerlando (mafioso), 1, 16, 43

Alcamo, Vittorio (Judge), 211, 213

allegiance, 52, 207, 227

alliance, 86, 166

allies, 11, 114, 137, 175

Andreotti, Giulio (Senator), 54–57, 66, 143, 180, 195, 210

anthropology: moral, 6; political, 10, 241; social, 20

anti-mafia, 29, 34, 65, 105, 117, 119, 181, 238–40; activism, 19, 70-71, 86, 96, 106, 110, 120, 181; campaign, 179, 210; groups, 193, 196; iconography, 69, 98; judges, 10, 12, 24–25, 32, 35, 38, 48, 51–52, 63, 65, 96, 98, 101, 103, 128, 188-89; photography, 12, 68–71, 74; prosecutors, 17, 32, 50, 60, 156

assassination, 7, 47, 52, 54, 63, 67, 124, 133, 152, 180, 184, 191, 193, 225

association: national, 47, 191; secret, 54

atheists, 64, 87

authorities, 15, 46, 115, 117–18, 149, 155, 164–66, 182, 185, 230, 232–33; corrupt, 135; legal, 186; legitimate, 186; local, 28, 34, 65, 70, 113, 117–18; patriarchal, 157; prosecuting, 69; public, 7, 207; supreme, 99

Italian Socialist Party, 54, 107, 195
Italian society, 3, 10, 23, 78, 164, 193
Italian state, 10, 28, 34, 51, 138, 152, 163, 180, 199–200, 242
Italian Supreme Court, 52, 56, 58
Italy, 7–9, 12, 25–26, 28, 30, 44, 56–59, 90–92, 100–101, 107–10, 137–38, 151–52, 195–96, 199–201, 240–41; mainland, 24; northern, 48, 138, 153; southern, 96, 150, 160

J

Jesse's tree, 89
judges, 22, 29, 37, 46, 48, 50–53, 57–58, 66–68, 85–90, 92–98, 100–102, 108–10, 126–28, 145–46, 153–54, 163–65, 167–72, 211–12, 215–16; independence, 101; irresponsible, 101; martyr, 102; slain, 91
judiciary, 3, 12, 19, 29–30, 34–35, 55–57, 164, 186, 210, 242
jurists, 37, 44, 46, 170, 190–91, 194, 197, 212, 233
justice, 21–22, 32, 35, 57–58, 60, 63, 66–68, 90, 92–96, 98–99, 102, 106, 108, 156–57, 186–89; anti-mafia, 3, 15, 190; archaic, 189; divine, 233; traditional, 190
justice collaborators, 148, 156, 164, 168–69, 175, 208

K

killing techniques, 137, 141
kinship, spiritual, 157

knowledge: compartmentalized, 30; partial, 31; renewing, 30; shared, 12

L

land, 87–88, 138, 161, 181
landowners, 138, 181; large, 46, 138–39
Latin America, 18
La Torre, Pio. See Rognoni–La Torre Law.
law, 6–10, 14, 17–18, 20, 43, 46–47, 49–50, 56–57, 99–100, 146–49, 155, 166, 168, 190–91, 196–97
lawfulness, 64, 89, 91, 110
lawmakers, 203, 207
lawyers, 4–5, 14, 18, 22, 24, 29, 78, 92, 181, 240, 242
legacy, 21, 97, 126
legal: proceedings, 8, 12, 25, 27, 36; records, 139–40; system, 14, 37, 47, 52, 190; tools, 24, 240
Leggio, Luciano. See Liggio, Luciano.
legitimacy, 7, 22, 86, 155, 180–81, 196, 200
Liggio, Luciano (mafioso), 175, 194, 228
Livatino, Rosario (Judge), 67, 99–102, 114

M

mafia, 1–28, 30–35, 37–39, 43–63, 68–78, 106–10, 112–15, 117–20, 123–24, 135–43, 147–50, 152–55, 157–61, 173–76, 179–86, 190–96, 198–201, 206–13, 232–33, 235–42; Sicilian, 139,

sentences, prison, 58, 100, 186, 207
shrines, spontaneous, 26, 105, 113, 117
Sicilian-ness, 124
Sicily, 24–25, 27–28, 30–31, 59, 61–62, 87, 98–99, 108, 137–39, 150–52, 154–55, 159–60, 180–82, 209–10, 220–21; culture, 7, 45, 124; defending, 6; free, 137; law of silence, 61; magistrates, 44, 48; rural, 10; sixteenth-century, 156
Signorino, Domenico (Judge), 187
silence, 2–8, 11–14, 19–21, 29, 33–34, 50, 70–71, 108, 112, 123–24, 136, 154–56, 158–59, 168, 213–15, 233–34, 238–40, 242; acts of, 6, 24, 234, 239–41; categorize, 239; deadly, 2, 4, 6, 8, 10, 12, 14, 16, 18, 20, 22, 24, 26, 120, 238–40; heuristics of, 29, 130; law of, 50, 52, 130, 155, 182, 187, 203–4, 206; power of, 15, 240; tenacious, 155
silencing, 5, 15, 18, 24, 164, 186, 233
spectators, 26, 64, 117, 214
speech, 32–33, 44, 48–49, 98, 101, 145–46, 149, 151, 155, 160, 168–69, 233–34, 239; mayoral, 65; performative, 148; pope's, 99; unbridled, 171; use of, 4, 167
spies, 129
state: central, 7; foreign, 108; mental, 36; modern, 20, 81, 141, 239, 241; neoliberal, 241; republican, 138
subjugation, 14, 36, 50, 159, 170, 204, 207–8, 216, 233
superstitions, 38, 126, 158

symbols, 22, 25, 27, 63, 86–87, 225–26; objectified, 12

T

taboo, 143, 233
Terranova, Cesare (Judge), 31, 46, 225
terrorism, 15, 35, 62, 89, 127, 175, 180, 190–91, 196, 198, 236; accusation of, 184; right-wing, 48
terrorist attacks, 76, 106; alleged suicide bomb, 180; kamikaze, 185; political, 52; right-wing, 180
testimonies, 62, 67, 92, 100, 124, 134, 136, 172, 188, 192, 194–95; corroborated, 134; moral, 90; privileged, 27; reliable, 148; transient, 85; written, 27
traditions, 232, 241; oral, 228
tree, magnolia, 26, 86
trial, 18–19, 23–24, 45–46, 51–52, 54, 56–58, 60, 62, 100, 126–27, 146–47, 173–74, 192–93, 195, 208–11; Aiello, Michele (mafioso), 36–37, 59–60, 203, 205, 207, 209–11, 215; anti-mafia, 12, 17, 54, 59, 172; Friuli, 126; historical, 235; inquisitorial, 127; mafia, 12, 36, 176, 198, 241; Maxi (maxiprocesso), 23, 51, 53, 62–63, 123–24, 127–28, 134, 136–37, 142, 145–46, 166–67, 169, 171–73, 176; Penal, 51, 53, 60, 167; Sofri, 128; Spatola, 30, 48, 151
truth: moral, 58; psychological, 37

Printed by Printforce, United Kingdom